Marketing Planning

A STEP-BY-STEP GUIDE

JAMES W. TAYLOR

PRENTICE HALL

PRENTICE HALL
A member of Penguin Putnam Inc.
375 Hudson Street, New York, N.Y. 10014
www.penguinputnam.com

Copyright © 1997 by Penguin Putnam Inc.

Prentice Hall® is a registered trademark of Pearson Education, Inc.

Library of Congress Cataloging-in-Publication Data

Taylor, James Walter.
    Marketing planning : a step-by-step guide / James W. Taylor.
      p. cm.
    ISBN 0-13-242058-9 (cloth).—ISBN 0-13-242041-4 (pbk.)
    1. Marketing—Planning—Handbooks, manuals, etc.   I. Title.
    HF5415.13.T379   1996   96-26483
    658.8'.02—dc20   CIP

Printed in the United States of America

10 9 8 7 6 5 4 3   10 9 8 7

ISBN 0-13-242058-9 (C)   ISBN 0-13-242041-4 (PBK)

Contents

Introduction

SECTION ONE

Marketing Planning and Strategy: What It Is and Why It Is Needed

SECTION TWO

What We Know About What Makes Businesses Profitable

SECTION THREE

The Product Life Cycle: How the PLC Drives Your Markets

SECTION FOUR

Every Company Has Strengths and Weaknesses: How to Understand and Use Your Company's Strengths and Weaknesses

SECTION FIVE

How to Conduct a Focused Market Review

How to Conduct a Competitive Analysis

SECTION SEVEN

Analyzing Your Environment and Dealing with What is "Out There"

SECTION EIGHT

Where Do You Want to Get To? Developing Your Own Mission Statement

SECTION NINE

Marketing Intelligence and Your Customers

SECTION TEN

Sales Force Planning and Management

Advertising, Sales and Trade Promotion

SECTION TWELVE

All Competition Is Now Global

SECTION THIRTEEN

Technology—It Is Changing Everything You Do in Business

SECTION FOURTEEN

Pulling It all Together to Develop a Winning Strategic Marketing Plan

Introduction

WHY THIS BOOK WAS WRITTEN
AND WHAT IT WILL DO FOR YOU

This book is a complete guide to marketing strategy and planning. It is a world-class executive MBA course in the basic fundamentals: what makes businesses profitable; why businesses must grow; how to develop a strategy for successful growth; how to prepare a detailed marketing plan to execute that strategy; and how to put it to work for you.

After fifteen years as a working marketing manager, I have spent the last fifteen years as a marketing consultant and in both conducting executive seminars and teaching MBA courses at universities around the world. In doing so, I have talked with, and spent time with, several thousand working managers. I have learned a great deal about what executives and managers between the ages of twenty-five and sixty know and, more importantly, what they do not know. This guide has been developed based upon that knowledge. There are eight major areas where many working managers of all ages and experience frequently need the help that this guide provides.

Understanding What Makes Businesses Successful

First, many working managers do not truly understand how business in free markets works, the importance of growth, the part costs play in strategy, how markets grow and develop and change over time, or how an individual business develops a long term strategy to capitalize on this knowledge. While quite a few managers now understand the importance of market share in determining profitability, few understand that product/service quality offers a similar competitive advantage. The fact is that only a few companies can have large market shares, but quality is a competitive weapon available to every company. Sections One, Two and Three are constructed to provide this overall view of business, costs and competition in free markets at the end of the 20th Century. These three sections are the integrated course that every MBA program should include and that almost none actually do.

A Clear View of the World

Second, many managers have difficulty really seeing their own company, and its competitors, in an impartial, objective manner. Too often they view their companies as something unique and existing apart from everything else. In particular, many working managers struggle with specifics when it comes to how the external environment, including competitors, affects their own business and its profitability. Sections Four, Five, Six and Seven are specifically designed to help managers understand their own company and their competitors, objectively; how they all combine to constitute an industry and how that industry reacts with the everchanging economic, demographic, technical, political and ecological environments.

Badly Needed: A Sense of Direction

Third, when managers have truly mastered the material described above, the question always becomes, "Okay, what do we do now?" And the answer is to develop a mission statement, a sense of purpose, a defined direction. Getting that answer is incredibly difficult and it is the true art of management. An enormous amount of unhelpful material has been written about mission statements, which probably is why so many mission statements are exactly that, unhelpful. No author can actually show a manager how to write a mission statement; nevertheless it is possible to provide many examples, good and bad, from companies operating manufacturing and service businesses, big businesses and small businesses, from all around the world. The one thing I have learned with absolute certainty is that working managers like examples, lots and lots of examples. This book accommodates in Section Eight. But if a mission statement is going to be useful, it must be put into practice. It has to become the guts of the operations, and that is really hard to do.

The Customer Really Is King

Fourth, while this is changing now (at last!), I am simply amazed how many smart, successful working managers do not truly understand the importance of customers in their businesses. And why is this? Because they don't know much about their customers, so they cannot deal with them in an effective manner. Section Nine contains a number of suggestions about how to develop a much better understanding of your customers. However, the primary method of learning about them is still marketing research. On this point, large companies with large market research budgets have a distinct advantage over smaller companies. Section Nine evens things out by providing a detailed description of the marketing research process and how to manage it. In addition, this section includes examples of two actual marketing research projects designed to understand customer behavior.

How to Create Real Value with Your Marketing Budgets

Fifth, the sales force, advertising and sales promotion comprise the largest part of any company's marketing budget; how to manage these specific activities is not well understood by many managers and, therefore, much of the marketing budget is wasted. In addition, there are many rapidly changing factors in the way all three marketing activities are performed. Sections Ten and Eleven outline these changes and explain in great detail how to remove as much waste as possible and make these activities significantly more efficient. In addition, Section Ten describes forecasting methods that any company can use effectively, quickly and inexpensively, that produce results as good as those from the largest, most sophisticated computer forecasting systems.

You Must Understand that all Competition Is Now Global

Sixth, a topic sure to strike terror into the hearts of many managers is international business. The unknowns just seem to be overwhelming. But the effects of international business are inescapable for every manager of every business of every size. Therefore, Section Twelve deals with the topic head-on. After a very brief history of international trade to show why it is important, the section explains in considerable detail how to get more information and assistance with your international business on the premise that the more you know, the less you fear. Most of the important points about how international business differs from your domestic business are discussed. For example, in international business trade shows and exhibits are extremely important marketing and business tools. Accordingly, an extensive discussion of how to use them is presented. Finally, a self-administered questionnaire allows the reader to evaluate his/her readiness for international business, in order to identify the potential problems in advance.

The Future Is Here Now and You Must be Ready for It

Seventh is the revolution! There is no other way to describe it. There is an absolute revolution going on in the way we make things, store things, ship things and sell things (and it applies to services as well). Some managers have glimpsed a part of the revolution, but very few really grasp its overall significance. Section Thirteen describes the revolution and attempts both to show how the parts all fit together and to suggest what every manager should be doing about it. Of particular importance is electronic communication (the Internet) that permits the smallest company to compete on absolutely even terms with the largest company.

Avoid Paralysis by Analysis: Develop Your Own Strategic Marketing Planning System

Last, all of the data and analysis and thinking and questioning that have been done by the reader in the preceding thirteen Sections must come to some kind of closure, and decisions need to be made. Those decisions are the real strategy and plan, but they must be communicated to a lot of other people who are going to be responsible for their execution. That is the role of the plans book. Every company must create a plans book format that is suitable for its own needs. No author can come close to doing that, but provided in Section Fourteen are four examples of how actual companies have done that job. The companies—one large, one small, and two mid-sized—are in manufacturing and in services.

HOW TO USE THIS BOOK

Three Specific Features

There are three other things that I have learned about what is of special importance to working managers; each has been incorporated in this book. One is that managers all want some way to connect the reading material with their own situation. This guide uses Marketing Planning Pages to accomplish that task. Each manager is given lots of space to write down his/her own particular activities. Where appropriate, Marketing Planning Pages for four Brands, Markets, Industries, etc. have been provided so that an important detail is not lost by summarizing. If more Marketing Planning Pages are needed, it is easy to make copies.

Second, I have learned that working managers place a high premium on instructions about where to find more material on a particular subject of greater interest. At every point in this guide where space limits discussion, direction is provided to one or more additional sources of information on the topic.

The third thing is that working managers love examples, lots of them! The rationale is pretty straightforward: "Okay, I've got this idea. Now how can I use it. Oh, here is how someone else used it. That's interesting but it doesn't quite fit my situation so let's look at another example, and another, and another." This guide provides many examples of how other managers have dealt with similar situations.

How to Get the Most Out of This Book and Its Features

The first thing to be clear about is that this is not a book to be read and then put on your bookshelf. It is intended to be a working tool for working managers just like your telephone, your Week-At-A-Glance or FiloFax, or your computer.

Begin by reading through the book quickly to get an overview of the whole project that you are beginning. Also, become aware that the material in some Sections is directly related to that in other Sections. Then get a three-ring binder (that is how I like to work, but any organizing device will do) that will become the focus of your work. Go back to the beginning of the guide and re-read more carefully. Whenever a relevant idea occurs to you, make an entry in your binder. As you encounter each Marketing Planning Page, tear it out and put it in the binder. Your objective is to transform this book into a set of notes and Marketing Planning Pages that are specific to your business and to your situation. This will become the basis for your formal written Marketing Plans Book.

Even if you never get to a formal written plan (you should, however, because that is the best way to communicate your thinking), the material in the binder represents your organized thinking about how to develop the best marketing strategy for your business. And the thinking is the *most important part* of the marketing strategy and planning process! The formal written Marketing Plans Book is simply a mirror of that thinking.

Be sure to complete each Marketing Planning Page as you come to it. Do not set aside a particularly demanding or difficult Section to do later. The organization of the material in this book is derived from many years of experience as a working manager doing this job, as a consultant helping other managers do this job, and as an instructor explaining how to do the work. My observation is that doing the work in a particular order is important. What seems to happen is that successful completion of one step of the job frequently leads to important insights into the work that comes later.

FINAL THOUGHTS

You will know that you are 50% of the way to having a successful strategic marketing plan when this guide is in the wastebasket and you have a binder filled with notes, completed Marketing Planning Pages, spreadsheets with pro forma P & L's, etc. The other 50% comes from executing your strategy and your plans, and then revising the whole thing as the future with all of its inevitable surprises unfolds for you.

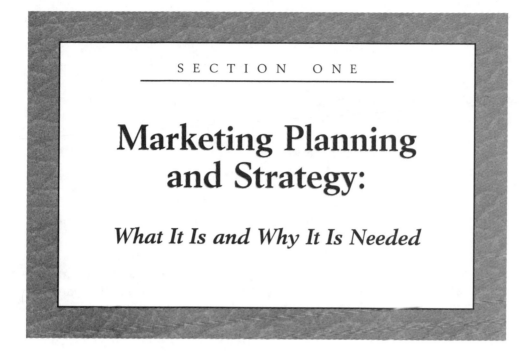

Marketing Planning and Strategy:

What It Is and Why It Is Needed

OVERVIEW OF SECTION ONE: Effective marketing strategy and planning takes time and money, and most of all, hard work. Section One addresses the reasons for undertaking this work, and provides a few cautionary tales about what may happen without planning and strategy. Since costs are always the most basic driver, Section One examines in considerable detail how costs affect strategy.

WHY DO MARKETING PLANNING?

This is an important question and should be dealt with up front. There are two useful ways to examine this question. One is the pragmatic approach that looks at what we have learned about the factors that have driven business success during the past decade or so. That will be dealt with in Section Two. The second way is to examine briefly some individual companies that have succeeded and some that have not. It is quite likely that the most important lesson learned about business success during the 1980s has been the importance of marketing planning and strategy. Big companies like Procter & Gamble and General Foods in consumer products, Motorola and Emerson Electric in industrial products, BancOne and Berkshire Hathaway in financial services showed the world how they used marketing planning and strategy to grow and profit in economic expansions and in economic recessions. You will find it very instructive to examine the annual reports of these companies over the past ten years or so. They have used well thought out marketing planning to grow their businesses profitably both in times of high inflation and stable prices. Many other less well known companies are also using superb business planning skills to re-invent themselves in order to remain competitive in the changing world of the 1990s.

However, there are some dramatic lessons that can come from studying companies that, for one reason or another, failed to develop marketing plans to guide them through the 1980s. Here are five examples of companies, large and small, from around the world that can teach you much about the importance of marketing planning. All of them were healthy, profitable companies at the beginning of the 1980s, but none of them fit that description at decade's end.

Let's begin overseas with Freddie Laker's Laker International Airlines. As the 1980s began, Laker's SkyTrain of Boeing 747's was chock full of people flying from New York to London for $99, and Laker International Airlines was on its way to becoming a multi-billion dollar business. Laker himself was so successful that he even became Sir Freddie along the way. However, Sir Freddie never had time to do any serious marketing planning. Whatever plans he had, he carried in his head; he gave whatever direction that plan required primarily by doing deals, many of which were worked out on the backs of envelopes and other scraps of paper. It was widely reported that Sir Freddie's top managers would gather together every night and search through the waste paper in his office looking for clues about the direction of the company.

Before the 1980s were half over, Sir Freddie had done so many deals in so many different directions that he was over-extended with his bankers and poorly positioned with his customers. Bankruptcy quickly followed and the Sky Train is gone.

Richardson-Merrill was a pharmaceutical and over-the-counter drug company as the decade of the 80s began. Its top management believed that its industry was too volatile to bother with marketing planning. As a result, it ran the company with a one-page annual pro forma Profit & Loss Statement!

Every single development in the pharmaceutical and OTC market during the 1980s caught Richardson-Merrill by surprise. As a result, almost all of its reactions were unplanned. By the middle of the 1980s, Richardson-Merrill was in so much financial distress that it was acquired in a hostile takeover, broken into parts, and the parts were auctioned off to the highest bidder. Richardson-Merrill is now simply gone.

In 1983, Moray Industries Ltd. was a $3 million company headquartered in Auckland, New Zealand. Moray fabricated and marketed a wide variety of items made of foam rubber designed to keep the wearer warm in and around water. They made "wet suits" for scuba diving, surfing, sailing and wind surfing, and the company was named after the aggressive eels that populate New Zealand seas.

The company was twenty-five years old and held a very large share of the New Zealand market. Unfortunately, New Zealand is a very small market. A decade earlier, Moray management understood that to grow to any reasonable size, it also had to have operations in Australia. The company proceeded to set up an Australian operation that was, in fact, by 1983 reasonably successful. But Moray management decided in 1983 that the real growth opportunities for its company were to be found in the huge U. S. market. Accordingly, they hired an experienced surfer (Graeme) and an experienced diver (Geoff), both with manufacturing experience, and sent them to Southern California to start Moray USA. After a year of losses in the U. S. and disorganization, New Zealand management hired a consultant to help the expatriate managers develop a marketing plan and strategy.

The consultant, the New Zealand management and the U. S. managers developed a very specific marketing plan that focused the company's limited resources on the best potential markets, surfing suits in Southern California and diving suits in Florida. The problem was that instead of making sales calls on dive shops in Florida, Graeme would go to Seattle because "someone up there telephoned with a question," and instead of making sales calls on surf shops in Southern California, Geoff would take off for Hawaii because "there was a terrific surfing contest going on there."

The real problem is that the American-based managers didn't want to have a marketing plan or strategy because it would interfere with what they really wanted to do. At the end of three years, Moray had lost something over a half million dollars on its U.S. operations, a staggering sum for a company of that size.

New Zealand managers finally closed down the U.S. effort, but by then it was too late. The company was taken over by an outside director and now operates in the New Zealand market as a much smaller Moray Industries Ltd.

In 1980, Knudsen, Inc. was a $400 million dairy and food products company headquartered in Los Angeles. The CEO used to say that the dairy business was too stable to bother with marketing planning. He felt that there were so many government regulations that there was little of substance that management could do to control the direction and fate of the company. He said marketing planning required a lot of time and money, and that it would never pay out. The marketing plan he carried around in his head was to buy a lot of other dairy companies that also operated in the same stable, uneventful environment. Accordingly, he managed Knudsen with a one-page annual pro forma Profit & Loss statement. (Does that sound familiar?)

Stable environment or not, by the mid 1980s Knudsen had acquired so many other dairy-based businesses, and acquired so much debt in doing it, that its bankers closed down the whole business in a devastating bankruptcy. All that is left of Knudsen today is the brand name on a few dairy products now manufactured by Kraft Foods.

In 1980, Quality Systems, Inc. was a Tustin, California-based software company with sales around $6 million. The company was three years old and very sharply focused on just two market segments, dental practices and bowling alleys. For these two target markets, Quality Systems produced turn-key computer operating systems.

The company had 60% gross margins and was privately owned. The owner/manager used to say that he knew he should have a marketing plan, but the business was growing so fast that there just wasn't time to develop one. He managed Quality Systems with a one page *quarterly* pro forma Profit & Loss statement!

Now that the 1990s are here, the owner/manager is still very busy. However, he is no longer concerned with rapid growth. These days he spends his time trying to recover from Chapter 11 bankruptcy.

So the major lesson from the 1980s for business people in the 1990s is that there are many, many reasons not to bother with marketing planning. And every one of them is a bad idea!

WHY DO MARKETING PLANNING?—TAKE TWO

There are five very fundamental factors why marketing planning is absolutely crucial for long term business success. If you haven't covered all five of these points in your business, then the only thing you have on your side is luck. In case you have forgotten, luck is a fickle partner and, sooner or later, abandons everyone.

Factor One—Tomorrow's Business is Different

Every manager has two sets of responsibilities. One involves managing TODAY'S business. The other involves managing TOMORROW'S business. There is a very large difference between TODAY'S business and TOMOR-ROW'S business. TODAY'S business depends exclusively on decisions that were made at some time in the *past*. TOMORROW'S business will depend almost exclusively on decisions that are being made today (or not made). As a result, TODAY'S business cannot be changed in any meaningful way. TODAY'S customers, competitors, products and services, plants, distribution channels, employees, etc. are all in place right now. But TOMORROW'S customers, competitors, products and services, plants, distribution channels, employees, etc. can be anything and anyone that the managers choose!

And that is the important point! TOMORROW'S business can be anything the managers choose. The chairman at Knudsen apparently never understood that he had a choice, and he never examined the alternatives available to Knudsen. The results were extremely unfortunate for both the employees and stockholders of the company.

Factor Two—Managing Tomorrow's Business is Different

Every manager accomplishes his or her responsibilities by allocating two scarce resources, time and money. Managers make decisions about how to spend the company's money and the time of its people. Every good manager makes decisions by conducting a series of small experiments to see what happens when a decision is made. The process goes like this:

Fully implement the decision

Identify a problem/opportunity

Gather important information

Analyze the information

Decide on some action (including no action)

Test the decision on a small scale

Get feedback about the results

Analyze the results

This decision-making process is widely used and it is usually effective. Here is how Procter & Gamble uses this process to manage its day-to-day business by making it official company policy.

However, this decision-making process is possible *only* because the variables involved in managing TODAY'S business are well-known and in place. (See Factor One on page 5.)

The decision-making process about TOMORROW'S business *must be* different from the process used with TODAY'S business because TOMORROW'S variables are not known. But much more important, the feedback about TOMORROW'S decisions is years and years away. The point here is that good managers make decisions about TODAY'S business by conducting small experiments. Good managers get to be very good at this process. Unfortunately, this decision-making process is completely inappropriate for decisions about TOMORROW'S business for which a completely different decision-making process is required, and the best choice is marketing planning. This is a fact that completely escaped the managers at Richardson-Merrill, much to their cost.

Factor Three—Speed of Change

The ONLY constant in life is CHANGE. Everything is always, and must be, changing. Understanding this inviolate fact is essential to understanding the need for marketing planning and strategy. Here is a small exercise that may demonstrate that point to you personally. In the space provided below, please:

WRITE DOWN THE NAMES OF THE FIVE PRODUCTS WHICH WILL BE MOST PROFITABLE FOR YOUR BUSINESS FIVE YEARS FROM NOW. (Use either total dollars or margins.)

1)_____

2)_____

3)_____

4)_____

5)_____

Exhibit 1-1

PROCTER & GAMBLE'S STATEMENT OF BUSINESS PRINCIPLES

1. *Plan all action in advance*—Always forecast business in relation to expenditure, always check that the business is reacting according to forecast, and always be ready to adjust plans as necessary.

2. *Base all actions on facts*—One fact is worth many judgments. Strive always to find the factual truth on a subject before acting. This applies to all fields of business: product, packaging, advertising, promotions, and expenditures.

3. *Always know the objective of your actions*—Know what advertising, individual promotions, and sales plans are intended to do and judge their success by whether they achieve objectives.

4. *Sell a better product*—Even if it costs more. It is not necessary to compete on price; we compete on product quality and marketing skill.

5. *Make a reasonable profit*—Profit related to field in which operating.

6. *Spend advertising and promotion money to build business*—If necessary, forego profit temporarily to build business, but only if adequate profit is assured when business is built.

7. *Spend big money only against proved techniques*—Never spend big monies (and hence potential profit) on large scale unless efficacy has been tested in small scale first.

8. *Spend some money to test possible improvements*—Unless new plans and techniques are tested now, future broad-scale progress is impossible.

9. *Wherever possible, limit our activities to those in which we are specialists*—We are product performance specialists and marketing specialists. We try to stick to those activities and do as little else as possible. (Let the firms who specialize in other activities perform them for us.)

10. *Generate competition between our own brands*—Only in this way can we properly meet the competition from other brands of other companies.

WRITE DOWN THE NAMES OF YOUR FIVE BIGGEST CUSTOMERS
FIVE YEARS FROM NOW.

1)_____

2)_____

3)_____

4)_____

5)_____

WRITE DOWN THE NAMES OF YOUR FIVE BIGGEST COMPETI-
TORS FIVE YEARS FROM NOW.

1)_____

2)_____

3)_____

4)_____

5)_____

HOW CONFIDENT ARE YOU THAT YOU HAVE ALL OF THIS
INFORMATION CORRECT? _____ (0 to 100%)

What this exercise asks you to do is to describe the absolute core of your
business just five years into the future. Five years is not a very long time at all
in the world of business. What were you doing five years ago? Does that seem
very long ago? No, probably not.

Now look at the level of confidence you expressed in your view of the
future core of your business. If you wrote down 90% or better, you might wish
to consider the following three facts about the speed of change.

Fact One: The first semi-conductor, and its properties, was discovered by
scientists at Bell Laboratories, in New Jersey, in 1965 and they began publishing their findings. It took seven more years before the first commercial applications appeared, and that was only in a relatively simple hearing aid. It took a
full decade for the properties of semi-conductors to become widely known.

Fact Two: The properties of the first "warm" conductors were discovered in Zurich in January, 1986. The first scientific article was submitted in April, 1986 and soon published. By December, 1986, the Swiss results had been confirmed by scientists in New Jersey, Texas, and Tokyo. In March, 1987, the first scientific conference was held at the Hilton Hotel in New York, and it lasted for three days and went all night, every night. It took fourteen months for the properties of warm conductors to become widely known.

Fact Three: On March 23, 1989, two scientists held a press conference in Salt Lake City, Utah to announce their results with cold fusion. By midnight of that same day, experiments were being conducted in ten other countries to validate their findings! Fourteen hours!

Factor Four—Too Many Variables

The variables that could affect TOMORROW'S business are literally limitless until some commitment has been made about what TOMORROW'S business will be. A serious management problem arises whenever managers who are good at managing TODAY'S business are confronted with too many variables. They invariably put off dealing with TOMORROW'S business and devote all of their energies to dealing with TODAY'S business. There is nothing malicious or mysterious about such behavior. Managers simply want to work in areas where they are comfortable using familiar tools that have proven their effectiveness before.

Marketing planning reduces the number of variables confronting managers by forcing them to make decisions about the future and, in doing so, eliminating most of the variables and the uncertainty surrounding them. Marketing planning, well done, requires a commitment from managers to the goals for TOMORROW'S business and thereby greatly increases their comfort level in dealing with new areas and new tools.

Remember, it is not enough to simply have a marketing plan. Managers must want to accomplish the goals in the plan That requires two things. One is to involve the appropriate manager in the development of the plans and strategy so that he or she can develop an "ownership" position in the marketing plans and their execution. The other thing to do is to tie managers' compensation to meeting the goals specified in the marketing plan. Because Moray's top management was unwilling to tie Graeme and Geoff's compensation to accomplishing the plan's goals, the two employees spent their time and efforts increasing their own levels of comfort instead of building a new business in the United States.

Factor Five—Communication

You now understand that a new decision-making process is required for dealing with TOMORROW'S BUSINESS, that a huge amount of new business variables must be dealt with, and that while this is happening, the world around you is changing at a breathtaking pace. One CEO nicely summed it up when he said, "We've got thirty-six different plants and businesses and it is hard enough to get them moving in any direction, let alone all moving in the right direction."

His point is well taken. However, the problem doesn't end there. Everyone in the organization must know clearly what that direction is if they are to make the maximum contribution. The *process* of marketing planning— that is, the work involved in examining where the company is, how it got there, who the competitors are, what is happening in the environment outside of the company, and a myriad of factors that can affect the future health of the company—and then making decisions about allocating the company's resources are both extremely valuable in managing the company. But the written marketing plans themselves are important because they are the device that *communicates* the direction for the business, and the reasons why, to the entire organization, and does it with a single voice. Marketing plans are the essential ingredient in ensuring that all key employees understand the goals of the business and how they are to be accomplished.

If you have the slightest doubt about the importance of communication inside your business, think about Freddie Laker for just a minute. How much would get done in your business if all of your managers had to sift through your wastepaper basket every night to figure out what they should do the next day?

WHY DEVELOP MARKETING STRATEGY?

The central fact of life that drives *every* marketing plan is a marketing strategy. The rest of this section is intended to demonstrate exactly why this is true, and why it is absolutely unavoidable.

Albert J. Crosson, the long-time CEO of Hunt-Wesson Foods, Fullerton, California, frequently points out that there are three all-important measurements in marketing planning: market share, sales volume and costs. But his real insight comes when he says, "I can sometimes control my market share, and I can usually control my sales volume, but I can *always* control my costs."

And it is with costs that we must begin because every business must control its own costs *and* because costs drive the marketing strategy of every business.

The first thing to know about costs is that they come in three types. One type is *fixed costs*, those that do not change in the short term when volume changes. The money you spend to build a plant is a fixed cost. The cost is the same (basically) if the plant is standing empty or if it is running at full capacity. By way of contrast, *variable costs* are completely sensitive to volume changes in the short term. The cost of materials that go into the products you make is a variable cost.

The third type is *semi-variable costs*. These have components of both fixed and variable costs. For example, your telephone bill has a component that reflects the cost of simply having the telephone and does not change with how much you use it, i.e., a fixed cost. But it also contains charges for each telephone call you have made. If you make a lot of calls, you have a lot charges, but if you make few calls, you have few charges, i.e., a variable cost.

Cost Structures Are the First Level of Strategy Drivers

Businesses with high *fixed costs* are volume-driven. That means that if your business has high fixed costs, your greatest leverage toward profitability is to drive up sales volume. By way of contrast, businesses with high *variable costs* are cost-driven. These businesses have the greatest leverage toward profitability in driving down costs. The simple example below makes this important point:

| | A HIGH FIXED COST BUSINESS | | A HIGH VARIABLE COST BUSINESS | |
	Now	*Future*	*Now*	*Future*
Revenues	$100	$200	$100	$200
Variable costs	20	40	60	120
Fixed costs	60	60	20	20
Profit	$ 20	$100	$ 20	$ 60

In this example, it is clear that the high fixed cost business benefits much more from increased volume than does the high variable cost business. But if the high variable cost business could focus on reducing costs, these results would appear:

	A HIGH FIXED COST BUSINESS		A HIGH VARIABLE COST BUSINESS	
	Now	*Future*	*Now*	*Future*
Revenues	$100	$200	$100	$200
Variable Costs	20	40	60	90
Fixed Costs	60	60	20	10
Profit	$20	$100	$20	$100

UNDERSTANDING THE BREAK-EVEN POINT IS VERY IMPORTANT Marketing strategies based solely on costs are usually too simplistic. To understand why, it is necessary to explore the idea of the break-even point which is that level of sales volume that produces neither profits nor losses. It is the point that is revenue-neutral. Break-even is calculated with this simple formula:

$$\text{Break-Even Point} = \frac{\text{Fixed Costs}}{\text{Unit Price} - \text{Unit Variable Costs}}$$

For example: suppose we have a plant lease that costs $100,000 a month, our unit selling price is $10 and our unit variable costs are $4. That would produce this break-even point:

$$\text{Break-even point} = \frac{\$100,000}{\$10 - \$4} = \frac{\$100,000}{\$6} = 16,666.67 \text{ units}$$

To prove this calculation, simply reverse the process.

Revenue:	*16,666.67 units @ $10 each*	*= $166,667*
Variable Costs	*16,666.67 units @ $ 4 each*	*= $ 66,667*
Fixed Costs		*= 100,000*
Total Costs		*= $166,667*

The important thing about break-even is what happens next when the break-even point is reached and exceeded. That is called the *Contribution Margin.* Here is what happens with our example above at break-even and then beyond.

At break-even:	*Sales price per unit*	*$10*
	Variable costs	*4*
	Fixed costs	*6*
	Margin	*$ 0*
Beyond break-even:	*Sales price per unit*	*$10*
	Variable costs	*4*
	Fixed costs	*0*
	Contribution margin	*$ 6*

The next refinement in marketing strategy development comes from understanding the relationship between *fixed costs* and *contribution margin.* All businesses are defined by their interaction. Obviously, there are four basic possible combinations of fixed costs and contribution margin.

HIGH FIXED COSTS AND HIGH CONTRIBUTION MARGIN The aerospace industry is an excellent example of this combination. The development costs that are required to get the first Boeing 757 are staggering, but when Boeing reaches the break-even point, the per unit profits from the contribution are also staggering. But this is not just a huge company combination. It is exactly the situation facing every software developer from giant Microsoft to tiny Berkeley Systems. The amount of time and money required to write and de-bug new computer programs is very large, but once that is accomplished, software companies sell a few dollars worth of plastic disk and printed manual for $100, $200, $300, or more.

The strategy indicated in this situation is two-fold. First, it should be to drive up volume because the per-unit profits when break-even is reached are so attractive. The second strategy is to drive down costs because that helps you reach break-even faster.

HIGH FIXED COSTS AND LOW CONTRIBUTION MARGIN The chemical industry is one example of this combination. The economies of scale are very great in that business and that, in turn, encourages large investments in large plants. Monsanto, Inc., one of the most profitable of the chemical companies, earns a Return On Sales of a miserly 2+%.

The supermarket industry is another good example of high fixed costs and low contribution margins. When a supermarket opens its doors for business, 90% of its costs are already in place. That is why the industry averages 1.5% Return On Sales in good years and 0.5%, or less, in bad years.

Clearly, the indicated strategy here is to drive up volume. There are two reasons for this. One is that the business *absolutely must* have enough volume to cover its high costs. Otherwise, it is bankrupt. The second reason is that driving costs down doesn't have much leverage. The exception would be when there is some sort of major break-through in reducing costs. That is what has happened in the office supplies business with the advent of super stores like Staples and Office Depot.

A great example of these forces at work can be seen in the Southern California supermarket business. When the 1980s began, there were fifteen significant supermarket chains in the area, but by the end of 1995, there were only four. Here is just one reason: a full page ad in the *Los Angeles Times* on Thursday (best food day) costs about $22,000 whether you have fifty stores, one hundred stores or two hundred stores.

LOW FIXED COSTS AND HIGH CONTRIBUTION MARGIN Professional businesses such as legal practices, accountancies, architectural firms, medical and dental practices are some good examples of this combination. (Gaining the qualifications to conduct a professional business are a personal cost just like getting a college degree to qualify for a job in a chemical company.) Starting a professional business requires a down payment on a lease and some furniture. Obviously, the strategy indicated here is to drive up volume. Incremental volume is extremely profitable in a well-run professional business. On the other hand, costs are already so low that much attention there just doesn't offer much chance of a big payout. Notice that this is a different reason for a lack of leverage in cost reduction than is true for high fixed cost and low contribution margin businesses.

LOW FIXED COSTS AND LOW CONTRIBUTION MARGIN This unattractive business situation is the one faced by many small retailers. You can open a women's dress shop, for example, with a down payment on a store lease, some fixtures bought on credit and some inventory secured on consignment. Although you can keep your costs low, Target, Ross, Mervyn's, K-Mart and other large scale stores all work to ensure that you will have low prices to compete with and, hence, low contribution margins.

The only strategy alternative here is to drive up volume in any way you can. That is why you see small retailers running virtually non-stop sales events.

WHY DEVELOP MARKETING STRATEGY—TAKE TWO

We have now examined how costs drive strategy for virtually all businesses and we have looked at the reasons why. In every instance, the primary strategy indicated was to drive up volume! That means increasing sales and that is what marketing is all about.

This is why businesses must grow or die. There is no standing still for any businesses. If your business is not growing, it is dying. It is as simple as that.

And that is why marketing planning and strategy is crucial for business success. Marketing planning and strategy is how you grow your business.

FINAL THOUGHTS

If it would help to have a very clear, very simple explanation of why every successful growing business must have a marketing plan and a marketing strategy, you could do no better than to recall this exchange from *Alice in Wonderland*.

> *"Would you tell me, please, which way I ought to go from here?" said Alice.*
>
> *"That depends a good deal on where you want to get to," said the Cat.*
>
> *"I don't much care where . . . ," said Alice.*
>
> *"Then it doesn't matter which way you go," said the Cat.*

What We Know About What Makes Businesses Profitable

OVERVIEW OF SECTION TWO: An extraordinary amount of data about what makes businesses successful has been uncovered in the past twenty years. But very little of that vital information has been made available to working managers. Section Two remedies that problem. This section explains why market share was the primary competitive tool of the 1980s, why quality is the competitive tool of choice for the 1990s, and why customer value will be the most important competitive tool of 2000 and beyond.

IS MANAGEMENT AN "ART" OR A "SCIENCE"?

There are still some managers around who think that the "art of management" is exclusively that, an "art." They believe that success in business comes solely from long experience with an industry and having excellent business judgment. (The more thoughtful of these managers will also give some credit to luck.) The idea that business success actually has some general rules to follow would be anathema to most of them.

16

Most such managers are really counting on luck for their success. But the best managers of the 1990s understand that the work of the PIMS (for the *Profit Impact of Marketing Strategy*) has demonstrated that there truly are general rules that differentiate successful businesses from unsuccessful businesses, and that the "art" of management is really the skillful application and implementation of those rules. The PIMS project can be traced directly back to General Electric's attempts to understand the differences between their successful and unsuccessful divisions. In the 1970s, the project was moved to the Harvard Business School and the scope of the project was widened to include non-General Electric businesses. The current PIMS project is a database of the performance of over 3,000 different businesses from every corner of the industrial world that extends back as far as twenty years, and is headquartered at the non-profit Strategic Planning Institute, 1030 Massachusetts Avenue, Cambridge, Massachusetts 02138.

For a detailed account of the PIMS project, it is well worth reading *The PIMS Principles* by Robert D. Buzzell and Bradley T. Gale (New York: The Free Press, 1987). (ISBN 0-02-904430-8)

The main results of the work that has been done on the PIMS database are the discovery and testing of eight fundamental rules of successful business strategy. Understanding these has to be the basis for all successful marketing strategy and planning. They are as follows:

1. Business situations behave in a *regular* and *predictable* manner. What this means is that managers do not have to rely solely on experience and luck in developing successful marketing strategies and plans. It is possible to decide on the elements of a good plan in advance. You don't have to guess.

2. *All* business situations are basically alike in obeying the laws of the market place. That means that companies that make consumer products, industrial products, service companies and raw material suppliers are all governed by the same basic rules. Have you ever worked for the guy who said to you, "Kid, you gotta work in this business for thirty years before you understand it." Well, he was wrong.

3. The rules of the market place account for about 80% of the difference in profitability in similar appearing businesses. These general rules, or laws, truly are powerful in their impact on profitability.

4. There are nine primary factors that influence profitability. They are listed below in their order of importance. Each will be discussed in more detail later in this section. All the factors except Investment Intensity are positive, i.e., the more you have, the more likely you are to be profitable.

    Investment Intensity

    Productivity

    Market Share

    Market Growth Rate

    Product/Service Quality

    New Product Development/Differentiation From Competitors

    Vertical Integration

    Cost Push

    Current Effort on These Factors

5. The interaction between these factors is complex. For example, vertical integration tends to improve profitability in slow growing markets, but it depresses profits in rapidly growing markets. (For more discussion of the characteristics of slow growing and rapidly growing markets, see Section Three.)

6. Product or service characteristics don't matter. So the same rules apply to all products and services.

7. Strategic characteristics tend to assert themselves over time, and if the fundamentals are sound, the strategy will be successful. If the fundamentals are not sound, the strategy will fail. Two well-known companies make this point extremely clear. As the 1980s began, John F. Welch, Jr. helped General Electric Company devise an exceptionally strong and appropriate strategy. As a result, GE has continued to grow its sales and profits steadily for over fifteen years through recessions, expansions, wars, new competition and a few experiments that didn't quite work out. At about the same time, James D. Robinson, III, was devising a fundamentally flawed strategy for American Express Company. No amount of continual acquisitions, divestitures, changes in direction, re-organizations, replaced managers and excuses could keep AmEx from heading straight toward extinction. By 1993, even the AmEx board of directors had finally figured out that Robinson's strategy was fundamentally flawed and fired him.

By 1995, General Electric was recording sales in excess of $60 billion combined with record profits. On the other hand, American Express was desperately trying to survive with a market share of the consumer credit card market of a mere 16.3%, a far cry from its dominant position at the beginning of the 1980s.

8. The strategy signals are "robust." This is simply a scientific term that means the strategy signals are easy to detect. This will be demonstrated later in this section.

THE NINE PRIMARY STRATEGY FACTORS

The single most important factor impacting profitability is *Investment Intensity*. And it is the only negative factor, i.e., all other things being equal, the *more* money you have to invest in your business, the *less likely* you are to be profitable. What is very important to understand here is that this finding is exactly contrary to usual economic theory.

Conventional economic theory says that when you want to improve your profit levels you invest in a lot of new plants and equipment to lower your costs, i.e., to improve your profits, you increase your investment. However, what happens in the real world is exactly the opposite. Here is a typical scenario.

The management of the third or fourth largest company in an industry, say Company X, comes under pressure to improve its profits. Accordingly, the management follows conventional economic theory and invests in a brand new plant full of state-of-the-art machinery. Because the Engineering Department can always be counted on to promise the largest savings from building the largest possible plant, the largest affordable plant will get built. And, because the Finance Department can always be counted on to point out that money will never be cheaper than it is now, the big new plant will be built immediately.

Now the new plant is built and it is only operating at about 50% of capacity but producing about as much product as the old plant did. Unfortunately, the reduced costs promised by the Engineering Department were predicted on operating the plant at 90% of capacity. (It is not unusual for the new plant to operate with higher costs than the old plant.) When confronted with this problem, the management decides to increase sales sharply, immediately, and it tries to do so by cutting prices.

Since the largest companies in the industry, Y and Z, cannot afford to lose customers due to Company X's price cut, they immediately cut their prices to match X's new prices. Every other company in the industry follows suit. Now the whole industry is operating at a new, lower price level, but the total demand for the industry's output has not changed. Since Y and Z are now under considerable profit pressure, they also decide that they need to match X's state-of-the-art plant. Since they also have Engineering and Finance Departments, they also build the largest possible plants and they build them immediately.

Now the industry's capacity has increased enormously, but demand has not changed at all. That gives the industry's customers enormous leverage against their suppliers. At this point, the industry has made a very large investment in new plant and equipment, without gaining cost reductions, while price levels have fallen dramatically and there is no way to raise the prices. This is exactly how increased investment leads to reduced profits, just the opposite of economic theory predictions.

If you want to watch a real-time example of this phenomenon in action, watch the European automobile industry as the 20th century draws to a close. Almost every native European car manufacturer is investing heavily in new plants and equipment to "modernize" their plants and lower their costs. Ford and Chevrolet are rapidly expanding their European operations to get ready to fend off the new native competition. Chrysler, meanwhile, circles the outside, trying to figure out how to get back into the game. Finally, the major Japanese car manufacturers are all busily expanding their European operations so as not to be frozen out of the market by import restrictions.

So the capacity for manufacturing automobiles in Europe is expanding at breakneck speed, but no one expects the market to grow more than 2% annually, and some think that may be optimistic. Fiat, Peugeot and Volvo may not survive this application of conventional economic theory.

Productivity is the second most important factor influencing profitability. This is pretty easy to understand. If one company has annual sales of $500,000 per employee and another has annual sales of $2,000,000, it is not hard to guess which company is more likely to be profitable.

Market Share is the next most important factor. Here is dramatic evidence from the PIMS database:

Companies with Market Shares	Average Return on Investment
Under 7%	9.6%
7% to 14%	12.0%
14% to 22%	13.5%
22% to 36%	17.9%
Over 36%	30.2%

Please understand that having a big market share does not simply mean being a big business. If that was all that was involved, General Motors would be 100 times more profitable than it is. The concept here is to have a large share of a specific, defined market. Section Ten will explore the idea of how to define markets and measure market share.

The source of the higher profits generated from larger market shares is threefold. One source is *volume effects*. Large market shares can be translated into large purchases from outside vendors which, in turn, can produce volume discounts. Another source is *bargaining power*. If volume effects reflect the ability of a large market share company to control relationships "backward" with suppliers, bargaining power reflects the ability of a large market share company to control relationships "forward" with competitors and customers. For a real life example, go to your local supermarket and look at the prepared soup section. In the United States, Campbell Soup will give you a demonstration of bargaining power. In Europe, Knorr will provide the same lesson. The third source is the *experience curve*. There is a very large body of evidence that there is a specific, predictable downward relationship between costs and each doubling of production of a particular good or service.

For a more detailed discussion of experience curves, see *Developing Winning Strategic Plans*, 1995 by James W. Taylor (Alexander Hamilton Institute, Inc., 70 Hilltop Road, Ramsey, New Jersey). (ISBN 0-86604-256-3)

Market share is a good example of the robust nature of these strategy signals. In the beginning of the PIMS research it was thought necessary to construct an involved measure of "relative market share." Then it was discovered that the same relationships were revealed with straightforward percentage shares of markets. Now it is known that it is enough to simply know the ranking of the company in the market regardless of percentage share. At companies such as General Electric, 3M, and Lear Sieglar, this strategy factor has been translated into action by setting criteria that they will only engage in markets where they can be either the number one or number two company.

Market Growth Rate is the next most important factor. Simply, rapidly growing markets tend to be more profitable than slow growing markets. This idea, discussed in greater detail in Section Three, is that in rapidly growing markets, demand exceeds capacity, but in slow growing markets capacity exceeds demand. Thus producers have the greater power when demand exceeds supply and customers have the greater power when capacity exceeds demand.

Product and Service Quality is next in importance. The evidence is that high quality products and services generate higher profits than lower quality products and services. Here are the PIMS findings on the effects of quality:

Product Quality	Average Return on Investment	Average Net Profit
Low	13%	6%
Average	17%	8%
High	30%	14%

To make this point even more dramatic, here is the Average Return on Investment from the *lowest* quality producers and the *highest* quality producers, by type of industry, in the PIMS database.

Industry	Lowest Quality Average ROI	Highest Quality Average ROI
Consumer Durables	16%	32%
Consumer Non-Durables	15%	32%
Capital Goods	10%	21%
Raw Materials	13%	35%
Supplies	16%	36%

The basic driver that produces greater profits from high quality products and services is surprisingly simple. Customers will pay more for high quality products and services. The concept of quality is such an important competitive strategy that we will return to it in detail later in this section.

A concept embodied in the idea of *New Products and Differentiation* is the next most important factor in explaining differences in profitability. The basic driver here is that truly differentiated products do not have ready substitutes and therefore are at least partially insulated from the price pressures of the market. One way to get truly differentiated products and services is to develop and introduce successful new ones. That way competitors are always playing catch-up. No one plays this game better than 3M. In 1994, 30% of their $15 billion in sales was generated by products and services introduced in the *past four years!* (And its goal is 35%.) Think about what would have to happen in your company if 30% of your sales came from products and services introduced in the past four years; you will then begin to have some insight into the enormity of 3M's accomplishments.

Next factor in importance is *Vertical Integration*. The general idea here is that the more you control of the channel of distribution, from raw materials forward to the final customer, the more profitable you are likely to be. However, this is an example of the complexity of the interdependency of these strategic factors. Vertical integration will increase your profitability in a mature, slow growing market, but it can be expected to severely reduce your profits in a rapidly growing market.

Then comes *Cost Push*. This simply is your ability to pass your costs onto your customers. If one company gets a 10% increase in material costs and can raise its prices 10% it will most likely be more profitable than a company with a 10% increase in costs without that capability. This factor is so important to General Electric that it has made it one of its criteria for evaluating its interest in a market.

And finally, there is *Current Effort on the Eight Factors Above*. The interactions between these factors are complex but beyond our space in this book. However, two of these factors are at the heart of any marketing strategy and planning activity, and hence deserve a more detailed examination. They are market share and quality.

Market Share Drives Profitability

While market share drives profitability, gaining market share in mature markets (and, as Section Three explains, most markets are mature) is a very slow process. Analysis of the PIMS database indicates that market share gains (and losses) are multi-year events. When actions are in place that lead to increases (or to decreases) in market share, the increases (or decreases) tend to continue for up to four years.

Gaining market share is also an expensive activity in mature markets. The five usual ways to do this are new products, improved quality levels, more salespeople, more advertising and/or more sales promotion. Researchers have examined the PIMS database to determine the effects of increased levels of investment in these market share gaining strategies. To accomplish this, they first searched for businesses that had made substantial increased investments in one, or more, of these share building activities. Then they divided the businesses by industry because the different marketing activities have different levels of effectiveness by industry. The table below shows the rate of change in market share (not share point changes!) in businesses that have made large investments in one, or more, of these share building activities.

RATE OF CHANGE IN MARKET SHARE

Market Share Building Activities	Consumer Products Businesses	Raw Materials Businesses	Industrial Products Businesses
New Products	+2.8%	+2.7%	+2.9%
Product Quality	+4.0%	+2.1%	+4.3%
Sales Force	+6.6%	+1.3%	+6.4%
Advertising	+3.0%	+1.4%	+3.2%
Sales Promotion	+3.7%	+1.9%	+4.2%

In spite of these limitations, gaining market share must be a consideration in the development of any marketing strategy and plan. Marketing Planning pages 2-1 through 2-4 on pages 26–29 are designed to help you organize your ideas about gaining market share, market by market. But before you do that, it may be worth looking at some major points made by Mark J. Chussil, Manager of Strategy Development for Sequent Computer Systems.

MARKET SHARE DO'S AND DON'TS

- Prepare a very specific list of the advantages that you expect to gain from growing your market share. Do not simply assume that a bigger market share will automatically improve your business. And be sure that you have considered and factored in the probable response of your competitors. If you are in a mature market, your competitors are not likely to give up business to you without a struggle.

- Prepare a very specific estimate of the costs of gaining the market share. Do not simply assume that a bigger market share wil be more profitable. Managers frequently want to believe that an increased market share will automatically solve their profit plan problems.

- Prepare a very specific plan covering what you will do with your new market share (assuming you can get it). Will this change out manufacturing position? Our raw materials position? Can we gain distribution? Will we be able to negotiate better media discounts? Will we need to increase our sales force? Our customer service? Have a plan to leverage the gains from your new market share position.

- Measure and monitor your market share just as closely as you do financial performance. Make sure that market share is a part of your marketing planning and strategy process. Develop market share forecast just like you make your financial forecasts. And remember that changes in sales levels are not changes in market share. Make very sure that you have defined your markets correctly so that you are measuring your share of the "right" market.

- And finally, remember Procter & Gamble's Statement of Business Principles, Point #7. (Exhibit 1-1 on page 7.) Never start spending on a major market share improvement project unless it has been thoroughly tested and proven on a small scale.

Marketing Planning Page 2-1

MARKET ONE—MARKET SHARE STRATEGY

Market One Definition: _____

_____

_____

Competitors Ranked by Market Share   *Estimated Share*

No. 1:_____   _____

No. 2:_____   _____

No. 3:_____   _____

No. 4:_____   _____

No. 5:_____   _____

No. 6:_____   _____

No. 7:_____   _____

What would you have to do to move your position up one place in this market?

_____

_____

_____

Approximately, how much would it cost to move your position up one place?

_____

Approximately, how long would it take to move your position up one place?

_____

Which specific benefits would you receive from moving your position up one place?

No. 1 benefit: _____   Profit value: $____

No. 2 benefit: _____   Profit value: $____

Marketing Planning Page 2-2

MARKET TWO—MARKET SHARE STRATEGY

Market Two Definition: _____

_____

_____

Competitors Ranked by Market Share	*Estimated Share*
No. 1:_____	_____
No. 2:_____	_____
No. 3:_____	_____
No. 4:_____	_____
No. 5:_____	_____
No. 6:_____	_____
No. 7:_____	_____

What would you have to do to move your position up one place in this market?

_____

_____

_____

Approximately, how much would it cost to move your position up one place?

_____

Approximately, how long would it take to move your position up one place?

_____

Which specific benefits would you receive from moving your position up one place?

No. 1 benefit: _____   Profit value: $____

No. 2 benefit: _____   Profit value: $____

Marketing Planning Sheet 2-3

MARKET THREE—MARKET SHARE STRATEGY

Market Three Definition: _____

_____

_____

Competitors Ranked by Market Share   *Estimated Share*

No. 1:_____   _____

No. 2:_____   _____

No. 3:_____   _____

No. 4:_____   _____

No. 5:_____   _____

No. 6:_____   _____

No. 7:_____   _____

What would you have to do to move your position up one place in this market?

_____

_____

_____

Approximately, how much would it cost to move your position up one place?

_____

Approximately, how long would it take to move your position up one place?

_____

Which specific benefits would you receive from moving your position up one place?

No. 1 benefit: _____   Profit value: $____

No. 2 benefit: _____   Profit value: $____

Marketing Planning Page 2-4

MARKET FOUR—MARKET SHARE STRATEGY

Market Four Definition:_____

_____

_____

Competitors Ranked by Market Share	*Estimated Share*
No. 1:_____	_____
No. 2:_____	_____
No. 3:_____	_____
No. 4:_____	_____
No. 5:_____	_____
No. 6:_____	_____
No. 7:_____	_____

What would you have to do to move your position up one place in this market?

_____

_____

_____

Approximately, how much would it cost to move your position up one place?

_____

Approximately, how long would it take to move your position up one place?

_____

Which specific benefits would you receive from moving your position up one place?

No. 1 benefit: _____	Profit value: $____
No. 2 benefit: _____	Profit value: $____

QUALITY AS A COMPETITIVE ACTIVITY

Not every company in a market can be number one or number two! And getting there can be very expensive! What is a business that is not number one or two to do to compete aggressively? There is a very significant answer for that question. Every company, regardless of market position, can use quality as a major competitive strategy. Consider these results from an analysis of the relationship between quality and profitability in the PIMS database.

PRODUCT QUALITY AND PROFITABILITY

Quality Level	Average Return on Investment (ROI)
Low	13%
Medium	18%
High	30%

As a matter of fact, quality is a partial offset for market share and that is very good news for every company that is not now number one or two in its markets. The table below shows the relationship between market share and quality in the PIMS database. (But, note that at EVERY level of market share, the businesses with the highest quality levels are the most profitable.)

THE RELATIONSHIP BETWEEN MARKET SHARE AND QUALITY

| Quality Level | Market Share Level | | |
| | High | Medium | Low |
	Return On Investment (ROI)		
HIGH	38%	29%	20%
MEDIUM	27%	20%	13%
LOW	21%	14%	7%

The key concept here is that of "Customer Value." Customer Value is defined as the right level of quality as defined by the customer (however the customer defines it), provided at the right price (however the customer defines it). Therefore, every business, no matter what share of market it holds, should be giving serious consideration to developing a customer value strategy.

Developing, or improving, your Customer Value is beyond the space limits here, but you can find an excellent handbook in Bradley Gale's *Managing Customer Value—Creating Quality & Service That Customers Can See*, published in 1994 by The Free Press, a division of Simon & Schuster, Inc., 1230 Avenue of the Americas, New York, NY 10020. (ISBN 0-02-911045-9)

The first point that Bradley Gale makes is that the old way of measuring quality that businesses used in the 1960s, 1970s and 1980s hides too much and fails to provide a direction for improving quality. As an example, this is the way we used to measure customer satisfaction in customer surveys:

"Would you say that you were Very Satisfied with the Quality of Hunt's Tomato Ketchup, Somewhat satisfied, Neither satisfied or dissatisfied, Somewhat dissatisfied, or Very dissatisfied?"

Very satisfied	[ ]
Somewhat satisfied	[ ]
Neither satisfied or dissatisfied	[ ]
Somewhat dissatisfied	[ ]
Very dissatisfied	[ ]

There are two serious problems with this approach. First, it doesn't tell you how to improve your product or service. Even a simple product like ketchup has a number of "determinate attributes" that customers use to make purchase decisions. They are:

Brand
Flavor
Color
Thickness
Package
Price

Each one of these attributes plays some part in every customer's decision process, but they are not all of equal importance to every customer. However, unless you know which attributes are important to your customers and how your product or service rates on each determinate attribute, you have no "blueprint" for improving your customer value.

Second, the importance of the determinate attributes may differ for the customers of your competitor's product, but you would have no way of knowing that without the detail determinate attribute rankings.

To develop a strategy for improving your customer value vis-a-vis your competitors, you need a fact-based matrix similar to the one shown in Exhibit 2-1 below.

Exhibit 2-1

CUSTOMER VALUE COMPETITIVE ANALYSIS

Determinate Attribute	Your Customers Attribute Importance	Your Score	Competitor #1 Customers Attribute Importance	Their Score	Competitor #2 Customers Attribute Importance	Their Score
Flavor	60%	XX	80%	YY	35%	ZZ
Thickness	20%	XX	15%	YY	15%	ZZ
Price	20%	XX	5%	YY	50%	ZZ

Three more thoughts about creating customer value matrices.

1. The customers you are interested in surveying are the "heavy" users of the product category. Section Nine will discuss the importance of segregating customers in terms of their purchase value.

2. The next step involves developing a matrix that shows how your customers, and your competitor's customers, score brands that they don't buy on each of the determinate attributes.

3. Also in Section Nine, you will learn how to uncover determinate attributes and how to create the kinds of scores needed for a Customer Value Competitive Matrix.

THE NEXT STEPS IN CUSTOMER VALUE COMPETITION

If you are new to the idea of developing customer value, you will soon discover that it is simply not just a marketing activity. To be truly successful in establishing a competitive advantage through delivering superior customer value requires a company-wide effort. That, in turn, means that you will sooner or later have to have some way of organizing and focusing all of the company's resources on creating customer value.

While there are lots of consultants, seminars and books that offer to provide you with that guidance, the single best source of a structure for focusing on delivering customer value is undoubtedly the criteria and program organized around the Baldrige Awards. This program was established to identify those U.S. companies that excel at delivering customer value. The program is managed by the U.S. Department of Commerce and is administered by the American Society for Quality Control. The awards themselves were named for former Secretary of Commerce, Malcolm Baldrige.

The award criteria provide an exceptional framework for organizing your company and for focusing its resources on delivering customer value. The Award Criteria Goals are as follows:

> The Criteria are designed to help companies enhance their competitiveness through focus on dual, results-oriented goals:
>
> - delivery of ever-improving value to customers, resulting in marketplace success; and
> - improvement of overall company performance and capabilities.

In turn, the Award Criteria are built upon a set of core values and concepts that are the foundation for integrating customer and company performance requirements. The 1995 Baldrige Award Criteria identify the following core values and concepts:

Customer driven quality

Leadership

Continuous Improvement and Learning

Employee Participation and Development

Fast Response

Design Quality and Prevention

Long-Range View of the Future

Management by Fact

Partnership Development

Corporate Responsibility and Citizenship

Results Orientation

The Examination Items that are used to evaluate a company's standings on each of these core values and concepts provide an excellent structure for evaluating your own company and its ability to deliver customer value. To get a set of the Baldrige Award materials, write to:

NATIONAL INSTITUTE OF STANDARDS AND TECHNOLOGY
Route 270 and Quince Orchard Road
Administration Building, Room A537
Gaithersburg, MD 20899

Marketing Planning Pages 2-5 through 2-8 are designed to help you organize what you know about your own customer value position and your primary competitors' customer value position.

Marketing Planning Page 2-5

CUSTOMER VALUE STRATEGY—MARKET ONE

Market One Definition: _____

_____

_____

Determinate Attributes in This Market: _____

_____

_____

_____

IMPORTANCE OF DETERMINATE ATTRIBUTES

Attribute	*Our Customers*	*Competitor #1*	*Competitor #2*	*Competitor #3*

SCORES ON DETERMINATE ATTRIBUTES

Attribute	*Our Customers*	*Competitor #1*	*Competitor #2*	*Competitor #3*

Marketing Planning Page 2-6

CUSTOMER VALUE STRATEGY—MARKET TWO

Market Two Definition: _____

_____

_____

Determinate Attributes in This Market: _____

_____

_____

_____

IMPORTANCE OF DETERMINATE ATTRIBUTES

Attribute	Our Customers	Competitor #1	Competitor #2	Competitor #3
_____	_____	_____	_____	_____
_____	_____	_____	_____	_____
_____	_____	_____	_____	_____
_____	_____	_____	_____	_____
_____	_____	_____	_____	_____
_____	_____	_____	_____	_____

SCORES ON DETERMINATE ATTRIBUTES

Attribute	Our Customers	Competitor #1	Competitor #2	Competitor #3
_____	_____	_____	_____	_____
_____	_____	_____	_____	_____
_____	_____	_____	_____	_____
_____	_____	_____	_____	_____
_____	_____	_____	_____	_____

Marketing Planning Page 2-7

CUSTOMER VALUE STRATEGY—MARKET THREE

Market Three Definition: _____

_____

_____

Determinate Attributes in This Market: _____

_____

_____

_____

IMPORTANCE OF DETERMINATE ATTRIBUTES

Attribute	*Our Customers*	*Competitor #1*	*Competitor #2*	*Competitor #3*
_____	_____	_____	_____	_____
_____	_____	_____	_____	_____
_____	_____	_____	_____	_____
_____	_____	_____	_____	_____
_____	_____	_____	_____	_____
_____	_____	_____	_____	_____

SCORES ON DETERMINATE ATTRIBUTES

Attribute	*Our Customers*	*Competitor #1*	*Competitor #2*	*Competitor #3*
_____	_____	_____	_____	_____
_____	_____	_____	_____	_____
_____	_____	_____	_____	_____
_____	_____	_____	_____	_____
_____	_____	_____	_____	_____

Marketing Planning Page 2-8

CUSTOMER VALUE STRATEGY—MARKET FOUR

Market Four Definition:_____
_____
_____

Determinate Attributes in This Market: _____
_____
_____
_____

IMPORTANCE OF DETERMINATE ATTRIBUTES

Attribute	Our Customers	Competitor #1	Competitor #2	Competitor #3
_____	_____	_____	_____	_____
_____	_____	_____	_____	_____
_____	_____	_____	_____	_____
_____	_____	_____	_____	_____
_____	_____	_____	_____	_____
_____	_____	_____	_____	_____

SCORES ON DETERMINATE ATTRIBUTES

Attribute	Our Customers	Competitor #1	Competitor #2	Competitor #3
_____	_____	_____	_____	_____
_____	_____	_____	_____	_____
_____	_____	_____	_____	_____
_____	_____	_____	_____	_____
_____	_____	_____	_____	_____
_____	_____	_____	_____	_____

SECTION THREE

The Product Life Cycle:

How the PLC Drives Your Markets

OVERVIEW OF SECTION THREE: Probably the single most important concept in business is the idea of the Product Life Cycle. It is the engine that drives markets. It is the closest thing there is to a universal law of business. Section Three examines the Product Life Cycle in great detail and explains how to use the concept in developing marketing strategy.

WHAT IS THE PRODUCT LIFE CYCLE (PLC)?

The PLC is a concept, a theory, but it is a theory in its most useful form. It is a theory that works. Basically, the PLC concept says that *every* market goes through a series of specific phases that are analogous to biological phases of life. For example:

Biological Phase	*Product Life Cycle Phase*
Birth	Market Development
Growth	Market Expansion
Adolescence	Market Turbulence

39

Biological Phase	*Product Life Cycle Phase*
Maturity	Market Maturity
Old Age	Market Decline

The PLC is a theory that can never be proven scientifically, but it has been studied so thoroughly in so many industries, markets and countries over the past thirty years that anyone who ignores the concept does so at grave risk to his or her business. Note that the PLC is NOT the business cycle. The business cycle is a reflection of the entire economy and it is driven solely by expectations and psychology. The PLC is a reflection of the demand for a specific product or service that satisfies a specific need. At any one time, there can be only one business cycle, but there are thousands of PLCs.

If you were to diagram the PLC, the vertical axis would be sales, in units or inflation-adjusted dollars, and the horizontal axis would be time. The primary reason that the PLC has been verified so widely is that each point at which one phase ends and a new one begins is an inflection point. That is a point at which the *rate of change changes*. In this way, historical data on markets and their development can be studied with great precision.

This a very important point. There is nothing in the PLC concept that tells you exactly when a market phase will end and a new one will start. Furthermore, there is no one instant when a market changes from one phase to the next. The great value of the PLC is that it can tell you what is "normal" market behavior in the phase your market is in now, AND it can tell you what kind of market behavior to *anticipate* when the next phase does actually arrive. Those are two advantages for marketing planners and strategists that are simply beyond valuation.

In spite of the virtually absolute evidence of the existence of the PLC, it is continually amazing to observe the number of business people who are not aware of it, or at least act as if they have never heard of it. Here is one very large, very expensive (for the participants) example to illustrate the point.

Jet Aircraft Come to Commercial Aviation

In the late 1950s, commercial airlines in the United States began taking delivery of their first jet aircraft. It was a huge gamble for the industry because the new Boeing 707s and McDonnell-Douglas DC-7s each cost many times as much as the propeller-driven airplanes they replaced. After some initial fumbling getting used to the new aircraft, the gamble paid off hugely. Growth in the airline travel market grew explosively! So did the airlines' demand for jet aircraft.

By the middle 1960s, the airlines were straight line forecasting the growth in the market since the introduction of jet aircraft. Their forecasts seemed to go straight up. The demand they predicted was truly awesome. It became quite clear to the airlines that the first generation of jets didn't carry enough passengers in each airplane to permit the airlines to handle the predicted growth. The predictions were for absolute gridlock at the nation's airports with all of the landings and take-offs.

The airlines looked at the predicted growth in the market and sat down with the aircraft manufacturers to plan the next generation of jet airplanes. The results of these efforts were the monsters of the sky like the Boeing 747, a plane that could carry three times as many passengers as the Boeing 707. And the price of the new generation of jets was also huge. Once again, confident from their last big win, airlines played "bet the farm" and ordered hundreds of the new, very expensive aircraft.

Just when they began to be delivered, growth in air travel slowed dramatically. The airlines suddenly found that they had no use for the new airplanes, and perhaps worse, no money to pay for them. Aircraft orders were canceled or postponed. If that was not possible, the new airplanes were delivered to vast airfields in the deserts of the Southwest to wait until somebody could figure out what to do with them.

The airlines bled red ink everywhere. The aircraft manufacturers fared no better. Seattle (Boeing's headquarters) became a major depressed area and for a long time, a large outdoor sign at the city limits of Seattle delivered this message:

"Will the last person to leave Seattle please turn out the lights?"

What happened? How could so many hard-working, intelligent business people create such a nightmare? After all, these were mostly the same people who had created the jet travel revolution in the first place.

What happened is that two fundamental facts of the marketplace were either overlooked, or not understood, or perhaps both. One fact of marketing life that was ignored was market segmentation. (See Section 10 for more on this topic.) Every market is composed of segments, sub-sections that combine to make up the total market. While the end use behavior of these market segments may seem to be the same, the forces driving the behavior can be very, very different!

The air travel market consists of three major segments: business-related travel, vacation travel and unplanned travel (where some unforeseen emergency requires the traveler to be someplace fast). Today, depending on fare levels at the time, the market is about 50% business-related travel, 45% vacation travel and 5% unplanned. During the 1960s, when the airlines and the manufacturers were planning the next generation of jets, the size of the segments was quite different. Business-related travel accounted for, perhaps, 80% of the demand, vacation travel about 15% and unplanned travel always seems to account for about 5%.

Not understanding different market segments, the airline industry failed to understand what was driving growth in each. What was driving growth in the business-related market segment was that the speed of jet air travel had forever altered the time/value relationship of business travel. Now it was cost efficient to conduct meetings face to face that used to be held on the telephone or by correspondence. But there is a limit to the number of face-to-face meetings that business people need to hold, and that limit was reached just about the time that the second generation jets were delivered.

The second fact of the market place that was overlooked was the PLC. Since each segment of the market has its own PLC, it was inevitable that growth in demand would slow down sooner or later, a factor that was never considered! Anyone in the industry who understood the PLC would have also understood that the explosive growth of the 1960s was not sustainable.

Because airline management in the 1960s did not understand the limits to growth imposed by the PLC, or that different market segments are driven by different factors, the industry lost staggering amounts of money in the 1970s. You can calculate your own total by reviewing airline annual reports from the period.

If that was the bad news, the worse news appears to be that, having learned nothing from the debacle described above, the major airlines and aircraft manufacturers are, as of this writing, beginning to plan for the next round of monster new jet aircraft, ones carrying 600 to 800 passengers. The justification for the need for these new aircraft designs are two, both necessary. One is that air passenger traffic in the Far East is now growing rapidly. The other is that take-off and landing slots at airports are now limited and that may impede growth in the industry.

The problem here is that whatever significant growth there is in air traffic is occurring in Asia, but the overcrowded airports are in Europe and the United States. And this time around, each new plane will cost in excess of $1 *billion*.

First Thing: How to Define a Market

In order to use the PLC successfully, you must be able to observe, and understand, the signals that the market is giving you. That, in turn, raises the question of "What market to observe?" There is absolutely no hard and fast answer to this question beyond the fact that the total market is *always* the wrong market. It is always some segment of the total market. And, as Section Ten will point out, much of market segmentation is an art as much as it is a science.

This is the basic problem. If you define your market too broadly, you won't be able to detect the correct signals because they will be buried in an ocean of conflicting information. But if you define your market too narrowly, you will never even be aware of many of the signals the market is sending you. Here is a way to think about this problem.

Suppose that you own and manage a good-sized automobile customizing business in Dallas, TX. You have observed a number of Toyota owners bringing their two-door automobiles to you to be customized into convertibles. You are beginning to wonder if there might be a market for customized convertibles in the Southwest. So you begin to collect some market data (see Section Five for assistance in how to do this job). If you collect market data on the generic product class, i.e., automobiles, you will be studying too broad a market. But if you just study the market at the brand level, i.e., Mustang convertibles, you will probably be looking at too narrow a market to get a good answer to your question. In this case, the best bet is to study the product class, i.e., all convertibles.

In this example, it was pretty easy to see the most likely market definition. Seldom will you find it that neat. Remember, there are no rules about how to do this job.

What follows here is a discussion of the major signals, characteristics, and conditions that exist at each phase of the PLC. You should study them and understand exactly why they are happening. If there are variations on the signals, you should also understand them and the factors that make them possible.

Marketing Planning Pages 3-1 through 3-8 on pages 56–63 are designed to help you organize what you know about your markets and their PLCs. Remember that your task here is to understand what phase of the PLC exists in your markets right now, what, if any, abnormalities exist, and what you can anticipate when the next phase arrives.

Market Development Phase

Somewhere, somehow, some person(s) gets an idea for a new product or new service and takes the first steps to turn the idea into a business. And a new market may begin to develop. The process that begins is one of attempting to find a way to solve a problem for a group of customers, and doing it at a profit. The difficulty is that exactly what the need is, and exactly how it might be satisfied, is seldom very clear. That means the Market Development Phase is one characterized very strongly by experimentation.

In turn, this major reliance on experimentation at this point in the PLC leads to these primary characteristics:

1. Sales are very small, if indeed, there are any sales at all. For many products and services under development there are no sales at all for long periods of time as in-home or in-use tests take place. Therefore, revenues are small or nonexistent.

2. Unit prices are high because both manufacturing and marketing costs are high. Manufacturing costs are high because no one knows exactly how to best manufacture the new product or produce the new service. In addition, since volumes are low, each unit must support a large part of the organization's fixed manufacturing costs. Marketing costs are high because no one knows exactly who might want this new product or service, how they might use it, what they might pay for it, etc. The small volume also means that each unit must support a large part of the organization's fixed marketing costs.

3. Distribution is very limited. Wholesalers and retailers don't know what to do with the new thing either.

4. During the Market Development Phase, there are frequent major changes in the product/service concept. This is a direct outgrowth of its experimental nature.

5. There is seldom any meaningful direct competition during Market Development.

6. It is easy to see why the Market Development Phase is a time of large cash requirements. The money may come from other deep pockets in an existing company, or from venture capitalists, or from personal savings, or from bank loans, or from stock sales, but it must come from some place.

The overriding business concern during Market Development is to get some direct feedback from potential customers about what they like and dislike about the new concept. At Minnesota Mining and Manufacturing, Inc. (3M), a brilliantly successful player at Market Development, this job is called, "Make a little, sell a little, make a little." The work that takes place in the Market Development Phase will be considered in greater depth in Section Twelve.

At some point, *if it ever happens*, sales begin to grow rapidly and the Market Expansion Phase begins. It is important to understand the emphasis on *if it ever happens*. The earliest systematic study of the new product success or failure question, conducted by the Department of Commerce in 1948, concluded that four out of five new products *fail*! There have been many similar studies since.

All new product failure/success studies must deal with a number of very sticky definitional problems. What is a new product or service? What is simply a minor variation of an existing product? What is success? What is failure? A moment's thought and you can see that some tricky problems are lurking here. Nevertheless, when all of the studies are taken as a whole, the answer is surprisingly consistent. Four out of five new products fail, and nothing has changed in the almost fifty years since the first Commerce Department study.

While those average numbers are very intimidating, they are only averages. A recent study by the non-profit Conference Board found extreme differences between companies. It allowed each participating company to provide its own definitions of "new" or "variation" and "failure" or "success." The highlights of its findings are worth reviewing.

A metal equipment manufacturer	100 successes	0 failures
An electric components manufacturer	25 successes	0 failures
A petroleum products company	9 successes	0 failures
A chemical company	0 successes	20 failures
A heating equipment manufacturer	0 successes	11 failures
A sporting goods manufacturer	0 successes	6 failures

Market Expansion Phase

The signal for the Market Expansion Phase is *always* a rapid increase in sales. In fact, that is the definition of the beginning of the phase.

The first major change signaled by the beginning of the Market Expansion Phase is an expansion of distribution. People in distribution, wholesaling and retailing are skilled at finding things that people want to buy and then supplying them. That is their basic reason for existence.

So when sales start to increase rapidly, a lot of wholesalers and retailers begin stocking the new product. In turn, that means that even more potential customers are exposed to the new product and sales increase even faster. All of this increasingly rapid and expanding total market attracts even more distributors who provide more distribution, etc. The cycle feeds itself.

The second major change that marks a Market Expansion Phase is the entrance of new competitors. There seems to be nothing in the world so loved by business people as a rapidly growing market (and for some very good reasons). The Japanese consumer electronics products company, Casio, has built its entire strategy on spotting new Market Expansion Phase opportunities and entering the market rapidly.

The new competitors produce two major effects. One is that each new competitor adds advertising, sales force and sales promotion spending to the total amount of money being spent against the new industry. All of these new marketing dollars fuel the increase in the market size even more. Thus, new competitors have an effect similar to expanded distribution, with one large difference. The additional marketing dollars tend to benefit the earliest entrants into the market more than later entrants because the early arriving companies have better and wider distribution. (See the Packard-Bell example below.)

The second major effect is that new competitors entering a growing market during the Market Expansion Phase *almost* always enter the market with some major new feature or improvement on the basic product or service. Only rarely will a company be foolish enough to try and "buy its way in" with only low prices, but with no product advantage.

In 1995, Packard-Bell sold more personal computers than any other company in the world. More than Compaq, more than Apple, more than IBM. The PC market is now in the Market Expansion Phase, driven by the demand from the newly formed SOHO (small office, home office) market segment. Packard-Bell has accomplished this feat with some of the lowest prices in the industry. But Packard-Bell is not buying its way into the market. It was the first PC manufacturer to distribute through department stores and consumer electronic stores. It was the first company to deliver its computers with the operating systems and other software already installed. It was the first company to offer a toll-free telephone support line. It was the first to include an internal CD-ROM drive and it was also the first to offer computers driven by Intel's high powered Pentium chip. No, Packard-Bell did not "buy its way into the market."

What is happening is that the new entrants have studied the market, to some degree, and they believe that they have found some group of potential customers who are not fully satisfied with the version of the product or service that is being offered by the original entrants (a market segment). These companies then create one, or more, features to appeal to that group of customers. In other words, they attempt to create a "niche" in the market for themselves. In this way, the future structure of the industry is being formed by customers and competitors.

Not all of them succeed, usually. Sometimes the customers really don't want the offered features. Sometimes the group of customers wants the features very much, but the group is too small to provide the basis for a successful business. The important point here is that this is the time during which market segments are formed. Each of the market segments, sub-markets, niches, whatever they are called, will persist until the market begins to decline. Therefore, capturing as many of these segments as possible, as early as possible, is an important element of strategy in the Market Expansion Phase.

It is obvious that later entrants into a rapidly growing market would search for unmet customer needs to provide a reason for potential customers to buy their products in place of the early entrants' products. What is not so obvious is the need for early entrants to also keep searching for unmet needs and to continue to introduce new features and/or new variations of the original new product or service. But if they can do this, they will be able to keep competitors out of the market and they will build large market shares which will pay off very handsomely as the future unfolds.

The third major effect to anticipate is that prices will decline. Costs decline because companies learn how to manufacture and market more and more efficiently, and the total unit base to cover fixed costs expands. As costs decline, competitors will lower their prices to avoid holding a price umbrella over the market that would tend to attract even more new competitors. You can expect competitors to try to maintain their margins as costs come down, but readily pass along the newly found lower costs to customers in the form of lower prices.

NOTE: The price behavior discussed above will NOT occur in markets where patents, proprietary technology, or other real barriers to entry exist. When the original entrants do not face potential competition, there is no incentive whatsoever for them to pass the effects of their declining costs on to their customers. This is what creates what economists call "monopoly profits."

The most important thing about the Market Development Phase is that it is the one time in which the demand exceeds the supply of the product or service; sooner or later, that situation will reverse itself. Therefore, the most important business task during the Market Expansion Phase is forecasting demand as accurately as possible.

If you forecast too low, you won't develop enough capacity and the competitors will simply take customers away from you. But if you forecast too high, you will end up with too much capacity when the Market Expansion Phase ends, and your costs will be higher than those of your competitors.

The biggest problem in attempting to forecast accurately at this time is the problem of market definition. As an example, consider the market for Personal Computers (PCs). There are at least five quite different markets (market segments):

- Scientific users
- Educational institutions
- Business users
- At home use
- SOHO

All five markets are growing at different rates because different factors are fueling the growth. Then extend the problem just a little more and decide whether laptop computers are competitors in each of these markets. How about work stations? How about word processors? There are no absolute answers to these questions, and your best protection is your extensive knowledge of your customers and how they use your products and services.

If you want to study a real time case history, watch the U.S. cruise ship business. Between 1981 and 1991, it grew 10% to 20% annually. Then growth slowed sharply. 1994 business was up only 1% over 1993. By 1995, the U.S. cruise ship business had 105,000 berths available. But it also has twenty-three brand new ships on order, to expand the fleet, for delivery by 1998. These new ships will add 41,000 new berths to the business's inventory, a stunning 39%

increase in capacity just as the industry demand curve peaks out. (Or does it? Watch for fascinating developments.)

Market Turbulence Phase

As we have just seen in the example of the cruise ship business, at some point in time, the *rate* of growth in the market begins to slow down. What is happening then is that a slowing in demand is allowing capacity to catch up with demand. This is very important to understand because all during the Market Expansion Phase, the excess demand over capacity allowed all kinds of weak competitors to survive. But as the demand overhang relative to the available capacity diminishes, real competition increases and the weakest competitors are forced out of the market. The reason that this phase is called "Turbulence" is that it is not always clear exactly which competitors are the weak ones. Here are some of the most important developments you will encounter as a market passes through this phase.

Prices will "soften." In the Market Expansion Phase, when prices came down, it was evident from the published price lists. But when prices come down during Turbulence, it is rarely reflected on published price lists. Instead, individual customer deals are developed, i.e., off-invoice deductions, one free with one, etc. In actual fact, the transaction prices in the market decline, but it is extremely difficult to obtain documentation of this development. These price declines can be steep and serious.

The price softening activity, however, is not always hidden from view. By 1995, the U.S. cruise ships were already slashing published fares to fill up berths. For example, Royal Caribbean's ship, Sovereign of the Seas, was selling per person fares, double occupancy, for $1,099 in 1994 and only $848 in 1995. The high fixed-cost nature of the business will demand more fare wars before all of the new excess capacity can be worked out.

Competitors will also attempt to re-define the product offering so as to re-orient the competitive arena. This means introducing added services like extended warranties, toll-free technical support telephone numbers, customer service centers, product use seminars, etc.

Distributors' margins and profits begin to shrink as manufacturers attempt to push the softening prices onto the distributors. As a result, distribution begins to contract during this phase.

Most important, competitors will begin to leave the market, resulting in market re-structuring. What is of great importance is how the withdrawal takes place. It can be either orderly or catastrophic.

Orderly withdrawal can be expected when a competitor has:

1. A continued interest in the market in some other form (as RCA had in the home electronics market when it withdrew its video disk players).

2. When there is some alternate use for the productive capacity. (Since all of RCA's video disk recorders were manufactured in Japan, it was easy for RCA to withdraw from the market by simply not renewing its production contracts.) For orderly withdrawal to occur, BOTH conditions must exist.

You can expect a competitor to stage a catastrophic withdrawal when:

1. The competitor has a real need for cash.

2. The competitor has no further interest in the market.

3. There is no alternative use for the competitor's productive capacity.

For catastrophic withdrawal to occur, it is enough for ONE of these conditions to exist. If TWO exist, catastrophic withdrawal is almost guaranteed.

But Turbulence seldom lasts very long. The weak competitors are money losers, and bankers can always be counted on to quickly terminate their activities.

The most important business task for strong competitors entering Market Turbulence is to decide in advance how you are going to deal with it. The one event occurring during Turbulence that you can anticipate without fail is the decline in prices and the disposition of inventories. The decision that must be made in advance is between maintaining your volume or your margins. You can't expect to do both and it is much better to conduct this discussion with your top management before the price wars begin.

If you choose to protect volume, you must communicate to all of your sales people and all of your customers that you will meet (or beat) all competitive offers PERIOD. After the six- carload order that your best customer just bought for 35% off-invoice from a competitor is already rolling, it is simply too late to counteroffer.

If you choose to protect margins and let volume slide temporarily (remember: Turbulence never lasts very long), then it is important to communicate this to production, distribution, and financial people so they can plan accordingly. It is very important to communicate exactly what you are doing, and why, to your sales force. There are few things as discouraging to a sales-person as seeing order after order from good customers lost to prices that are too high.

Market Maturity Phase

The rate of market growth will slow down one more time, and Market Turbulence will have ended and Market Maturity begun. Please understand that during this discussion, it sounds as if one phase ends overnight and a new one begins in the morning. This is clearly not true. Sometimes it takes years to move from one phase to the next. What is important is that you are aware of the process and what is *going* to happen.

When Market Maturity sets in, sales growth is no longer responding to increasing direct demand, and sales must come from one of three sources:

1. New household formations (99% of all U.S. households have a refrigerator. How many need two?)

2. Replacement (Auto and truck tires wear out)

3. Technological improvements (Color TV for black & white)

Mature Markets have three major characteristics and each one of them has significant implications for marketing planning and strategy. Since most markets are mature, these are the conditions under which most competition takes place.

1. Prices are low because costs are low. The competitors who survived Turbulence are almost always low-cost, efficient producers. All of the high-cost producers have been driven out of the market by the thrifty bankers. This fact has created real barriers to entry in the market. Why would a new, high-cost producer want to enter a mature market domi-nated by low-cost producers?

NOTE: This fact drives economists bonkers. They think barriers permit high prices. Nothing could be further from the truth. Prices in mature mar-kets are about as low as it is possible to be and still attract capital investment.

But there is an important caveat here. The barriers to entry in mature markets can be breached by new technology that alters the costs of production. None of the wood ski manufacturers survived the introduction of metal skis, and none of the metal ski manufacturers survived the introduction of fiberglass skis. This is an important point to remember when you are conducting your analysis of the Technological Environment (see Section Seven).

2. Point number two is closely related. In mature markets, competition among producers is only very rarely price competition. The market is growing slowly and major market share gains can only come from competitors' sales. Most of the competitors are low-cost producers. The profits in the industry are at a level that will still attract investment capital in the industry. And if one competitor tries to buy market share with low prices, every other major competitor will meet those prices at once since they cannot afford to lose the volume. (However, producers are usually more than happy to let distributors compete with each other on price.)

If a price war should happen, a real problem develops. Every competitor's revenues are now lower because everyone's prices are lower, but their costs didn't decrease. Thus, they now have profits below the levels necessary to attract investment capital. The only way out is for some competitor to raise prices, but who would do that? Nobody would follow because they would all be grabbing for the price increaser's customers.

This is why competition is seldom price competition in mature markets. But it has happened, on both small and large scale agendas. If you want to study what was probably the most grand example of price cutting to gain volume in a mature market, look at the world bulk chemical market in the 1970s and 1980s. The competitors had to completely change their businesses to get out from under.

But that does not mean there is no competition in mature markets. Quite the contrary, there is intense competition! But it is on secondary characteristics because all of the competitors adequately fill the basic need that the market developed to serve in the first place. For example, all banks accept deposits and honor checks written by their depositors. This is the basic need. So competition takes place with additions like longer open hours, mail deposits, etc.

NOTE: This fact drives people like Ralph Nader crazy. They keep saying, "Why don't you stop giving us all of these "flavors" and just give us low prices?" They don't understand that the prices are already low and it is the "flavors" that keep them low.

3. Third, in mature markets, the competitors tend to be well defined, in place and in order. The evidence on this point is a little less clear than on the first two points, but it is still strong and you should know about it.

As discussed in Section Two, the world's largest research project into business success factors is the PIMS study (Profit Impact of Marketing Strategy). This project finds that in a typical mature market, the competitors and their market shares are arranged as follows:

The leader	33% share of market
No. two competitor	17% share
No. three competitor	12% share
No. four competitor	7% share
	69% of total market

First of all, you can see why only the top three or four competitors in any one industry are of importance (see Section Six). Second, increasing your share points in mature markets is an extremely slow and expensive proposition. Third, if left to themselves, market shares will tend to drift toward this pattern, a ratio of 0.6 between competitors.

More evidence: Campbell Soup recently conducted a study of all the consumer products markets they compete in, and they found this was the typical situation:

The leader	40% share of market
No. two competitor	30% share
No. three competitor	17% share
No. four competitor	10% share

General Electric has studied its individual industrial products markets and has discovered similar results. GE will now only compete in markets where it is number one or two.

Here are the market shares from consumer batteries in 1992 as an example:

Eveready	44% share of market
Duracell	33% share
Ray-o-vac	14% share
Kodak	7% share

Obviously, there is a great deal of distance from perfect convergence in these examples, but that is acceptable since the purpose is to understand the general structure of mature markets and how they got that way. (That is the point made in the beginning of Section Two.)

NOTE: The market structure described above gives economists huge ulcers. They call such markets "concentrated" and ascribe all sorts of terrible things to them. For a good example, study the U.S. Department of Justice's proceeding against the four largest ready-to-eat cereal manufacturers in the United States during the late 1970s and early 1980s. In real life, what economists see as evil is really a well organized, highly rational, and extremely efficient market.

The basic business tasks in a mature market are two. First is to pursue competitive advantages over time by focusing on continually upgrading and improving your products and services. The small, incremental, continual improvement is usually the most powerful competitive weapon in mature markets. The second task is to continually monitor and understand your markets. While the discussion here has presented mature markets as unchanging, that is not correct. Mature markets are continually changing, although not as dramatically as expanding markets. (Dozens of brands of "natural cereals" entered the ready-to-eat cereal market in the 1970s because American eating habits changed.) Your job is to follow those changes closely and continually. Adjust and adapt your products and services to meet those changes continually. This was a task that IBM forgot to do all during the 1970s and 1980s, and you know what it cost that company.

Above all, DO NOT START A PRICE WAR!!

Market Decline Phase

Finally, at some point, total market sales begin to decline on a year-to-year basis. Some new product, new service, new technology is taking your customers away from you. Declining markets are not necessarily unprofitable, but they do demand more careful planning and strategy than, say, mature markets, because there is little room for error when things begin to shrink.

There are three major events that take place in declining markets. They are:

1. Product lines get narrower. In a mature market, competitors were anxious to provide a "flavor" for every possible market segment. In a declining market, many of those segments become too small to serve profitably. Competitors narrow their product lines to "strawberry," "chocolate," and "vanilla." Finally, only vanilla is offered.

2. Prices decline. Whether they "soften" or "crash" depends upon whether departing competitors leave on an orderly basis or a catastrophic one. The criteria are exactly the ones discussed under Market Turbulence.

3. Competitors abandon the market.

There are three fundamental strategies available to companies in declining markets. They can 1) fight the decline, 2) "milk" the market by minimizing investment, or 3) abandon the market quickly. The basic business task here is to recognize the signs of a declining market as early as possible, and to decide as quickly as possible what strategy you wish to follow. There is nothing as pathetic as a company in a declining market acting as if it was business as usual.

Recognizing the Product Life Cycle in Your Markets

Marketing Planning Pages 3-1 through 3-8 are designed to help you recognize the PLC in your markets. Marketing Planning Pages 3-1 to 3-4 are to be used when you have access to good data on total industry sales. Marketing Planning Pages 3-5 to 3-8 are useful when reliable data are not available and it will be necessary to use your judgment and estimate the situation.

Marketing Planning Page 3-1

DESCRIBING THE PRODUCT LIFE CYCLE FOR BRAND A

Definition of the market for Product A _____

_____

Year	*Total Market Sales*	*Change In Units From Previous Year*	*Percentage Change From Previous Year*
_____	_____	_____	_____
_____	_____	_____	_____
_____	_____	_____	_____
_____	_____	_____	_____
_____	_____	_____	_____
_____	_____	_____	_____
_____	_____	_____	_____
_____	_____	_____	_____
_____	_____	_____	_____
_____	_____	_____	_____
_____	_____	_____	_____
_____	_____	_____	_____
_____	_____	_____	_____
_____	_____	_____	_____
_____	_____	_____	_____
_____	_____	_____	_____
_____	_____	_____	_____
_____	_____	_____	_____

Marketing Planning Page 3-2

DESCRIBING THE PRODUCT LIFE CYCLE FOR BRAND B

Definition of the market for Product B _____

_____

Year	Total Market Sales	Change In Units From Previous Year	Percentage Change From Previous Year

Marketing Planning Page 3-3

DESCRIBING THE PRODUCT LIFE CYCLE FOR BRAND C

Definition of the market for Product C _____

_____

Year	Total Market Sales	Change In Units From Previous Year	Percentage Change From Previous Year
_____	_____	_____	_____
_____	_____	_____	_____
_____	_____	_____	_____
_____	_____	_____	_____
_____	_____	_____	_____
_____	_____	_____	_____
_____	_____	_____	_____
_____	_____	_____	_____
_____	_____	_____	_____
_____	_____	_____	_____
_____	_____	_____	_____
_____	_____	_____	_____
_____	_____	_____	_____
_____	_____	_____	_____
_____	_____	_____	_____
_____	_____	_____	_____
_____	_____	_____	_____

Marketing Planning Page 3-4

DESCRIBING THE PRODUCT LIFE CYCLE FOR BRAND D

Definition of the market for Product D _____

_____

Year	Total Market Sales	Change In Units From Previous Year	Percentage Change From Previous Year

Marketing Planning Page 3-5

ESTIMATING THE PRODUCT LIFE CYCLE FOR BRAND A

(Circle X's that Apply to the Market Now)

Market Characteristics	Phase in the Product Life Cycle				
	Development	Expansion	Turbulence	Maturity	Decline
Total Market Sales					
Growing slowly	X			X	
Growing rapidly		X			
Sales rate slowing			X		
Number of Major Competitors					
None or a few	X				
Many		X			
Three or four				X	
Fewer than before			X		X
Prices in Constant Dollars					
Stable	X			X	
Declining		X	X		X
Distribution					
Increasing		X			
Decreasing			X		X
Not much change	X			X	
No. of Major Product Changes Recently					
Many		X			
A few	X				
None of importance			X	X	X
How Product is Being Sold					
On basic benefits	X				X
On major features		X	X		
Secondary characteristics				X	

Marketing Planning Page 3-6

ESTIMATING THE PRODUCT LIFE CYCLE FOR BRAND B

(Circle X's that Apply to the Market Now)

Market Characteristics	Phase in the Product Life Cycle				
	Development	Expansion	Turbulence	Maturity	Decline
Total Market Sales					
Growing slowly	X			X	
Growing rapidly		X			
Sales rate slowing			X		
Number of Major Competitors					
None or a few	X				
Many		X			
Three or four				X	
Fewer than before			X		X
Prices in Constant Dollars					
Stable	X			X	
Declining		X	X		X
Distribution					
Increasing	X				
Decreasing		X			X
Not much change	X			X	
No. of Major Product Changes Recently					
Many		X			
A few	X				
None of importance			X	X	X
How Product is Being Sold					
On basic benefits	X				X
On major features		X	X		
Secondary characteristics				X	

Marketing Planning Page 3-7

ESTIMATING THE PRODUCT LIFE CYCLE FOR BRAND C

(Circle X's that Apply to the Market Now)

Market Characteristics	Development	Expansion	Turbulence	Maturity	Decline
Total Market Sales					
Growing slowly	X			X	
Growing rapidly		X			
Sales rate slowing			X		
Number of Major Competitors					
None or a few	X				
Many		X			
Three or four				X	
Fewer than before			X		X
Prices in Constant Dollars					
Stable	X			X	
Declining		X	X		X
Distribution					
Increasing		X			
Decreasing			X		X
Not much change	X			X	
No. of Major Product Changes Recently					
Many		X			
A few	X				
None of importance			X	X	X
How Product is Being Sold					
On basic benefits	X				X
On major features		X	X		
Secondary characteristics				X	

Marketing Planning Page 3-8

ESTIMATING THE PRODUCT LIFE CYCLE FOR BRAND D

(Circle X's that Apply to the Market Now)

Market Characteristics	Development	Expansion	Turbulence	Maturity	Decline
Total Market Sales					
Growing slowly	X			X	
Growing rapidly		X			
Sales rate slowing			X		
Number of Major Competitors					
None or a few	X				
Many		X			
Three or four				X	
Fewer than before			X		X
Prices in Constant Dollars					
Stable	X			X	
Declining		X	X		X
Distribution					
Increasing		X			
Decreasing			X		X
Not much change	X			X	
No. of Major Product Changes Recently					
Many		X			
A few	X				
None of importance			X	X	X
How Product is Being Sold					
On basic benefits	X				X
On major features		X	X		
Secondary characteristics				X	

Every Company Has Strengths and Weaknesses:

How to Understand and Use Your Company's Strengths and Weaknesses

OVERVIEW OF SECTION FOUR: One absolutely inviolate rule of business is that successful plans must be built on the company's strengths, not its weaknesses. But it is not always clear to everyone what a company's strengths and weaknesses are. Section Four shows you how to identify them, and how to get everyone to share that knowledge.

NOBODY DOES EVERYTHING WELL

Every manager has learned to do some things well. Over time, each of us must learn to be good at something, or we become only marginal members of society. By the same token, every manager also realizes that he or she is not good at everything and cannot do some kinds of tasks well. This is a very important point to understand because we are going to expand it into a major basis for developing strategy. Therefore, stop for a minute right here and list five things that you do well in your work, and five things that you do not do very well.

THINGS I DO WELL AT WORK

1)_____

2)_____

3)_____

4)_____

5)_____

THINGS I DO NOT DO WELL AT WORK

1)_____

2)_____

3)_____

4)_____

5)_____

The reason that it is important to understand your strengths and weaknesses is because of the way we deal with them. We all seek out opportunities to demonstrate our strengths by working on tasks where we have high chances of succeeding. We also all avoid like the plague those assignments that call for skills we do not have because we wish to avoid failing. Simple as that: we seek success based on our strengths and avoid failure by limiting the exposure of our weaknesses.

There is a fantasy taught in many business schools that the way managers deal with their own weaknesses is to hire subordinates who are good at the very things where the manager is weak. Total rubbish! What really happens is that managers hire people who are also good at the same things they are good at, for the simple reason that it minimizes the likelihood of conflict with the employee. If you doubt this, think about working for a boss who was really good at something you were terrible at. Do you see the problem? Right, you would hate to go near your boss for fear that his or her strengths would spotlight your weaknesses.

But there is a worse scenario. Imagine that you worked for a boss who was just terrible at something you were really good at ! Now, not only do you not want to be around your boss for fear of showing his or her ineptness, but he or she wouldn't want *you* to be around for exactly the same reason. Now carry it a step further. Your boss's boss knows you are good at what your boss is not, and begins to ask you questions in meetings and bypassing your boss!

Exactly so. People get hired into organizations because of their similarities, not their differences. If that were not true, organizations would simply self-destruct.

Now the point is that as organizations grow, they tend to collect similar thinking, similar skilled and similar behaving people. This growing group of people is what gives every company its own unique personality. This is what the pop management gurus like to call the company's "culture." Whatever you wish to call it, this personality or culture is a real thing and understanding your company's strengths and weaknesses is vital to developing a successful marketing strategy for the simple reason that the strategy must be built on your strengths, not on your weaknesses.

Let's illustrate this point with an example with which everyone will be familiar. In Armonk, New York, Tom Watson, Chairman of IBM decided long ago that, because leasing mainframe computers was a very important decision for companies to make, it was very important to IBM's success to project a personality of stability, reliability, trustworthiness, etc. Accordingly, he built an organization with people who had such virtues as strengths. In turn, even a dress code evolved. You know how IBM people, both men and women, have presented themselves: blue suit or dress, white shirt or blouse, quiet tie or scarf, black shoes, etc. They show up on time, with everything prepared and they are very serious about their work.

Much, much later, in Cupertino, California, Steve Jobs was building an entirely different personality for his Apple Computer Company. Steve Jobs didn't have a chance of taking away IBM's corporate customers and he probably didn't care about it. His customers would be the extremely bright young men and women who understood, and loved working with, computers. What you wore to work, or when you did your work, had no real bearing on doing brilliant work. What mattered was actually doing the brilliant work, and doing it fast. So Apple developed a personality totally different from that of IBM because it valued creativity and flexibility over everything else.

This is not to say that one was right and the other wrong. In the early 1980s, Steve Jobs almost bankrupted Apple because he couldn't get the kind of discipline from his company that IBM had in abundance. And in the early 1990s, it looked as if John Akers, then IBM chairman, might bankrupt IBM because he couldn't get IBM people to respond flexibly as the market for computers rapidly changed direction, an activity at which Apple is superb.

To re-emphasize the earlier point about hiring similarities, not differences, imagine this scenario. A successful Apple salesperson shows up at IBM to apply for a job dressed in jeans, a flowered sports shirt, a corduroy jacket and boots. Will he get the job? Will he be successful if (by some quirk of fate) he actually gets hired? No, of course not. Now reverse the direction and have a successful IBM salesperson show up at Apple to apply for a position. Same outcome, right?

The point of all this is that companies learn to be good at some things over time because their people are good at some things. (In the current jargon of management consultants, they are called "core competencies.") These things are your company's strengths, and you must understand them accurately and use them carefully. At the same time, companies develop weaknesses because there are some things that their people are not good at. These things are your company's weaknesses, and you must understand and deal with them appropriately. And, if you think that none of this applies to your company because it is all about big companies, all you have to do is remember that just a little over fifteen years ago, Apple Computer was two guys working in a garage.

Finally, a word of warning about corporate culture gurus. They will tell you that they can help you change the culture, or personality, of your company, but you should be very wary of those promises. The only way to change a corporate culture is to change the people. And that is a very difficult thing to undertake. Just ask Louis Gerstner, the current CEO at IBM!

THREE EXAMPLES OF COMPANIES THAT FAILED TO UNDERSTAND THEIR STRENGTHS

Perhaps all of this discussion sounds too obvious for anyone to overlook, but it isn't. Here are three examples of large, mostly well-managed companies that have come to grief, or close to it, because they didn't understand their strengths and weaknesses (or at least acted as if they didn't since only the top insiders know for sure).

Texas Instruments

The transistor and the principles of semi-conductors were discovered by Bell Laboratories, but it took Texas Instruments to make those inventions commercially valuable. It engineered useful applications for the first integrated circuits in 1958, for the first micro-processor in 1971, etc. The company is absolutely magnificent at engineering. Unfortunately, it is not too magnificent at marketing.

In the early 1970s, Texas Instruments engineered the first hand-held calculators and launched a huge market. But it had no idea how to compete and was quickly forced into a tiny market segment.

Later in the decade, it engineered the first digital wrist watches. Again, it had no idea how to compete in the market and was left with only scraps for its efforts.

By the end of the 1970s, Texas Instruments was awash in its own calculators and watches, so it tried opening its own retail stores to sell just its own products. Another marketing fiasco!

The company entered the 1980s with some idea about entering the "home computer market," whatever that might be. By the middle of the decade, it had once again demonstrated it had no talents for marketing whatsoever and took a $330 million write-off on its efforts to market home computers. It closed the 1980s with another write-off on an educational toy called Speak and Spell.

Fortunately for everyone, as the 1990s advance, there seems to be growing evidence that Texas Instruments has finally learned a two-decade lesson, e.g., their people are superb engineers and bad marketers. The company now seems willing to focus all its efforts on engineering, and once again it is turning in a magnificent performance. Texas Instruments is the only U. S. company that gained market share against the Japanese in semi-conductors in the 1990s.

Sears Roebuck

For thirty years after World War II, Sears Roebuck was the world's largest, most profitable retailer. Its sales growth was fueled by U. S. population growth. At one point, Sears sales equaled *1% of the total Gross National Product of the United States*. For thirty years, Sears developed a wonderfully efficient control system. Electronic cash registers in over 800 stores around the U. S. linked the stores immediately with headquarters in Chicago. Therefore, all merchandising decisions were made in Chicago and merchandise was dispatched to the stores where no one was required to make any decisions.

By the middle 1970s, Sears growth was beginning to slow down as the growth of the U. S. population slowed. But, as Sears growth slowed, K-Mart (a new form of retailer brilliantly formed out of the old five-and-dime store company (S. S. Kresge) was demonstrating explosive growth and beginning to challenge Sears' number one position. K-Mart pioneered the concept of promotional merchandising. Virtually all K-Mart buying was done locally to reflect local market tastes. Any merchandise that didn't sell immediately was marked down and sold out. In this way, cash was turned over fast and was a major source of profits.

Without any apparent understanding of its own strengths or K-Mart's strengths, Sears decided to emulate K-Mart and become a promotional merchandiser. So Sears told the employees in the stores to order merchandise on their own decision for their own markets. However, nobody in the stores did anything. They waited for Chicago to decide for them, just like always. When headquarters couldn't get the stores to order on their own, they ordered merchandise for the stores, just like the old days.

But when the headquarters-ordered merchandise arrived in the stores, it didn't sell. It just piled up on the floor and in the warehouses. Inventories ballooned. In the stores, the employees stood around looking at the ever-increasing piles of merchandise and waited for someone from headquarters to tell them what to do.

After the *first two money-losing quarters in the history of Sears*, management gave up trying to be a promotional merchandiser.

Sorry to say, simply returning to its old department store concepts did not solve Sears' problems as the 1980s unfolded. The decade was marked by overbuilding of shopping centers so that the historical anchor tenants like Sears saw their sales and profits per square foot falling steadily. In addition, specialty stores took customers away from department stores at a rapid rate.

Instead of seriously trying to understand its strengths, weaknesses and the changing market place, Sears management hired a management guru to guide the company out of its troubles. This guru took the position that companies can compete in only one of two ways. Either they must differentiate themselves from their competitors, or they must undersell their competitors with lower prices.

Since Sears had decided that it could not successfully differentiate itself from the specialty stores like The Limited, Victoria's Secret, Lane Bryant, etc., it had only the low price alternative left. So it decided to become a discount merchandiser (does this story sound familiar yet?) and stopped having sales events. Instead it substituted everyday low prices in all of its stores.

But Sears had not bothered to understand its weaknesses either. It didn't know that its costs were too high to permit it to be a discount merchandiser. As a result, Sears "everyday low prices" were substantially higher than those of its competitors. So its sales failed to increase, but its margins shrunk.

Sears' response was to cut prices even more. To offset the continuing shrinkage in its margins, it fired thousands of store-level employees. But the new price reductions were still too little to compete. Furthermore, the stores were filled with overpriced merchandise, but there were no sales clerks in case a customer should actually wander into the store!

It will be some sort of miracle if Sears survives the 1990s. The sell-off of the parts of Sears has already begun.

Humana Hospitals

Humana is a major hospital-operating company headquartered in Louisville, Kentucky. By 1985, Humana had revenues of $2,875,140,000 and profits of $216,220,000 from operating 87 hospitals with 17,706 licensed beds. It earned these profits by providing outstanding hospital services and health care. However, the costs of these services were passed on to other payers.

About this time, Humana began to experience declining capacity utilization, which in the hospital business means fewer patients in the beds for fewer days. To pump up occupancy in its hospitals, Humana elected to start a medical insurance business and called it the Health Services Division.

By 1992, Humana was still experiencing falling occupancy in its hospitals, but expenses in its new division exceeded the industry average by 36%, and profits at the once-healthy company were in free fall. Once again, top management failed to understand its strengths and weaknesses.

Humana was successful earlier in its hospital business because it offered participating doctors state-of-the-art facilities and outstanding patient care. After all, it is the doctors who bring the patients to the hospital. But in the health insurance business (which it began with the Health Services Division), success depends on minimizing hospital and doctor costs. Thus, Humana set its two major operating companies at war with each other the instant it decided to enter the new business.

WHAT TO DO NEXT

To understand the strengths and weaknesses of your company you must develop two instruments. One is a list of the business factors that are important to success in your industry, and the other is a rating system for evaluating your company on each of these factors.

Business Factor Lists

Start with the business factor lists. What you are trying to do is to develop a profile of the factors that are important to success in *your industry*. There is no one ideal way to develop this list, but here are some suggestions. Marketing Planning Pages 4-1 through 4-6 on pages 76–81 are designed to give you a starting point. These pages list items in six different areas that are significant to many businesses. You may not need all of them; discard those that you don't need. Decide if you need additional pages to cover other areas in your business. If so, make up new pages that look like the existing pages.

Then go through the items on each page and cross out those items that are not applicable to your business. Follow that by adding new items that are necessary to describe your particular situation. Take your lists to the key managers in each functional area, explain what you are trying to do, and ask for their help. This can be a real opportunity to increase your insights into your own business. If the question arises about whether an item should be included or not, it is generally better to include than to exclude.

A Rating System

The other tool you need to complete this exercise is a rating system. All kinds of systems work perfectly well. One to ten; A, B, C, D, E; Excellent, Good, etc. are examples. Marketing Planning Page 4-7 will help you with this task.

What is important here is that you develop a clear, written description of what each level of rating means. You are going to ask key managers in your company to rate your company on each of the items on your business factor lists and it is extremely important that they all use the *same criteria*.

The first thing to understand is that these ratings are not about some ideal standard. The point of reference for all of your ratings is your *competition* today. Your objective is to identify your strengths and weaknesses vis-a-vis your current competitors because that is how your strategic opportunities are defined. In Section Five, you will begin to understand how your industry has developed by profiling the total industry sales, your own sales and the sales of your main competitors. The rating system is crucial to developing this understanding, but there are a lot of potential pitfalls in creating and using a rating system. First of all, you will find that your managers want to use *other criteria* to do the ratings. For example, you may find a manager saying something like, "I used to work in the XXX industry and compared with that, we are . . ." You must firmly, but gently, not allow this kind of rating because it is simply irrelevant. You don't compete with industry XXX and it doesn't make any difference to you what it does.

The next problem you will encounter is that your managers will want to use different criteria for evaluating strengths than for evaluating weaknesses. What is most likely is that they will substitute some sort of historical evaluation for strengths. Something like "We do this a lot better than we used to do it" is a warning that your system is not being followed. With weaknesses, some normative criteria are likely to appear, as in "We really ought to be doing better here." Neither of these situations is permissible. You can't develop a dynamic, forward-looking strategy by competing with the past or with some vague standard of perfection. A successful business strategy will earn profits only if it is successful in competing against today's competitors in today's market serving today's customers. The better you understand your position, the better your strategy is going to be, and that is the message about ratings that you must communicate to your managers.

WHO DOES THE RATING? Again, there is no single correct answer here. You certainly need all of the key managers, but how wide to cast your net beyond them is a judgment call. Yes, you want an accurate, widely based understanding, but at the same time you don't want to involve so many people that the task becomes unwieldy.

Here is one fact of life to consider. Your top level managers will evaluate differently from lower level managers. Top managers, by nature of their jobs, will bring a much broader perspective to the evaluations. For example, top level managers will consider the company-wide level of employee training and skills, while a plant manager will respond to the specific level of skills of the machinists working in that plant. Top level managers are likely to produce optimistic ratings, (i.e., "We are just great here") while those of lower level managers are more likely to be pessimistic (i.e., "We have a lot of problems here."). In the same vein, top level managers may find it harder than lower level managers to acknowledge weaknesses. You will also find that managers in different sections of the company see themselves differently than others in the company see them.

All of these viewpoints have value for you, but be aware of the inherent biases as you select the managers to participate in your analysis. Always remember that an accurate assessment is your goal. You want a broad-based, but also detailed evaluation of your operations. With all of this in mind, try your hand at creating specific descriptions for a rating system using Marketing Planning Page 4-7.

Gathering the Data

When you have selected your list of evaluators, distribute the Business Factor Lists and the Ratings Description with a short memo that makes three points.

1. Give a clear description of what you are trying to do, why it is important to the future of the company, and your expectations for everyone's best efforts.

2. Ratings should be made only of the items about which the rater has first-hand knowledge. If there is a doubt, the item should be left blank.

3. The results are completely confidential. As you are surely aware, there is a lot of room for gamesmanship in this exercise. You want to do everything possible to minimize it.

Summarizing the Results

When you have all of the forms returned, prepare a summary of each item on each list. From now on, ignore the functional areas and use only the individual items. Count the number of "A's" given to each item. Prepare a table and/or a graph that ranks all the items from most A's to fewest A's. Then do the same thing for A's and B's.

Then look at the other end of the scale and prepare similar summaries of the E-rated items (if any), and the E and D-rated items (combined).

Distribute copies of all the summaries to all the raters and schedule a review meeting.

The Review Meeting

You want to accomplish three things at the Review Meeting: 1) determine the accuracy of the ratings profile; 2) identify weaknesses and develop specific assignments to deal with them; and 3) begin to isolate your strengths.

The meeting should begin with a group assessment of the accuracy of the composite ratings. This may go quickly, as in, "Yeah, that's us all right," or it may lead to some major disagreement(s). If disagreements arise, it is extremely important that you gain insights into the dynamics that are fueling the disagreement(s) because you may be witnessing the manifestation of other management problems within your company.

When you arrive at a consensus agreement that you finally have an accurate profile of your company, focus on the E and/or D items because they represent your weaknesses. They also represent significant opportunities for your competitors to take business away from you. Therefore, you want to move quickly and surely against these problem areas. When consensus is reached that an item, or group of items, is truly a weakness, assign responsibility to someone for developing a plan to deal with the problem. Set a deadline for a report and recommendations. Don't leave the room until every weakness has some one specifically assigned to it with a timetable for action. Too often, weaknesses are only dealt with when some awful crisis occurs. This is one time when you can deal with them in a calm environment with lots of options.

As you think about what to do with weaknesses, be sure you include the possibility of having someone else do it for you. This is called "outsourcing" these days. The basic idea is that letting someone else do something you are not good at brings you two major benefits. One is that your weakness now becomes a strength because the job is being performed by a state-of-the-art supplier (why else would you hire that person?). And the other is that it frees up capital and executive time to devote to your strengths, or "core competencies," as these things are called today. Both are good reasons.

Many companies in electronics and apparel outsource their entire manufacturing operations to someone who can do a better job. But it also works in things as mundane as shoes. Nike owns no plants whatsoever and earned a sparkling 16% ROA in 1992.

But don't limit your search to just major operations. Last year, DuPont turned over all of its photocopy machines and their maintenance to Lanier, and they now pay Lanier a flat fee for each copy from a particular machine. DuPont figures they will save over $14 million a year. Kodak used to spend $40 million a year cooking for 40,000 employees at its headquarters in Rochester, New York. Now Marriott FoodSystems does the same job at a lower cost on contract.

The third task for the review meeting is to develop insights into your strengths, both in existing form and in potentially new and dynamic forms. The existing items of strength are relatively easy. Those are the individual items with high scores in terms of A ratings. Examine each one to make sure that you are fully exploiting these advantages. If some are not being fully exploited, assign someone to develop a plan to accomplish that goal and assign a deadline for reporting back. This is the stuff that really gives you competitive muscle in the market and you must take full advantage of all of it.

The subject of potential strengths is a little more tricky. What you are searching for here are "clusters" of strengths that may give you new competitive advantage in the market if you can organize and exploit them properly. Start with a blackboard and ask for suggestions of highly rated items that might seem to go together in some way. An example might be: highly trained assembly workers, low return rate, quality control procedures, employee ownership. These clusters may be molded into future competitive advantage and provide the foundations for future strategy.

Once such clusters begin to appear, return to the high-scoring B items and look for those that could strengthen a cluster if the item were upgraded to an A status. For every B item that is judged to strengthen a cluster, assign someone to develop a plan for upgrading and a deadline for submission.

The final thing to do at the Review Meeting is to have everyone attempt to write short descriptions of each cluster. This will go a long way toward sharpening everyone's insights into what your future competitive advantages may be.

Don't worry about the C items, or the other B items, just now. You can't do everything all at once. If you try, nothing will get done. What you have done here is twofold: identified your most significant areas of competitive disadvantage and moved to correct them, and identified your current areas of strength and moved to fully exploit them. In addition, you have developed insights into what may become your future strategic advantages. Just make sure you follow through with this new focusing of your activities.

Marketing Planning Page 4-1

BUSINESS FACTOR ITEMS — MARKETING AREA

Item	Rating				
	A	B	C	D	E
Sales growth	____	____	____	____	____
Market share	____	____	____	____	____
Distribution	____	____	____	____	____
Size of sales force	____	____	____	____	____
Effectiveness of sales force	____	____	____	____	____
Sales training	____	____	____	____	____
Selling expenses	____	____	____	____	____
Prices	____	____	____	____	____
Customers	____	____	____	____	____
Advertising effectiveness	____	____	____	____	____
Advertising budget	____	____	____	____	____
Warehouses	____	____	____	____	____
Inventory levels	____	____	____	____	____
On time delivery	____	____	____	____	____
Distribution expenses	____	____	____	____	____
Market growth rate	____	____	____	____	____
Gross margins	____	____	____	____	____
Product quality	____	____	____	____	____
_____	____	____	____	____	____
_____	____	____	____	____	____
_____	____	____	____	____	____
_____	____	____	____	____	____
_____	____	____	____	____	____
_____	____	____	____	____	____
_____	____	____	____	____	____

Marketing Planning Page 4-2

BUSINESS FACTOR ITEMS—PRODUCTION AREA

Item	Rating				
	A	B	C	D	E
Plant capacity	——	——	——	——	——
Plant location(s)	——	——	——	——	——
Age of plant(s)	——	——	——	——	——
Age of equipment	——	——	——	——	——
Condition of P & E	——	——	——	——	——
Ability to expand capacity	——	——	——	——	——
Skill of labor force	——	——	——	——	——
Labor turnover	——	——	——	——	——
Union relations	——	——	——	——	——
Scrap rate	——	——	——	——	——
Quality control	——	——	——	——	——
Supplier relations	——	——	——	——	——
Raw material sources	——	——	——	——	——
_____	——	——	——	——	——
_____	——	——	——	——	——
_____	——	——	——	——	——
_____	——	——	——	——	——
_____	——	——	——	——	——
_____	——	——	——	——	——
_____	——	——	——	——	——
_____	——	——	——	——	——
_____	——	——	——	——	——
_____	——	——	——	——	——
_____	——	——	——	——	——

Marketing Planning Page 4-3

BUSINESS FACTOR ITEMS—FINANCIAL AREA

Item	A	B	C	D	E
			Rating		
Profitability	___	___	___	___	___
Cash flow	___	___	___	___	___
Retained earnings	___	___	___	___	___
Current assets	___	___	___	___	___
Current liabilities	___	___	___	___	___
Long term debt	___	___	___	___	___
Stockholder's equity	___	___	___	___	___
Bad debt ratio	___	___	___	___	___
Inventory turnover	___	___	___	___	___
Return on sales	___	___	___	___	___
Credit line	___	___	___	___	___
Bank relations	___	___	___	___	___
Debt/equity ratio	___	___	___	___	___
Per share book value	___	___	___	___	___
Stock price	___	___	___	___	___
Return on investment	___	___	___	___	___
Net margins	___	___	___	___	___
Productivity	___	___	___	___	___
_____	___	___	___	___	___
_____	___	___	___	___	___
_____	___	___	___	___	___
_____	___	___	___	___	___
_____	___	___	___	___	___
_____	___	___	___	___	___
_____	___	___	___	___	___

Marketing Planning Page 4-4

BUSINESS FACTOR ITEMS—ADMINISTRATIVE AREA

Item	Rating				
	A	B	C	D	E
Headquarters facilities	——	——	——	——	——
Branch office facilities	——	——	——	——	——
Office employee skill levels	——	——	——	——	——
Office employee turnover	——	——	——	——	——
Administrative expenses	——	——	——	——	——
Age of office equipment	——	——	——	——	——
Office employee training	——	——	——	——	——
Data processing capability	——	——	——	——	——
Inter-office communications	——	——	——	——	——
————————————	——	——	——	——	——
————————————	——	——	——	——	——
————————————	——	——	——	——	——
————————————	——	——	——	——	——
————————————	——	——	——	——	——
————————————	——	——	——	——	——
————————————	——	——	——	——	——
————————————	——	——	——	——	——
————————————	——	——	——	——	——
————————————	——	——	——	——	——
————————————	——	——	——	——	——
————————————	——	——	——	——	——
————————————	A	B	C	D	E

Marketing Planning Page 4-5

BUSINESS FACTOR ITEMS—MANAGEMENT AREA

Item	Rating				
	A	B	C	D	E
Top management experience	____	____	____	____	____
Middle-level management experience	____	____	____	____	____
Supervisory management experience	____	____	____	____	____
Top management depth	____	____	____	____	____
Middle management depth	____	____	____	____	____
Supervisory management depth	____	____	____	____	____
Open communications	____	____	____	____	____
Effective communications systems	____	____	____	____	____
Managers' access to information	____	____	____	____	____
Well-defined responsibilities	____	____	____	____	____
Cohesiveness of top management group	____	____	____	____	____
Management compensation plan	____	____	____	____	____
Decision speed	____	____	____	____	____
Top management turnover	____	____	____	____	____
Middle management turnover	____	____	____	____	____
Strategic planning ability	____	____	____	____	____
Plans execution	____	____	____	____	____
Board of directors	____	____	____	____	____
_____	____	____	____	____	____
_____	____	____	____	____	____
_____	____	____	____	____	____
_____	____	____	____	____	____
_____	____	____	____	____	____
_____	____	____	____	____	____
_____	____	____	____	____	____
_____	____	____	____	____	____

Marketing Planning Page 4-6

Business Factor Items—Technology/R&D Area

Item	Rating				
	A	B	C	D	E
Age of R & D facilities	___	___	___	___	___
Age of product technology	___	___	___	___	___
Age of process technology	___	___	___	___	___
Product patents	___	___	___	___	___
Process patents	___	___	___	___	___
Basic innovation	___	___	___	___	___
Engineering abilities	___	___	___	___	___
Ability to work with customers	___	___	___	___	___
R & D personnel experience	___	___	___	___	___
R & D management	___	___	___	___	___
R & D budgets	___	___	___	___	___
R & D project timeliness	___	___	___	___	___
_____	___	___	___	___	___
_____	___	___	___	___	___
_____	___	___	___	___	___
_____	___	___	___	___	___
_____	___	___	___	___	___
_____	___	___	___	___	___
_____	___	___	___	___	___
_____	___	___	___	___	___
_____	___	___	___	___	___
_____	___	___	___	___	___
_____	___	___	___	___	___

RATING SYSTEM DEFINITIONS

Definition of A rating: _____

_____

(Example: Nobody is better. Unquestioned leader. Best in the industry. Stronger than anybody. Have more than any other competitor.)

Definition of B rating: _____

_____

(Example: As good as the best competitors. At the leading edge of technology. Equal to the strongest. More than most competitors.)

Definition of C rating: _____

_____

(Example: Average for industry. Adequate for now. Acceptable to most customers. Does not seem to be a problem.)

Definition of D rating: _____

_____

(Example: Most of competition is better. Competitors use this against us. Fairly far behind industry.)

Definition of E rating: _____

_____

(Example: A major problem. Must be corrected at once. Worst in industry. Is costing us significant sales, high returns, lost man-hours, etc.)

BENCHMARKING

Up to this point you have been comparing your company to your industry in general. Now it is time to raise the hurdle. Pick the best performing company that operates generally in your kind of business. For example, if you manufacture high technology products, select Motorola, or if you are in retailing, select Wal-Mart Stores, or if you are in a service business, select McDonald's. The idea is to focus on one company that regularly produces truly outstanding results year after year.

Then assemble a team of one each of your best people from operations, finance, marketing, sales, research & development, etc. Give them the task of analyzing your profit and loss statement, item by item, against your selected benchmark company. For every item where you are not equal to, or better than, your benchmark target, ask your team to prepare a plan for improving that item. Make sure that there is a timetable and a budget included in the plan for each item.

How to Conduct a Focused Market Review

OVERVIEW OF SECTION FIVE: To the greatest extent possible, strategies and plans must be developed based on historical facts. Those facts are most likely in the form of numbers. Therefore, a crucial question in strategy development and marketing planning concerns where you can find existing numbers that describe your markets accurately. Section Five addresses this problem very specifically. You will be shown how to gain access to the vast amount of data available and useful in your planning. In addition, Section Five will show you how to use your new found data to identify the markets with the most potential for growth.

WHERE STRATEGY DEVELOPMENT STARTS

In 1992, Dun & Bradstreet, the credit reporting company, questioned thousands of managers in growing businesses about the most important factors in succeeding with a growing business. By an overwhelming margin, the number one factor cited in managing a successfully growing business is how well you know your business, your markets and your industry. This means that your marketing plan and marketing strategy must be developed from a thorough, accurate understanding of three major interrelated factors:

- The historical growth trends for the total market for each of your products and/or services
- The historical sales trends for each of your products and/or services
- The historical sales trends for each of your major competitors'** products and/or services

We are only concerned with the three or four largest competitors in your industry because these are companies that set the trends for the entire industry and define what activities are permissible. Section Six will show you how to examine these competitors in much greater detail.

Your objective is to obtain a firm, clear, widely shared view of where you stand in each market in which you compete, how you got to that position, and how your competitors got to their positions. In turn, that means you will have to re-create some history before you can begin developing marketing plans and marketing strategy.

DEFINING THE MARKET THROUGH SIC CODES

Before you can begin a search for historical data, you will have to define the markets in which you compete in some operational method. One widely used and very useful method of defining markets is on the basis of Standard Industrial Classification codes. The federal Office of Management and Budget classifies *every* business in the United States into eleven divisions and ninety-three major groups. The major groups are further refined into narrower groups. All of this structure is organized around numerical categories with very specific definitions.

Example: In Division D, Manufacturing, you will find Major Group (SIC Code) 35, Industrial and Commercial Machinery and Computer Equipment; within Major Group 35, you will find SIC Code 358, Refrigeration and Service Industry Machinery. Inside this code, you will find SIC Code 3581, Automatic Vending Machines, defined as "establishments primarily engaged in manufacturing automatic vending machines and coin-operated mechanisms for such machines." Delving further into this code, we find that those establishments are defined as:

- Lock, coin-operated
- Mechanisms for coin-operated machines
- Merchandising machines, automatic
- Vending machines for merchandise: coin-operated

All of this information is available in a book called the *Standard Industrial Classification Manual* 1987. You can find a copy in your local business library, or you can buy your own copy from National Technical Information Service, 5285 Port Royal Road, Springfield, Virginia 22161.

If you are operating an existing business, you have already been assigned one, or more, SIC codes for reporting purposes to the Internal Revenue Service and other government agencies. If you don't know your SIC code classification(s), your financial or accounting people will know.

The advantage to using SIC codes to define markets is that there is a massive amount of data available that has been collected along those guidelines. The major disadvantage is that the SIC classifications tend to be organized around producing goods and services, rather than around customers, and your planning and strategic efforts must always be organized around, and focused on customers. We will examine how to organize marketing data around customers when we discuss market segmentation in Section Ten, but for now, understanding your SIC code data is a very useful place to begin.

COLLECTING SECONDARY DATA

To understand what has happened in the past, you must gain access to data that was collected in the past, i.e., historical data. That means it must be data someone else has collected for some other purpose, and data collected by someone else is usually referred to as "secondary data."

Remember two important things when you begin to collect secondary data. First is to collect data in units if at all possible. Inflation creates incredible distortions in monetary measures. In addition, the distortions are not evenly distributed. Markets within the U. S., as well as different countries, frequently experience differing rates of inflation. This monetary inflation will camouflage exactly what the customers are actually doing. Your goal is to find data in inflation-proof quantity data, i.e., cases, tons, bottles, quarts, liters, kilometers, etc.

Here is a recent example of how financial data would lead to one conclusion while volume data leads to quite a different conclusion.

SALES OF TOMATO KETCHUP IN U. S. FOOD STORES

Year	$ Millions	Lbs. Millions
1985	511	706
1986	515	693
1987	506	679
1988	513	680
1989	526	669
1990	532	661

If you only had the dollar data, you would conclude that the retail market for tomato ketchup in the U. S. was growing slowly, if erratically. However, the real picture is that the market is in a steady, long term decline.

If your business has only currency as a measure of activity, you must use a "deflator" to wring the effects of inflation out of your data. Be sure to use one that is as "close" to your industry as possible. A deflator is a government-sponsored method of measuring price changes, such as the well-known Consumer Price Index (CPI). It (and all of its component indices) is published by the Bureau of Labor Statistics, U. S. Department of Labor. The same Bureau also publishes the Producer Price Index (PPI) and all of its component indices for businesses that do not sell to consumers.

Where to Find Secondary Data

There are three major sources of secondary data that will prove valuable in the planning activities. Broadly defined, they are:

- Government agencies
- Trade associations and trade publications
- Private research firms, including computer databases

You should learn the advantages and disadvantages of each of these sources in terms of your business.

GOVERNMENT AGENCIES Governments at all levels collect a wide variety of data for purposes of taxing, controlling, regulating and setting policies. The major problem of working with government data is that there is no ONE place that you can turn to for a complete listing of available data. While most of what follows concerns U. S. government data sources, keep in mind that state, county and city governments also collect data that may be useful to you.

The most central focus for U. S. government data is the Government Printing Office. It also operates retail book stores in major cities around the country. Locate the one closest to you and pay a visit. You will find it full of buried treasures.

The library at a university or college in your area may be a designated U. S. Government Repository and that means the library will receive every government document printed. A telephone call to any library in your area should reveal the Repository closest to you. More than likely, some one person in that library will have specific responsibility for that government data. This is a person you want to get to know because he or she can be of immense assistance if you so allow. Try to explain your goals rather than specify exactly the data you think you are looking to find. Searching for secondary data is a skill that you can highly develop; surprisingly, serendipity can also play a role.

TWO ABSOLUTELY ESSENTIAL SOURCES OF GOVERNMENT DATA Every year, the Bureau of Economic Analysis of the U. S. Department of Commerce compiles a *Survey of Current Business 19XX* and a companion volume, *Business Statistics 19XX*. This report provides concise summaries of current conditions, and forecasts for the future, for hundreds of the U. S.'s most important industries. The *U. S. Industrial Outlook 19XX* surveys approximately 350 industries every year, and it is one of the government's best selling reports. It comes as a 650-page book, on CD-ROM, or as a set of 3 $1/2$" or 5 $1/4$" diskettes. You can get all of these publications from the Superintendent of Documents, your local GPO bookstore, or you can try to borrow a copy from the library.

The other essential source is the *Current Industrial Reports (CIRs)*. These individual reports present data on more than 5,000 industrial products and they account for about 40% of all manufacturing activity in the U. S. In total, there are about 100 different CIRs. About one-third of them are sponsored by a trade association or a specific government agency. The other two-thirds represent direct reporting to the government. All CIRs are published annually, and some are published quarterly or even monthly. Some rely on survey data and some use complete census data.

Exhibit 5-1 is a list of the major product categories covered by *Current Industrial Reports*. Each of the listed reports contains considerable additional detail within the product category.

Exhibit 5-1

CURRENT INDUSTRIAL REPORTS

Processed Foods

Flour Milling Products (M20A)

Confectionery, Including Chocolate Products (M20C)

Fats and Oils: Oilseed Crushing (M20J)

Fats and Oils: Production, Consumption and Stocks (M20K)

Textile Mill Products

Woven Fabrics Production, Inventories and Unfilled Orders (M22A)

Consumption of Woolen and Worsted Systems (M22D)

Textured Yarn Production (MA22F.1)

Spun Yarn Production (MA22F.2)

Narrow Fabrics (MA22G)

Cotton, Man-Made Fiber Staple and Linters (M22P)

Carpets and Rugs (MQ22Q)

Broad woven Fabrics Finished (MA22S)

Broad woven Fabrics (Gray) (MQ22T)

Apparel and Leather

Men's Apparel (M23B)

Women's Apparel (M23H)

Gloves and Mittens (MA23D)

Brassieres, Girdles and Allied Garments (MA23J)

Sheets, Pillowcases and Towels (MQ23X)

Shoes and Slippers (M31A)

Shoes and Slippers—By Type of Construction and Price Line (MA31A)

Exhibit 5-1

CURRENT INDUSTRIAL REPORTS *(continued)*

Chemicals, Rubber and Plastics

Inorganic Chemicals (M28A)

Inorganic Fertilizer Materials and Related Acids (M28B)

Industrial Gases (M28C)

Paint, Varnish, and Lacquer (M28F)

Pharmaceutical Preparations, Except Biologicals (MA28G)

Asphalt and Tar Roofing and Siding Products (MA29A)

Sales of Lubricating and Industrial Oils and Greases (MA29C)

Rubber Supply and Distribution (MA30D)

Plastic Bottles (M30E)

Stone, Clay and Glass Products

Flat Glass (MQ32A)

Refractories (MQ32C)

Clay Construction Products (M32D)

Consumer, Scientific, Technical and Industrial Glassware (MA32E)

Glass Containers (M32G)

Fibrous Glass (MA32J)

Primary Metals

Iron and Steel Castings (MA33A)

Steel Mill Products (MA33B)

Inventories of Steel Shapes (M33-3)

Nonferrous Castings (M33E)

Magnesium Mill Products (MA33G)

Inventories of Brass and Copper Wire Mill Shapes (M33K)

Insulated Wire and Cable (MA33L)

Aluminum Ingot and Mill Products (M33-2)

Copper Base Mill and Foundry Products (DIS917)

Exhibit 5-1

Current Industrial Reports *(continued)*

Intermediate Metal Products

Commercial Steel Forgings (MA34C)

Plumbing Fixtures (MQ34E)

Steel Power Boilers (MA34G)

Closures for Containers (MA34H)

Steel Shipping Barrels, Drums and Pails (MQ34K)

Heating and Cooking Equipment (MA34N)

Aluminum Foil Converted (MA34P)

Machinery and Equipment

Farm Machines and Equipment (MA35A)

Office, Computing and Accounting Machines (MA35R)

Construction Machinery (MQ35D)

Mining Machinery and Equipment (MA35F)

Selected Air Pollution Equipment (MA35J)

Internal Combustion Engines (MA35L)

Air Conditioning and Refrigeration Equipment (MA35M)

Pumps and Compressors (MA35P)

Tractors except Garden Tractors (MA35S)

Vending Machines (MA35U)

Metalworking Machinery (MQ35W)

Electric Lamps (MQ36C)

Fluorescent Lamp Ballasts (MQ36C)

Electric Housewares and Fans (MA36E)

Major Household Appliances (MA36F)

Motors and Generators (MA36H)

You can deal directly with the U. S. Government by writing to:

U. S. GOVERNMENT PRINTING OFFICE
Superintendent of Documents
Washington, D. C. 20402

Ask for the current "United States Government Information for Business" catalog (it's free) and ask to be placed on the mailing list for business publications (also free). Also see Section Twelve.

Before we leave the U. S. Government, there is another source of information that may help. Federal Information Specialists are available at the Federal Information Center (800-688-9889) to assist you in finding government information and data.

TRADE ASSOCIATIONS AND TRADE PUBLICATIONS One of the most important functions that a trade association performs for its members is to collect data about the association's markets and then make that data available to its members and sometimes even to non-members for a small charge. The best single source of data on associations is the *Encyclopedia of Associations* published annually by Gale Research, Inc., (1-800-877-GALE), 835 Penobscot Bldg., Detroit, Michigan 48226. You should also be able to find the *Encyclopedia* in any library with a good business section.

Trade publications often do this same job of gathering market information and disseminating it to the industry the publication serves. Many have research departments specifically to gather data. Write or telephone the publication's offices and ask for the data you need. The single best source of information about trade publications is *Business Publication Rate and Data Service* published by Standard Rate & Data Service (SRDS), 3004 Glenview Road, Wilmette, Illinois 60091. This volume includes the names, addresses and personnel of virtually all of the trade, business and professional magazines published in the U. S.

SRDS is in the business of supplying up-to-the-minute information about the costs (and other information) of advertising in each of these magazines and publications. The SRDS volumes are sold mostly by subscription to advertising agencies. However, they become outdated within months and you may be able to buy a back issue directly from SRDS at a much reduced price. (Any volume less than two years old is fine for your purposes.) Or you may find a local advertising agency that will give you a set it was going to throw away anyway. Some larger business libraries will have these volumes in their stacks. It just takes a telephone call to find out.

PRIVATE RESEARCH FIRMS   There are two types of private research firms that may be of interest to you. One undertakes exactly the kind of industry data collection process that you are engaged in and does it on speculation. The firm packages all of the collected data, usually along with written analysis, comment and sometimes forecasts, in bound volumes for sale. It also re-sells similar reports done by other research firms.

Two of the best of this type of firm are listed below.

FIND/SVP
625 Avenue of the Americas
New York, NY 10011
(800) 346-3787 [In New York, (212) 645-4500]
Fax: (212) 807-2676

Find/SVP publishes a bi-monthly catalog which is called *The Information Catalog*. Telephone or fax them for your own copy of a current *Information Catalog*.

BUSINESS TREND ANALYSTS, INC.
2171 Jericho Turnpike
Commack, NY 11725
Tel: (800) 866-4648 or (516) 462-2410
Fax: (516) 462-1842

You can telephone or fax for a current copy of its catalog *Off the Shelf.*

Both of these companies will also undertake custom projects designed specifically for your information needs.

The second type of research organization does primarily custom research. This type will work with you from beginning to end to locate exactly the information you need to develop your marketing plans and strategy. There are hundreds of these firms scattered all across the U. S. Look in your local Yellow Pages under Marketing Research, or write to the American Marketing Association, 250 South Wacker Drive, Chicago, IL 60606 and request a copy of its Marketing Services Guide which lists member companies engaged in marketing research.

Or you can telephone Charlie Walker, at C. A. Walker & Associates, Inc., 3800 Barham Boulevard, Suite 516, Los Angeles, CA 90068, Tel: (213) 850-6820, Fax (213) 850-7603 . Over the last twenty-five years, his company has successfully completed hundreds of industry studies.

ON-LINE COMPUTER DATABASES There are now a number of sources of information that can be accessed by going on-line with your own computer, modem and telephone line. One of the best is:

DIALOG INFORMATION SERVICES, INC.
2440 El Camino Real
Mountain View, CA 94040

For a fee, you enroll in its service. You will receive a number of manuals to help you use the service and a personal code number that allows you access to the database by telephoning its computer from your computer. Additional charges are based on the number of minutes you are connected to its computer. This service is available to you twenty-four hours a day, seven days a week.

Dialog currently comprises over 450 databases containing over 330 million articles, abstracts and citations. Dialog offers:

The complete text of articles from more than 2,500 journals, magazines, and newsletters.

The complete text of over 60 leading U. S. and international newspapers.

References to and abstracts of articles from more than 100,000 international publications on science and technology.

Financial profiles and background information on more than 12 million U. S. and 1 million international companies.

You can get more information from Dialog's Customer Service at (800) 334-2564.

A similar service (but restricted and less expensive) is offered under the *Knowledge Index* label. *Knowledge Index* is administered by CompuServe® and you can obtain further information at (800) 848-8199.

The Internet

Also on-line is the rapidly expanding source of information contained in the Internet. The possibilities of doing business on the Internet will be explored in Section Thirteen, but it should be noted here that the Internet can be a fast, efficient way to search for secondary data all around the world. It is growing so fast that by the time this book reaches print, all kinds of things will have changed. But here is one place to start that is unlikely to change for the next several years. The U. S. Government came on-line in mid 1995 with its own "home page" on the World Wide Web. The site includes links to dozens of federal agencies and to information on business, health, safety and the environment. It is called Fedworld and the "address" (URL) is what follows inside the parentheses: (http://www.fedworld.gov/) Give it a look.

MORE SOURCES OF SECONDARY DATA Here are four additional sources of secondary data that can be helpful. They are all very different.

BUSINESS INFORMATION—SECOND EDITION
Michael R. Lavin
The Oryx Press
4041 North Central at Indian School Road
Phoenix, AZ 85012

STATISTICS SOURCES 19XX
Gale Research, Inc.
P. O. Box 33477
Detroit, MI 48232

BUSINESS INFORMATION SOURCES
Lorna M. Daniells
University of California Press
2120 Berkeley Way
Berkeley, CA 94720

BAKER LIBRARY MINI-LISTS
Publications Office
Baker Library
Harvard Business School
Soldiers Field
Boston, MA 02163

TWO CAUTIONS ABOUT USING SECONDARY DATA We have already discussed the first caution, gathering data in units and not in financial measures if at all possible. The inflation effects in monetary measures can mask vitally important trends. If you can't avoid financial measures, make sure that you carefully "deflate" the numbers.

The second caution involves another way that secondary data can mislead you. The information was collected originally by someone else for some purpose other than yours. Therefore, it is very important that you know exactly what is included in the data, what is not included and how it was collected. In addition, you must have very carefully defined your markets (See Section Ten) so that you are completely aware of how the secondary data fits your needs and how it doesn't.

Organizing Your Data

Marketing Planning Pages 5-1 through 5-4 are examples of how you can begin to organize and analyze your data. When you have completed as many of these pages as you need, go back and look at the three challenges to your knowledge at the beginning of this chapter. Then return to the data and ask what it can tell you about the answers to those questions. Write down your conclusions in narrative form.

Marketing Planning Page 5-1

RECENT HISTORY OF MARKET FOR BRAND A

Source of these market data: _____

Definition of these data: _____

Your definition of this market: _____

....

	19____	19____	19____	19____	19____		
Total Industry Sales	____	____	____	____	____	____%	% Change from 1st Yr to 5th Yr
	100%	100%	100%	100%	100%		
Your Sales	____	____	____	____	____	____%	% Change from 1st Yr to 5th Yr
Your Share of Market	____	____	____	____	____	____Pts	& Points of Change from 1st Yr to 5th Yr
Competitor No. 1 Sales	____	____	____	____	____	____%	% Change from 1st Yr to 5th Yr
Competitor No. 1 Share of Market	____	____	____	____	____	____Pts	& Points of Change from 1st Yr to 5th Yr
Competitor No. 2 Sales	____	____	____	____	____	____%	% Change from 1st Yr to 5th Yr
Competitor No. 2 Share of Market	____	____	____	____	____	____Pts	& Points of Change from 1st Yr to 5th Yr
Competitor No. 3 Sales	____	____	____	____	____	____%	% Change from 1st Yr to 5th Yr
Competitor No. 3 Share of Market	____	____	____	____	____	____Pts	& Points of Change from 1st Yr to 5th Yr

ANALYSIS _____

_____

_____

Marketing Planning Page 5-2

RECENT HISTORY OF MARKET FOR BRAND B

Source of these market data: _____

Definition of these data: _____

Your definition of this market: _____

....

	19____	19____	19____	19____	19____		
Total Industry Sales	____	____	____	____	____	____%	% Change from 1st Yr to 5th Yr
	100%	100%	100%	100%	100%		
Your Sales	____	____	____	____	____	____%	% Change from 1st Yr to 5th Yr
Your Share of Market	____	____	____	____	____	____Pts	& Points of Change from 1st Yr to 5th Yr
Competitor No. 1 Sales	____	____	____	____	____	____%	% Change from 1st Yr to 5th Yr
Competitor No. 1 Share of Market	____	____	____	____	____	____Pts	& Points of Change from 1st Yr to 5th Yr
Competitor No. 2 Sales	____	____	____	____	____	____%	% Change from 1st Yr to 5th Yr
Competitor No. 2 Share of Market	____	____	____	____	____	____Pts	& Points of Change from 1st Yr to 5th Yr
Competitor No. 3 Sales	____	____	____	____	____	____%	% Change from 1st Yr to 5th Yr
Competitor No. 3 Share of Market	____	____	____	____	____	____Pts	& Points of Change from 1st Yr to 5th Yr

ANALYSIS _____

_____

_____

Marketing Planning Page 5-3

RECENT HISTORY OF MARKET FOR BRAND C

Source of these market data: _____

Definition of these data: _____

Your definition of this market: _____

....

	19___	19___	19___	19___	19___		
Total Industry Sales	____	____	____	____	____	____%	% Change from 1st Yr to 5th Yr
	100%	100%	100%	100%	100%		
Your Sales	____	____	____	____	____	____%	% Change from 1st Yr to 5th Yr
Your Share of Market	____	____	____	____	____	____Pts	& Points of Change from 1st Yr to 5th Yr
Competitor No. 1 Sales	____	____	____	____	____	____%	% Change from 1st Yr to 5th Yr
Competitor No. 1 Share of Market	____	____	____	____	____	____Pts	& Points of Change from 1st Yr to 5th Yr
Competitor No. 2 Sales	____	____	____	____	____	____%	% Change from 1st Yr to 5th Yr
Competitor No. 2 Share of Market	____	____	____	____	____	____Pts	& Points of Change from 1st Yr to 5th Yr
Competitor No. 3 Sales	____	____	____	____	____	____%	% Change from 1st Yr to 5th Yr
Competitor No. 3 Share of Market	____	____	____	____	____	____Pts	& Points of Change from 1st Yr to 5th Yr

ANALYSIS _____

_____

_____

Marketing Planning Page 5-4

Recent History of Market for Brand D

Source of these market data: _____

Definition of these data: _____

Your definition of this market: _____

	19____	19____	19____	19____	19____		
Total Industry Sales	_____	_____	_____	_____	_____	____%	% Change from 1st Yr to 5th Yr
	100%	100%	100%	100%	100%		
Your Sales	_____	_____	_____	_____	_____	____%	% Change from 1st Yr to 5th Yr
Your Share of Market	_____	_____	_____	_____	_____	____Pts	& Points of Change from 1st Yr to 5th Yr
Competitor No. 1 Sales	_____	_____	_____	_____	_____	____%	% Change from 1st Yr to 5th Yr
Competitor No. 1 Share of Market	_____	_____	_____	_____	_____	____Pts	& Points of Change from 1st Yr to 5th Yr
Competitor No. 2 Sales	_____	_____	_____	_____	_____	____%	% Change from 1st Yr to 5th Yr
Competitor No. 2 Share of Market	_____	_____	_____	_____	_____	____Pts	& Points of Change from 1st Yr to 5th Yr
Competitor No. 3 Sales	_____	_____	_____	_____	_____	____%	% Change from 1st Yr to 5th Yr
Competitor No. 3 Share of Market	_____	_____	_____	_____	_____	____Pts	& Points of Change from 1st Yr to 5th Yr

ANALYSIS _____

_____

_____

FINDING OUT WHERE YOU ARE STRONG

The next step in understanding your position in the market is understanding where you are within individual geographic markets. Every company is stronger in some geographic markets and weaker in others. You want to identify those markets where you are strong and those where you are weaker. In addition, markets themselves differ from each other in their potential for the sales of your products or services.

Therefore the first step is to develop a MARKET DEVELOPMENT INDEX (sometimes called a Category Development Index). To do this, you follow six steps:

1. Gather total sales in your product category (or some closely related data) on a geographic market-by-market basis.

2. Identify the number of households in each of these markets.

3. Divide sales in the market by the number of households in the market to create a sales-per-household figure for each market.

4. Total the sales and the households in your total geographic area.

5. Divide total sales by total households to obtain an average sales-per-household number for your entire market.

6. Divide each individual market's sales per household number by the average sales per houschold number for your total market

Exhibit 5-2 is an example of how this process works. The example assumes that the product is sold through Hardware and Building Supply Stores in the northeastern United States only. The data are from the 1992 *Survey of Buying Power* published in *Sales & Marketing Management* magazine every August. You can obtain a copy of this very useful data source from:

BILL COMMUNICATIONS, INC.
355 Park Avenue South
New York, NY 10010
(212) 592-6200

Exhibit 5-2

A SAMPLE MARKET DEVELOPMENT INDEX

Markets	Hardware and Bldg Supply Store Sales (in 000's)	Total Number of Households (in 000's)	Sales per Household	Market Development Index
Boston	$1,388,102	1,409.5	$984.81	87
Hartford	421,158	428.3	983.32	90
New Haven	398,312	307.5	1,295.32	118
Bridgeport	375,908	303.7	1,237.76	116
Providence	302,406	347.9	869.23	79
Worcester	268,074	265.2	1,010.83	92
Portsmouth	244,921	131.6	1,861.10	170
Springfield	237,694	222.2	1,069.72	98
New Bedford	184,560	189.4	974.44	89
Manchester	156,468	129.2	1,211.05	111
Portland	143,395	96.3	1,489.04	136
New London	123,907	94.2	1,315.36	120
Burlington	81,789	51.8	1,578.93	144
Bangor	75,196	54.8	1,372.18	125
Pittsfield	73,036	53.9	1,355.02	124
Lewiston	43,874	40.8	1,075.34	98
Total Markets	$4,518,900	4,126.3	1,095.15	100

As you can see from the exhibit above, a sale to a household in Portsmouth is likely to be much more valuable than a sale to a household in Providence.

The next step is to create a *Brand Development Index*. You do that exactly the way you created a *Market Development Index* except that you substitute *your own sales* for the industry sales. Exhibit 5-3 extends the example in Exhibit 5-2 to an individual company level.

Exhibit 5-3

A SAMPLE BRAND DEVELOPMENT INDEX

Markets	Our Company Sales (in cases)	Total Number of Households (in 000's)	Sales per Household (in cases)	Brand Development Index
Boston	3,832	1,409.5	2.71	66
Hartford	1,690	428.3	3.94	96
New Haven	1,802	307.5	5.86	143
Bridgeport	1,004	303.7	3.30	80
Providence	1,821	347.9	5.23	128
Worcester	1,731	265.2	6.52	159
Portsmouth	1,368	131.6	10.39	254
Springfield	864	222.2	3.88	95
New Bedford	367	189.4	1.94	47
Manchester	513	129.2	3.97	97
Portland	477	96.3	4.95	121
New London	409	94.2	4.34	106
Burlington	206	51.8	3.97	97
Bangor	170	54.8	3.10	75
Pittsfield	98	53.9	1.81	44
Lewiston	207	40.8	5.07	124
Total Markets	16,859 cases	4,126.3	4.08	100

Even a casual inspection makes it clear that our hypothetical company is much more likely to make a sale in Portsmouth than in Pittsfield. The real value of this analysis comes when you combine your *Market Development Index* with your *Brand Development Index*. Exhibit 5-4 shows what happens when we do that with the data from Exhibits 5-2 and 5-3.

Exhibit 5-4

A Market Development Index and Brand Development Index Analytical Structure

Market	Market Development Index	Brand Development Index
Boston	87	66
Hartford	90	96
New Haven	118	143
Bridgeport	116	80
Providence	79	128
Worcester	92	159
Portsmouth	170	254
Springfield	98	95
New Bedford	89	47
Manchester	111	97
Portland	136	121
New London	120	106
Burlington	144	97
Bangor	125	75
Pittsfield	124	44
Lewiston	98	124

As Exhibit 5-4 illustrates, there are four possible combinations of sales and market potential:

High Market Development and High Brand Development
High Market Development and Low Brand Development
Low Market Development and High Brand Development
Low Market Development and Low Brand Development

This classification system has very important implications for developing marketing strategy. Clearly, your best opportunities for growth lie in those markets where there is a heavy demand for your type of products and/or services AND you have a strong position, e. g. a large market share. This is the definition of a High Market Development Index AND a High Brand Development Index. (Portsmouth is a good example of such a market in Exhibit 5-4.) These are the markets you want to deal with first in developing your strategy and plans.

At the absolute opposite pole are those markets where there is relatively little demand for your type of products and/or services AND you have a small market share. This, of course, is the definition of a Low Market Development Index AND a Low Brand Development Index. (Boston is a good example of such a market in Exhibit 5-4.) These markets represent your poorest opportunities for growth.

This raises a very important question: what are the trends in these development indices? The very best markets are those where BOTH total demand AND your sales are growing rapidly.

Marketing Planning Pages 5-5 through 5-8 are designed to help you organize your sales and market data, and to do it in a format that makes it easy for you to spot recent trends.

Marketing Planning Page 5-5

MARKET AND BRAND DEVELOPMENT INDICES — BRAND A

Market	*Market Development Index*					*Brand Development Index*				
	19XX	*19XX*	*19XX*	*19XX*	*19XX*	*19XX*	*19XX*	*19XX*	*19XX*	*19XX*
_____	____	____	____	____	____	____	____	____	____	____
_____	____	____	____	____	____	____	____	____	____	____
_____	____	____	____	____	____	____	____	____	____	____
_____	____	____	____	____	____	____	____	____	____	____
_____	____	____	____	____	____	____	____	____	____	____
_____	____	____	____	____	____	____	____	____	____	____
_____	____	____	____	____	____	____	____	____	____	____
_____	____	____	____	____	____	____	____	____	____	____
_____	____	____	____	____	____	____	____	____	____	____
_____	____	____	____	____	____	____	____	____	____	____
_____	____	____	____	____	____	____	____	____	____	____
_____	____	____	____	____	____	____	____	____	____	____
_____	____	____	____	____	____	____	____	____	____	____
_____	____	____	____	____	____	____	____	____	____	____
_____	____	____	____	____	____	____	____	____	____	____
_____	____	____	____	____	____	____	____	____	____	____
_____	____	____	____	____	____	____	____	____	____	____
_____	____	____	____	____	____	____	____	____	____	____
_____	____	____	____	____	____	____	____	____	____	____

Marketing Planning Page 5-6

MARKET AND BRAND DEVELOPMENT INDICES—BRAND B

Market	*Market Development Index*					*Brand Development Index*				
	19XX	*19XX*	*19XX*	*19XX*	*19XX*	*19XX*	*19XX*	*19XX*	*19XX*	*19XX*

Marketing Planning Page 5-7

MARKET AND BRAND DEVELOPMENT INDICES—BRAND C

Market	*Market Development Index*					*Brand Development Index*				
	19XX	*19XX*	*19XX*	*19XX*	*19XX*	*19XX*	*19XX*	*19XX*	*19XX*	*19XX*
_____	____	____	____	____	____	____	____	____	____	____
_____	____	____	____	____	____	____	____	____	____	____
_____	____	____	____	____	____	____	____	____	____	____
_____	____	____	____	____	____	____	____	____	____	____
_____	____	____	____	____	____	____	____	____	____	____
_____	____	____	____	____	____	____	____	____	____	____
_____	____	____	____	____	____	____	____	____	____	____
_____	____	____	____	____	____	____	____	____	____	____
_____	____	____	____	____	____	____	____	____	____	____
_____	____	____	____	____	____	____	____	____	____	____
_____	____	____	____	____	____	____	____	____	____	____
_____	____	____	____	____	____	____	____	____	____	____
_____	____	____	____	____	____	____	____	____	____	____
_____	____	____	____	____	____	____	____	____	____	____
_____	____	____	____	____	____	____	____	____	____	____
_____	____	____	____	____	____	____	____	____	____	____
_____	____	____	____	____	____	____	____	____	____	____
_____	____	____	____	____	____	____	____	____	____	____
_____	____	____	____	____	____	____	____	____	____	____
_____	____	____	____	____	____	____	____	____	____	____

Marketing Planning Page 5-8

MARKET AND BRAND DEVELOPMENT INDICES — BRAND D

Market	*Market Development Index*					*Brand Development Index*				
	19XX	*19XX*	*19XX*	*19XX*	*19XX*	*19XX*	*19XX*	*19XX*	*19XX*	*19XX*

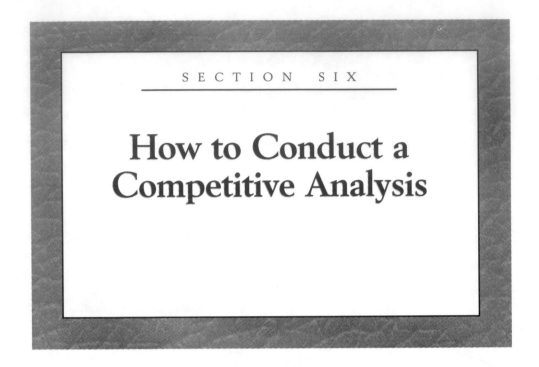

How to Conduct a Competitive Analysis

OVERVIEW OF SECTION SIX: This Section will show you how to develop a thorough understanding of your competitors and their behavior. In addition, Section Six will show you how to use the most sophisticated analytical tool for developing competitive strategy, the Served Market Concept.

THE COMPETITIVE ENVIRONMENT

The only good marketing strategy is one that you can successfully execute. And the only ones that you can successfully execute are those that your competitors will let you execute. Therefore, understanding your competitors is extremely important in developing a successful strategy.

Too often, managers make the mistake of believing that all of their competitors manage and operate in the same way that they do. Nothing could be further from the truth. Every company learns to manage in its own way. That is the entire point of Section Four. Companies develop strengths (core competencies, if you wish) because of the ways they learn to do things that work out successfully.

It is necessary to study only the three or four largest competitors in each of your markets. The reason is that they are the ones who make the decisions about what is acceptable behavior in the industry and what isn't. If you attempt to study more than that, no matter how interesting the companies may be, you will quickly make competitive analysis excessively burdensome.

The objective here is to develop written profiles of these competitors that specifically address each of these six points:

1. What are their strengths and weaknesses?
2. How do they manage/make decisions? Who is involved?
3. What are their real priorities?
4. How satisfied are they with their present position in the market?
5. What changes in that position are they most likely to attempt?
6. What two things could you do that would threaten them the most?

There are many open, ethical sources of information about your competitors. For example:

Annual reports and 10K reports from publicly traded companies

Government records, applications, licenses, etc.

The trade press

The general press*

Their own press releases

Their suppliers

Their customers

*NOTE: This is one place where computer database searching is particularly useful. Reason: companies always want to be well thought of in the individual communities where they have headquarters, plants, distribution centers, R & D labs, etc. As a result, local managers will frequently be very cooperative and open with local reporters and those stories end up in local media. Databases can give you great access to these local media. For example, one of the databases offered by Dialog/Knowledge Index is ABI/Inform's® Business Dateline® full text database covers of 180 U. S. and Canadian regional publications, daily newspapers, and news wire services. (See Section Five for more details about Dialog/Knowledge Index.)

Here are a variety of activities that you can undertake that will help you build these profiles:

A. The CEO (Chief Executive Officer) is the most important person in any competitor's company because he or she is the single person who makes the final strategic decisions. Take one of your application forms that would be appropriate to hiring a person at that level and fill it out for each competitor's CEO.

B. Take a map and indicate all of your competitors' plants, one color for each competitor. Vary circle size to reflect plant capacity. Then do the same thing for their distribution centers, sales offices, whatever is important for success in your industry.

C. Prepare an investment history for each competitor. What does each spend capital funds on? Where? When? How often?

D. Evaluate each competitor's products and/or services from a technical/cost/quality perspective.

E. Then do the same thing from a customer's point of view. How good is the quality? How good a value does it represent?

F. Analyze each of the following:

> Financial position and sources of borrowing
>
> Production capacities and age of facilities and equipment
>
> Sales force in size, training and effectiveness
>
> Company-wide training programs
>
> R & D expenditures
>
> New product development activities and success rates
>
> Management experience and depth
>
> Pricing policies
>
> Advertising and sales promotion spending

SERVED MARKET CONCEPT

Bruce Henderson, former Chairman of the Boston Consulting Group, first advanced the concept of the "Served Market," and it can be a very powerful tool in assisting you to think about your company, your industry and the future. The first idea in the Served Market Concept is that every successful company must be able to differentiate itself from all of its competitors. (A theme espoused throughout this guide.) Because each successful company is different in some meaningful way, each successful company has some combination of products/services and customers where the company has an absolute advantage over every other competitor. These customers are untouchable by competitors; they are "your" customers and yours alone.

By implication, your competitors also have combinations of products/services and customers that are exclusively theirs and are not available to you. But as you move away from these "central" clusters of products/services and customers, the ties between them weaken. When you reach the boundaries between competitors, neither has an advantage. Henderson's idea is that all real competition in an industry takes place at these boundaries of *no competitive advantage*. Exhibit 6-1 is an illustration of these ideas.

The great usefulness in the Served Market Concept comes when you attempt to address the following questions:

1. What combination of products/services and customers gives your company an absolute competitive advantage? In other words, how is your Served Market defined?

2. How are the Served Markets of your major competitors defined?

3. What are the characteristics of the boundaries between you and each of your competitors? Under what conditions do neither of you have a competitive advantage?

4. What actions could your company take to re-define these boundary areas of no competitive advantage?

Marketing Planning Pages 6-1 through 6-8 are designed to help you think about the answers to these questions for one market and one set of competitors. There are enough sets of Marketing Planning Pages here for four markets. If you operate in more than four, make additional copies.

Exhibit 6-1

THE SERVED MARKET CONCEPT ILLUSTRATED

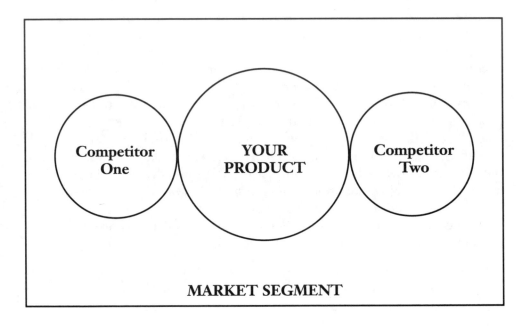

Marketing Planning Page 6-1

Using the Served Market Concept — Competitor A

What features or characteristics of your products and/or services give you an absolute competitive advantage over Competitor A? _____

_____

_____

_____

_____

_____

What are the characteristics of the customers that find the features or characteristics of your products and/or services better/more important/more useful than those of Competitor A?_____

_____

_____

_____

_____

_____

What are the features or characteristics of the products and/or services of Competitor A that give them an absolute competitive advantage over you?

_____

_____

_____

_____

_____

USING THE SERVED MARKET CONCEPT—COMPETITOR A

What are the characteristics of the customers of Competitor A that find the features or characteristics of their products and/or services better/more important/more useful than yours? _____

_____

_____

_____

_____

_____

How would you define the area of "no competitive advantage," the boundary area between you and Competitor A? _____

_____

_____

_____

_____

_____

What actions could your company take to re-define the boundary areas between your company and Competitor A? _____

_____

_____

_____

_____

_____

Marketing Planning Page 6-2

Using the Served Market Concept — Competitor B

What features or characteristics of your products and/or services give you an absolute competitive advantage over Competitor B? _____

_____

_____

_____

_____

_____

What are the characteristics of the customers that find the features or characteristics of your products and/or services better/more important/more useful than those of Competitor B?_____

_____

_____

_____

_____

_____

What are the features or characteristics of the products and/or services of Competitor B that give them an absolute competitive advantage over you?

_____

_____

_____

_____

_____

Marketing Planning Page 6-1, *continued*

USING THE SERVED MARKET CONCEPT—COMPETITOR B

What are the characteristics of the customers of Competitor B that find the features or characteristics of their products and/or services better/more important/more useful than yours? _____

_____

_____

_____

_____

_____

How would you define the area of "no competitive advantage," the boundary area between you and Competitor B? _____

_____

_____

_____

_____

_____

What actions could your company take to re-define the boundary areas between your company and Competitor B? _____

_____

_____

_____

_____

_____

Marketing Planning Page 6-3

USING THE SERVED MARKET CONCEPT—COMPETITOR C

What features or characteristics of your products and/or services give you an absolute competitive advantage over Competitor C? _____

_____

_____

_____

_____

_____

What are the characteristics of the customers that find the features or characteristics of your products and/or services better/more important/more useful than those of Competitor C? _____

_____

_____

_____

_____

_____

What are the features or characteristics of the products and/or services of Competitor C that give them an absolute competitive advantage over you?

_____

_____

_____

_____

_____

Using the Served Market Concept—Competitor C

What are the characteristics of the customers of Competitor C that find the features or characteristics of their products and/or services better/more important/more useful than yours? _____

_____

_____

_____

_____

_____

How would you define the area of "no competitive advantage," the boundary area between you and Competitor C? _____

_____

_____

_____

_____

_____

What actions could your company take to re-define the boundary areas between your company and Competitor C? _____

_____

_____

_____

_____

_____

Marketing Planning Page 6-4

USING THE SERVED MARKET CONCEPT—COMPETITOR D

What features or characteristics of your products and/or services give you an absolute competitive advantage over Competitor D?_____

_____

_____

_____

_____

_____

What are the characteristics of the customers that find the features or characteristics of your products and/or services better/more important/more useful than those of Competitor D?   _____

_____

_____

_____

_____

_____

What are the features or characteristics of the products and/or services of Competitor D that give them an absolute competitive advantage over you?

_____

_____

_____

_____

_____

Marketing Planning Page 6-1, *continued*

USING THE SERVED MARKET CONCEPT—COMPETITOR D

What are the characteristics of the customers of Competitor D that find the features or characteristics of their products and/or services better/more important/more useful than yours? _____

_____

_____

_____

_____

_____

How would you define the area of "no competitive advantage," the boundary area between you and Competitor D? _____

_____

_____

_____

_____

_____

What actions could your company take to re-define the boundary areas between your company and Competitor D? _____

_____

_____

_____

_____

_____

Marketing Planning Page 6-5

Using the Served Market Concept
Defining the Market—Brand A

Describe this market in words. _____

_____

_____

_____

_____

_____

_____

_____

_____

_____

_____

_____

_____

_____

_____

_____

_____

_____

_____

_____

_____

_____

Marketing Planning Page 6-6

USING THE SERVED MARKET CONCEPT
DEFINING THE MARKET—BRAND B

Describe this market in words. _____

_____

_____

_____

_____

_____

_____

_____

_____

_____

_____

_____

_____

_____

_____

_____

_____

_____

_____

_____

_____

_____

_____

_____

_____

_____

Marketing Planning Page 6-7

USING THE SERVED MARKET CONCEPT
DEFINING THE MARKET—BRAND C

Describe this market in words. _____

_____

_____

_____

_____

_____

_____

_____

_____

_____

_____

_____

_____

_____

_____

_____

_____

_____

_____

_____

_____

_____

_____

_____

Marketing Planning Page 6-8

USING THE SERVED MARKET CONCEPT
DEFINING THE MARKET—BRAND D

Describe this market in words. _____

_____

_____

_____

_____

_____

_____

_____

_____

_____

_____

_____

_____

_____

_____

_____

_____

_____

_____

_____

_____

_____

_____

_____

_____

YOUR OWN INEXPENSIVE
COMPETITIVE INTELLIGENCE SYSTEM

The one thing you want to avoid at all costs is setting up some big database that has to feed at regular intervals and has to produce some kind of report on a regular basis. If it becomes that big, it will soon be the basis for some little kingdom, budget wars, etc. Since competitors don't do interesting things on a regular timetable, regularly scheduled reports will soon be filled with trivia most of the time.

Here is a simple two-step system that will put you in charge of an effective, low cost, minimal time demands, competitive intelligence system that will let you keep up with your competitors and your industry.

1. Get yourself an Internet connection. If you aren't sure what this means, skip ahead to Section Thirteen. Then find a news scanning service that will let you build a set of key words to trigger items of interest to you. The names of your competitors, obviously, as well as brand names in your industry, processes, prominent people, etc., will be key words.

    Every day, several days, once a week, once every two weeks—you choose—you visit your screening service and review the articles that have been collected for you. Then you usually buy those of interest to you. Remember to specify a worldwide scan. Three of the most widely used are Dialog, Newsnet and Nexis. You can telephone them for current services at Dialog (415) 858-3785, Newsnet (800) 345-1301 and Nexis (513) 859-1611.

    An alternative service would be something like NewsPage from Individual, Inc. You select the topics you are interested in and at 8:00AM every day, you receive brief summaries on those topics you selected. After reviewing the briefs you can further opt for full-text articles. You can find NewsPage at [http://www.newspage.com]. (See Section Thirteen for more discussion of using the Internet for research.)

2. Select *one* individual in every major operating group, department, whatever, in your organization and designate that person as the company's competitive intelligence specialist for that area. Ask that individual to send you an E-Mail message anytime he or she comes across some piece of competitive intelligence that might be valuable to the management.

Be sure to acknowledge each submission with a copy to the individual's supervisor. Keep careful records of the submissions from each source. As time passes, you may have to replace a few of the people, but very quickly you will have a network of eyes and ears throughout the company filtering competitive intelligence back to you covering every aspect of the competitive environment.

Also remember to attend regularly the trade shows in your industry. These shows are great sources of competitive intelligence. (Section Twelve has additional discussion about Trade Shows.)

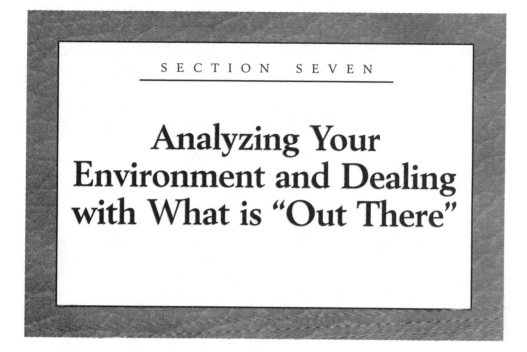

SECTION SEVEN

Analyzing Your Environment and Dealing with What is "Out There"

OVERVIEW OF SECTION SEVEN: History has repeatedly shown that the real threats to companies and industries usually come from outside the industry. That means you must constantly be on the watch for what is "out there" that can damage your business. But "out there" is a huge place! You can't watch everything. Section Seven shows you how to focus on the important parts of "out there."

THE REAL DANGERS FOR YOUR BUSINESS ARE "OUT THERE"

Up to this point, we have looked closely at how your industry has grown, how your position in the industry has changed, and how your major competitors' positions in the industry have changed. We have also examined in detail the activities that make your company a strong competitor and have attempted to isolate those activities in your company that put you at a competitive disadvantage. All of this work has been focused internally, within the industry and within your company. Now it is time to look outside of your industry and outside of your company, to look at what is happening "out there," in the "external environment."

The reason that the external environment is extremely important to your plans and strategy is that the real threats to your business, and the real opportunities for new business development, are most likely to come from outside of your industry, from "out there." Here is just one example, but it is one you have watched develop in your own hometown over the past two decades.

The 1980s saw wave after wave of bankruptcies sweep through the major department stores of the United States. When Macy's went into Chapter 11 bankruptcy it became quite clear that no company was big enough to be immune. As was pointed out in Section Four, Sears Roebuck, the biggest of them all, is teetering on the edge of bankruptcy, or major dismemberment at least. What has brought all of this misery to department stores? Specialty stores is the clear answer. And where did specialty stores come from? Here are the facts about two of the most successful specialty store chains, two that Macy's management really wishes would go away. The Limited, Inc. is a preeminent specialty store chain operating over 4200 The Limited stores, Victoria's Secret, Lane Bryant, and other stores. 1994 sales were $7.3 billion. Leslie Wexner, the founder and CEO of The Limited, Inc., never even worked in a department store. His total experience before he started The Limited, Inc. was a couple of years helping out in his parents' women's dress shop in Columbus, Ohio.

Another spectacularly successful specialty store chain is the Gap, Inc., which operates over 1,200 Gap, Gap for Kids, etc., stores. Its 1994 sales were around $3.7 billion. Donald G. Fisher, the founder and CEO of the Gap, Inc., never worked in retailing at all before starting the Gap. He made his first fortune as a real estate developer in and around San Francisco.

The point is that the managements of the department stores were so busy watching each other that they never saw the real threat coming. You have to watch "out there" all the time. But "out there" is a huge place, and you need a practical method for analyzing and observing the environment in which your business operates. This chapter will help you construct such a method that applies specifically to your business.

MONITORING YOUR EXTERNAL ENVIRONMENT

The simple fact is that you do not have time to watch everything that happens in the external environment. Therefore, the first step is to identify those environments that are most likely to affect your business and your strategy. For most businesses, these five are the key ones to watch and understand:

ECONOMIC ENVIRONMENT

TECHNOLOGICAL ENVIRONMENT

DEMOGRAPHIC/SOCIAL/CULTURAL ENVIRONMENT

POLITICAL ENVIRONMENT

ECOLOGICAL ENVIRONMENT

But each of these areas still covers an enormous amount of material. You need to narrow your focus still further. You can do that by following each of the three steps listed below for each environment.

1. Evaluate which dimensions of each environment are of particular importance to your own business. For example, the Kohler Company manufactures bathroom fittings, i.e., tubs, sinks, faucets, etc., and new single home starts are very important in its planning. In turn, the rate of new home starts is heavily influenced by interest rates. Therefore, any company selling to the new home market should be monitoring interest rates closely.

When you have decided which economic factors are crucial to your business, you should examine each one for immediate threats and/or opportunities.

2. Then you must make the most reasonable estimates of what are the most likely future developments for each of these factors in the short term and in the longer term. You should put those estimates in writing, along with the rationale for each of them, and circulate the estimates to all of your key managers for comment. When those comments have been received and, if necessary, the estimates revised, then it becomes important to insist that all managers make decisions that are consistent with those estimates. It is simply amazing to see the number of occasions when well-meaning managers can agree absolutely on a future estimate, and then turn around and act in exactly the opposite direction. For example, on one hand, a group of managers agrees that long term interest rates are sure to fall sharply in the next twelve months; then they authorize a major new plant to be financed with borrowing at today's interest rates. Don't let this happen in your company.

An Important Digression

Your job here is NOT to predict the future! You simply cannot do that with any degree of precision. One of the things that the whole world has learned very clearly in the past twenty or so, years is that nobody can predict the future with any useful accuracy. The 1970s started out with a lot of people promising to do just that. They had their own organization, THE WORLD FUTURISTS. The University of Southern California had a CENTER FOR THE FUTURE (which issued studies on the effects of zero population growth on Los Angeles just as the population of Los Angeles was exploding), and arcane forecasting methods like the Delphi technique (which came to be known as "pooled ignorance" in impolite circles).

All of that is gone now. No more world conferences among futurists, no more Center for the Future, and Delphi research is back on a shelf. Why? The really simple answer is that it didn't work. And the primary reason it didn't work is that events in real life that NO ONE can foresee actually occur and trash the best prepared of forecasts.

Having said that, it is also necessary to point out that there are still some people around who pretend to be able to forecast the future with great precision. They are usually called economists. Here are two thoughts that you may find useful if an economist offers to forecast the future with great accuracy for your company. Joan Robinson, the noted British economist, said, "The only good reason to study economics is to protect yourself from economists," and Robert Reich, the U. S. Secretary of Labor, has remarked that, "It seems that economic forecasting was invented to make astrology look good."

This DOES NOT mean that you don't have to prepare forecasts. It is one of life's smaller ironies that you absolutely must spend time doing something that is most likely to prove wrong. Section Ten is devoted to an array of simple, workable, inexpensive, but useful, forecasting methods for you to use in accomplishing this job. The reason you have to forecast, even if you know you most likely will be wrong, is that without forecasts you would have no way to measure your progress.

And those forecasts are based on certain assumptions about which events will, and will not, take place in the future, which leads to the third task.

3. Develop a monitoring system to continually test your assumptions about the future as the future unfolds. Here are two cautionary tales about the failure to do this.

No organization in the world spends as much time and money developing strategic plans as does the Pentagon. For obvious good reason, the Pentagon spent thirty years developing strategic plans in case of war in the Middle East. But when Saddam Hussein actually began a Middle East war, all of the thirty years of planning was completely useless. And the reason was starkly simple.

The Pentagon had always assumed that it would have a minimum of three months warning of any Middle East war. And that assumption was never reviewed.

A Thought for Managers

The old saying is that generals always fight the last war. Planning for the Middle East war was a good example of this truth. Does that maxim also apply to managers in your company? Are you fighting yesterday's marketing wars?

The other example can be found at American Express, Inc. All during the 1980s, AMEX CEO James Robinson had a failed view of turning AMEX into some kind of powerhouse financial organization. He bought and sold or closed insurance companies, banks, brokerages, etc. in pursuit of his vision. While he was chasing his dream, the cash cow at AMEX, the Travel Related Services Division and its familiar American Express Card, was under severe competitive pressures from VISA and MASTER CHARGE cards. The number of American Express cards issued fell, the amount of money purchased using the card fell and the number of establishments accepting the American Express card fell.

Finally, AMEX decided to tackle its competitors head on, and it began issuing its own credit card, OPTIMA. OPTIMA cards were issued primarily to holders of American Express cards because AMEX believed that it already had credit histories on these customers. This saved a lot of time and money in building a new credit card business.

And OPTIMA was a huge failure. It cost a $200 million write-off, and may have been the final straw that convinced the Board of Directors to fire James Robinson as CEO. How did all of this happen? Again, starkly simple. AMEX management had ASSUMED that the people to whom they issued OPTIMA cards would treat them the same way they treated their American Express Cards.

Nothing could have been more mistaken. American Express Cards are heavily used for business expenses, which are reimbursed by some company.

The OPTIMA card was used for personal expenditures and there is no company to re-imburse. It was the huge bad debt losses that did in OPTIMA.

The unfortunate part for AMEX is that, unlike the Pentagon, AMEX could have tested its assumption before committing major resources.

The Economic Environment

The economic environment is the most important environment for every business, but it is also the one that any one business is least likely to affect. The very first thing to understand about this environment is the business cycle (as measured by changes in the Gross National Product, i.e., the total value of all the goods and services produced by the U. S. economy in some period, usually one year). It is surprising and distressing how many business people and politicians do not seem to understand the existence of the business cycle. The evidence has been building continuously for hundreds of years now.

The business cycle (or economic cycle, if you prefer) has two parts: expansion and contraction. During the expansion phase, everything goes up. Sales go up, incomes go up, number of jobs goes up, exports go up, everything (almost) goes up. The longer things go up, the more people convince themselves that things will go up forever. But much worse than that, the longer that things go up, the more that marginal projects get approved because there is a sense that the "rising tide will lift all boats." What all of this fundamentally leads to is overcapacity throughout the economic system.

At some point, all of this overcapacity becomes apparent to many people and they stop their own expansion plans. Then sales fail to rise, incomes fail to rise, jobs are lost, exports decline, etc. And in this way, the contraction begins. The contraction phase is called a recession or a depression depending on some economists' definition. What a contraction really is, is a period of time necessary to work off, or through, all of the *excess* capacity created during the expansion.

For a good micro example of the process at work, just look at any major city near you. During the mid 1980s, ten, twenty, a hundred, commercial developers in your city looked at the increasing number of businesses, increasing number of employees, increasing incomes, etc. and decided that office space would soon be a premium because of all this expansion. So every one of those developers took their plans for new office buildings to the local bank and showed the banker the numbers on growth and expected demand. Since the bankers had been looking at the same numbers, and since the increasing businesses had been increasing the deposits in the banks, the bankers were all too happy to lend the money to finance each of these new office building complexes.

Some of these projects were always marginal. Like the one that was to be built way out on the outskirts of town because the land was really cheap, and it was a sure thing that the new Interstate highway would be routed right past the site. But, marginal or not, they all got built. Now, all at once it seems, instead of a shortage of office space, there is a great surplus of office space. More new space than there is new demand, and the excess capacity inevitably leads to falling prices. But the new projects weren't justified on falling prices and they weren't justified on 50% occupancy. As a result, the weakest projects went into bankruptcy and the banks became landlords of unwanted office space.

But eventually (and that is the key word, eventually), growth finally catches up with the excess capacity and the economy is once again operating at full capacity and things are growing again just fine, thank you.

Now take this limited example of commercial real estate and re-play it in every sector of the economy and you have the business cycle exactly. The business cycle is just as real and tangible as the book you are holding right now, and expansions will be followed by contractions as sure as the sun will rise again tomorrow morning. What is not at all clear is when expansions stop and contractions begin, and vice versa. If you attempt to manage your business without regard to the business cycle, e.g., build inventories in the face of a contraction, or neglect increasing the sales force in the face of an expansion, your chances of building a successful business are somewhere between slim and none.

However, you can greatly improve the odds of building a profitable, viable business if you manage it as if the business cycle is real and as if it matters. Therefore, your first task in understanding the economic environment must begin with your assumptions about the business cycle. Then go on to the specific economic factors most influential in your business. Write down your estimates. Make your estimates specific, i.e., +9%, not "up somewhat." Write down your assumptions underlying these estimates. If you operate in countries other than the U. S., do this task country by country. Marketing Planning Page 7-1 is designed to help you with this task.

Marketing Planning Page 7-1

THE ECONOMIC ENVIRONMENT

	1st Qtr	2nd Qtr	3rd Qtr	4th Qtr	Yr 1	Yr 2	Yr 3	Yr 4	Yr 5
	—	—	—	—	—	—	—	—	—

Change in Gross
National Product —   —   —   —   —   —   —   —   —

Rationale:_____

_____

_____

_____

_____

Economic Factor One (Definition): _____

_____

_____

_____

_____

Change in
Factor One: —   —   —   —   —   —   —   —   —

Rationale:_____

_____

_____

_____

_____

Marketing Planning Page 7-1

The Economic Environment *(continued)*

1st Qtr	2nd Qtr	3rd Qtr	4th Qtr	Yr 1	Yr 2	Yr 3	Yr 4	Yr 5
—	—	—	—	—	—	—	—	—

Economic Factor Two (Definition): _____

_____

_____

_____

Change in
Factor Two: — — — — — — — — —

Rationale: _____

_____

_____

_____

Economic Factor Three (Definition): _____

_____

_____

_____

Change in
Factor Three: — — — — — — — — —

Rationale: _____

_____

_____

_____

The Technological Environment

There are two ways that the technological environment can impact you. One way is that new methods of production can substantially alter the cost structure of the industry and thereby change the profitability of the competitors. For example, when Head and Hart both introduced metal manufacturing techniques into the ski industry, they put McGregor and all of the other wood ski manufacturers out of business. Then Japanese manufacturers introduced fiberglass manufacturing techniques and put both Head and Hart out of the ski business. Now there are no major manufacturers of skis remaining in the United States.

Be aware that changing manufacturing technology can take place among your suppliers and/or your customers, as well as among competitors. Bar codes and scanning technology in supermarkets throughout the United States have removed many profitable, but slower moving, brands from the shelves of America's food stores, with major implications for their manufacturers.

But the other threat from the technological environment is the more dangerous one. That is the threat that new products developed entirely outside of your industry may destroy the market for your products. It was pointed out in Section Four that Texas Instruments, Inc. created a whole new market with its electronic pocket calculators. It was not in the office supply or technical supply business, but its new product certainly destroyed the market for slide rules and came close to putting K & E, the main maker of slide rules, out of business.

A much larger drama has played out on the world stage since the end of World War II, and not once, but twice in the same industry. At the end of the war, 80% of all of the watches manufactured in the world were made in Switzerland and they all contained jeweled movements. But during WW II, British manufacturers had developed a device for timing the explosion of bombs that relied on an inexpensive, but quite accurate pin and lever device. TIMEX used that technology to develop a line of inexpensive watches which they distributed outside of the traditional jewelry store channels, and wrote a new page in the history of time keeping. The Swiss market share began a long slide.

But worse was yet to come. In the 1970s, Japanese manufacturers of medical equipment solved a problem of making their instruments legible in broad daylight with LED (light emitting diode) technology. Other Japanese manufacturers combined LED technology with transistors and the resulting digital watches had neither hands nor movements. The Swiss were paralyzed. They had no idea how to respond and their market share continued to decline.

By 1983, the Swiss share of the world watch market had shrunk to 30%, and the only two remaining large Swiss watch makers were losing huge quantities of Swiss francs. In a last ditch effort to save any of the once dominant Swiss watch business, the Swiss government forced a merger between the remaining two Swiss watch companies, Allgemeine Schweizerische Uhrenindustrie and Societe de Wuisse Pour L' Industrie Horlogere with the promise of a bail-out loan. The Swiss government also demanded a change in management.

The new management redefined watches as fashion accessories, rather than just time keeping devices, and the incredibly successful SWATCH was born. The Swiss market share is now 55% of the world market, and climbing.

The point is that neither the British bomb manufacturers nor the Japanese medical equipment manufacturers were trying to take the watch market away from the Swiss. The fact that their new technologies actually accomplished that goal is why you must be monitoring the technological environment continually. Marketing Planning Page 7-2 will help you with that task.

Marketing Planning Page 7-2

THE TECHNOLOGICAL ENVIRONMENT

New technology that could affect our customers' need for our product: _____

_____

_____

_____

_____

New technology that could significantly reduce our cost of manufacturing: _____

_____

_____

_____

_____

New technology that could change the way our suppliers do business: _____

_____

_____

_____

_____

New technology that could change the way our distributors do business: _____

_____

_____

_____

_____

The Demographic/Social/Cultural Environment

Whatever you want to call it, this is the environment that includes all those people around you, your customers, or your customers' customers. In any event, these are people that are the source of the final demand for all goods and services. And this environment has some real peculiarities. It is easy to see. Just walk down the street and look. Then compare what you see with what you can see about the economic environment.

It is easy to measure and lots of measurements are taken regularly. For example, every person in the world who will be twenty-five years old in five years is alive right now. Just count today's twenty-year olds, adjust for a simple mortality figure and you will know how many twenty-five year olds there will be in five years time. Compare that with your ability to foresee technological developments in five years time.

It is the slowest moving of all of the environments. Compared with the speed with which the political environment can change, the demographic/social/cultural environment is the slowest of turtles. Everybody in this environment has to live one year at a time. There are no breakthroughs. There are no leapfrogging events. It is just one day at a time, day after day.

Having said all of that, the demographic/social/cultural environment is the absolutely most difficult of all five environments to anticipate. You can see it, you can measure it accurately, it moves at a snail's pace and you can see it forever down the road ahead. But what it means for your business is incredibly difficult to determine. However, it can affect your business in either, or both, of two ways: through your customers or through your employees.

Here is an exercise to make that point about customers: These are the fertility rates in some of the leading developed countries using 1991 OECD data—the latest comparable data available. Fertility rates are the number of live births per woman of childbearing age in the country. A fertility rate of 2.1 is necessary for simple replacement and zero population growth.

Country	Fertility Rate
Germany	1.4
Italy	1.3
Japan	1.5
Spain	1.3
United Kingdom	1.8

Country	Fertility Rate
Canada	1.8
France	1.8
United States	1.8

Here are some of the direct implications of these data:

- The population of the developed world is getting smaller.
- The population of the developed world is getting older.
- Families are getting smaller.
- The labor force will be shrinking.
- Families have more money to spend on each child.

There are many other implications as well. Your assignment is to write down below five significant ways in which this worldwide direction in the demographic/social/cultural environment will affect the demand for your products and/or services.

1. _____
   _____
   _____
   _____

2. _____
   _____
   _____
   _____

3. _____
   _____
   _____
   _____

4. _____

_____

_____

_____

5. _____

_____

_____

_____

It is not easy, is it? Here is a little story about a company that not only could not understand what the changing demographic/social/cultural environment meant to its business, it didn't even *try* to understand it. The Singer Company used to be the world's foremost manufacturer of home market sewing machines. It had large market shares in the U. S., Canada and in Europe. It had two distinctive market segments that it served. One was younger women aged 16 to 24 who bought the inexpensive, introductory level machines. The other was slightly older young women, aged 25 to 29, who bought the top of the line machines with all of the features and the best margins.

Here are the key numbers that put Singer out of business.

In the United States

In 1970—46% of women 16 to 24 had a sewing machine at home

In 1980—18% of women 16 to 24 had a sewing machine at home

In 1970—79% of women 25 to 29 had a sewing machine at home

In 1980—30% of women 25 to 29 had a sewing machine at home

The market for home sewing machines simply stopped growing in the United States in 1972 and in Europe in 1974. However, Singer management did not find out about any of this until 1982, by which time the game was all over for Singer in the home sewing machine business. Most sewing machines sold for home use these days are made in Japan.

The other way that the changing demographic/social/cultural environment can affect your business is through your employees. That can happen in any, or all, of three different ways.

1. Simple availability: As the fertility rate exercise indicated, there are simply going to be fewer native-born workers available in the developed world in the future. Here is an example of what that means. Every January, in Japan, Coming of Age Day is celebrated by young Japanese who reach their 20th birthday in that year. It marks the time of becoming able to smoke, drink and vote legally. Here are some numbers to reflect upon:

   In January, 1970—2,400,000 Japanese celebrated Coming of Age Day

   In January, 1990—1,880,000 Japanese celebrated Coming of Age Day

   which, of course, means that Japan will have a half million fewer candidates for management jobs in 2000 than it had in 1980. How do you think it will be able to compete in the world market then?

2. Motivation. Everywhere in the world, money is losing its power as a motivator. Employees are increasingly unwilling to work overtime. Time away from work is increasingly important. And to add to the anxieties facing top management in Japan is the fact that right now Japanese middle managers, are the most dissatisfied with their jobs of any similar group in any developed country.

3. The interface with your customers. Banks are good examples of businesses where the interface between employees and customers can have a substantial impact on the success of the business. The Bank of America, for one, makes regular surveys of employees' attitudes. In the 1970s, it found that soaring rates of inflation were causing serious and widespread frustration and pessimism among its employees about their inability to progress in their lives. By the 1980s, the Bank found that deregulation and rapidly changing technology were causing rapidly changing job functions, which, in turn, were creating high levels of anxiety and frustration.

Marketing Planning Page 7-3 will help you organize your ideas about the demographic/social/cultural environment.

Marketing Planning Page 7-3

The Demographic/Social/Cultural Environment

The most significant factors affecting your customers are: _____

_____

_____

_____

_____

The most likely changes in those factors:_____

_____

_____

_____

_____

_____

The most significant factors affecting your employees are: _____

_____

_____

_____

_____

The most likely changes in those factors:_____

_____

_____

_____

_____

_____

The Political Environment

The political environment is the one that can change the fastest and, frequently, with immediate dramatic effects. There are two primary dimensions of the political environment that require your attention. One is new regulations for your industry (including de-regulation) that are made directly, or indirectly. The other dimension is governmental attitudes towards profits, investments and specific business expenditure. Marketing Planning Page 7-4 will help you organize your most important assumptions about the political environment.

The Ecological Environment

The "newest" of the environments that businesses must monitor is the ecological. To give you some sense of just how fast this has happened, here is the opening paragraph from an Earth Day speech given on April 22, 1990 by the newly elected Premier of the state of New South Wales in Australia. His words apply equally well to every developed country in the world.

> Environmentalism has come of age as a political issue. In a very brief period of time, the environment has matured from a radical issue on the fringes of politics into a mainstream concern shared by middle Australia.

The idea to take away here is that the environment truly has become an issue of significance to approximately half of all Americans. Decisions will be made in the 1990s that will affect the U. S. and U. S. businesses for decades to come.

One of the reasons you can safely anticipate environmental concerns sweeping through U. S. businesses is that the United States is so far behind the rest of the developed world. Here is just one example:

In 1978, the Federal Republic of Germany began an environmental labeling program. Today, it covers 3,500 products.

In 1989, Canada and Japan began similar environmental labeling programs.

In 1991, Norway, Sweden, Finland, France, Portugal, Austria, and New Zealand also began labeling programs.

As of 1995, the United States was the only member of the Organization of Economically Developed Countries without a labeling program.

Marketing Planning Page 7-4
THE POLITICAL ENVIRONMENT

In the immediate future, do you expect more or less governmental regulation of your production processes? If so, how will it affect your cost? Will it impact any of your competitors more than you? How will it be enforced? How much time will you have to comply? _____

_____

_____

_____

_____

_____

What are the probabilities that this will happen? _____

What will be the key signal that this event is becoming more likely? _____

In the immediate future, do you expect more or less governmental regulation of your marketing activities? If so, how will it affect your cost? Will it impact any of your competitors more than you? How will it be enforced? How much time will you have to comply? _____

_____

_____

_____

_____

_____

What are the probabilities that this will happen? _____

Marketing Planning Page 7-4

THE POLITICAL ENVIRONMENT (*continued*)

What will be the key signal that this event is becoming more likely? _____

_____

What is the most likely change in taxation by the government to affect your business in the immediate future? _____

_____

_____

Will there be changes in the investment tax credit in the immediate future? If so, how will that affect your business? _____

_____

_____

Do you expect that the government will change the way it treats research & development expenditures in the immediate future? If so, how will it affect your business?

_____

_____

Any other significant political changes you anticipate in the immediate future: ____

_____

_____

In answering the questions on this Planning Page, assume that the immediate future is the next one or two years. Then take a separate page and answer all the same questions for the longer term, say three to five years.

There really is no question that major sweeping environmental regulations are coming and that they will create major threats and major opportunities for businesses everywhere. But there are two major problems for business planners. One is sorting out, and reacting to real problems, not bogus issues. For example, in the United States in 1993, we threw away 80% more trash than we did in 1960, and that is in absolute ton measurements. As a consequence, we are running out of landfill, and this is a real problem.

By way of contrast, consider the much publicized problem of "global warming." This "politically correct" environmental concern is based *solely* on computer simulations of the weather and these are the same weather simulations that *cannot predict* as much as a single rainstorm tomorrow with as much as 50/50 accuracy. In the 1960s, similar simulations were predicting a new ice age because the whole planet was cooling off! Furthermore, a major 1991 study by the National Oceanic & Atmospheric Administration concluded that *all* of the warming that the computer models seem to be based on has occurred *at night*!

The point is that all environmental issues are not created equal and it will be worth your time to examine each one very carefully.

The second problem with developing strategies and plans around environmental issues is that there remains a very large gap between what people *say* are their environmental concerns and what they *actually do about them*. For example:

> 60% of all U. S. women 18 years and older say that people should not buy aerosol hair sprays because they damage the atmosphere, but fully half of those same women continue to buy aerosols in preference to the pump alternative.

> 58% of all U. S. men 18 years and older say aerosols should not be used because they damage the environment, but 87% of those same people buy and use aerosol shaving creams.

The best advice, apparently, is never ignore the ecological environment, but don't believe everything you see or hear either. Marketing Planning Page 7-5 is intended to help you focus on the most important issues affecting your business.

Marketing Planning Page 7-5

THE ECOLOGICAL ENVIRONMENT

Is there anything about your production processes that could cause concern among environmentalists? If so, what is it? _____

_____

_____

_____

What would be required to correct the problem? How much would it cost? _____

_____

_____

_____ _____

Is there anything about your products and/or services, or distribution system, that could cause concern among environmentalists? If so, what is it? _____

_____

_____

_____

What would be required to correct the problem? How much would it cost? _____

_____

_____

What could you do to make your packaging more "environmentally friendly"? ____

_____

_____

Marketing Planning Page 7-5

THE ECOLOGICAL ENVIRONMENT *(continued)*

Is there anything that any of your suppliers do that can cause serious environmental complaint? If so, exactly what is it? How would your suppliers respond to such an issue? How would it affect your business? What actions could you take? _____

_____

_____

_____

_____

Is there anything that your customers do with your products and/or services after they acquire them that could cause environmental problems? If so, what is it? What can you do about it? What would it cost to correct? _____

_____

_____

_____

_____

What communication system exists within your company that you can rely on 100% to bring ecological environmental concerns to your attention at the earliest possible time?_____

_____

_____

Who is the one person in your company that you can absolutely count on to have state-of-the-art knowledge about ecological issues and how they might affect your business? _____

_____

Where Do You Want to Get To?

Developing Your Own Mission Statement

OVERVIEW OF SECTION EIGHT: This Section deals with the most important function for every business, which is to develop a mission, a vision, a purpose.

Section One ends with this short piece from *Alice in Wonderland*:

"Would you tell me, please, which way I ought to go from here?" said Alice.

"That depends a good deal on where you want to get to," said the Cat.

"I don't much care where . . . ," said Alice.

"Then it doesn't matter which way you go," said the Cat.

The Cat's question is one that every growing business must answer, and answer better than Alice did. The answer to that question lies in the company's mission statement which must provide the answer to three fundamental questions:

1. What business are we in now?

2. What business do we want to be in?

3. How are we going to get there?

152

And it *may* answer a number of other questions as well.

Before we examine the subject of mission statements in depth, we must clear up some of the semantic jungle that surrounds these ideas.

Mission statements have been called:

Corporate Objectives

Vision

Management Statement

Corporate Philosophy

Foundations

Value Statement

Guiding or Operating Principles

Business Purpose or Principles

Corporate Goals & Values

Credo or Creed

Corporate Belief

and all of those terms, and more, mean exactly the same thing, the company's mission statement. As such, they all attempt to deal with the absolutely crucial question of where your company is going in the future as it unfolds.

Unless you are like Alice and don't care where you are going, you must have a mission statement (no matter what you choose to call it) because it sets the goals for your company to reach as the future arrives. If you don't have goals, there is no point to marketing planning or marketing strategy whose whole purpose is to figure out how to get from today to tomorrow.

Every book on planning and strategy, and every consultant specializing in this work, agree that the mission statement is the starting point of all planning and strategy. And they are absolutely correct. So they start their books or consulting assignments with developing mission statements, and that is where the trouble always begins.

Developing and writing a mission statement is almost always the *hardest* part of the marketing planning and marketing strategy process. The reason is easy to understand. When managers face changing conditions, they always want to hold open as many options for future action as they possibly can because they are unsure of what is coming next. They strive very hard to retain flexibility because they see this as the best way to be prepared for whatever the future brings.

While that is all understandable, it is also the wrong way to manage any organization. When all of the key managers retain all of their options for future action, the company simply stands still, or drifts without direction, at best. What a mission statement does is give shape to the future that the company has selected for itself. It is an expression of what the future will look like when it arrives.

In this way, the mission statement takes away a great deal of flexibility from managers because it says "this is what we are going to do," and (by implication) "what we are *not* going to do." So the first problem in its creation requires taking decision-making authority away from managers.

The second problem is that a mission statement embodies and expresses a reasonably specific view of the future. That is not an easy thing to acquire. However, if the work described so far in this book has been done completely and accurately, you will have developed some very powerful insights into your organization and into the most likely future of your company. Out of this body of knowledge and from your own experience must evolve some vision of things to come.

WHO WRITES THE MISSION STATEMENT?

The answer is absolutely clear! The Chief Executive Officer of the company must write the mission statement because he or she is the final decision-making person in the organization. The mission statement is the ultimate final decision because it commits the organization to a specific direction.

That does not mean that the CEO must write the mission statement alone. A newly appointed CEO at General Mills, Inc. conducted this task in a particularly classy manner. He gathered all of his top managers at an off-site meeting location for one week. The first thing on Monday morning, he divided the managers into small groups and gave them all the same assignment, to "define the characteristics of an outstanding company." On Wednesday, he gathered them all together, and they spent the day coming to a common agreement on the characteristics of an outstanding company.

Wednesday evening, he assigned new groups and gave them all the same, new assignment, to "describe the actions that General Mills must take in the next five years to elevate a very good company into an outstanding company." On Friday, the entire group reviewed the actions General Mills would have to take to reach the CEO's goals. Then the CEO went away with the results and wrote a mission statement that reflected the weeks' work.

The Mission Statement Must Be Written

The mission statement must be written for two reasons:

1. Because it is a communications device between the top management and many different audiences. Only a written form can guarantee accurate transmission of the message.

2. Because it is a long-term document. A written statement provides continuity over time.

MISSION STATEMENTS: A TESTIMONIAL

Although IBM is now a troubled company searching for a new direction that will lead it into the 21st century, for a very long time it was one of the best managed companies in the world. A large measure of that success was due to the brilliant leadership of Thomas Watson, Jr. When he retired from Chairmanship of IBM, this is what he had to say about the importance of mission statements:

> This, then, is my thesis: I firmly believe that any organization in order to survive and achieve success, must have a sound set of beliefs on which it premises all of its policies and actions.

> Next, I believe that the most important single factor in corporate success is faithful adherence to those beliefs.

> In other words, the basic philosophy, spirit and drive of an organization have far more to do with its relative achievements than do technological or economic resources, organizational structure, innovation or timing.

> All of these things weigh heavily on success. But, they are, I think, transcended by how strongly the people in the organization believe in its basic precepts and on how faithfully they carry them out.

MISSION STATEMENTS: SOME EXAMPLES

There is no formula, no "right way" to write a mission statement (although there are some wrong ones), so the remainder of this section is devoted to presenting a wide variety of mission statements from companies large and small operating in a broad spectrum of industries. As you read each one of them, ask yourself, "Just what is the management of this company trying to accomplish?"

A & W Brands, Inc., headquartered in White Plains, New York, is a tiny player among the soft drink giants of the world, Pepsi-Cola and Coca-Cola. Yet it achieves sales in excess of $100 million through 400 bottlers around the U. S. and the world, record operating income that is 20% of net sales, and has virtually no long-term debt. It accomplishes these outstanding results by focusing on smaller, *niche*, flavor markets. In other words, it has segmented the soft drink market and targeted those market segments ignored by the giants. Its brands include A & W Root Beer, Squirt, Vernors, Country Time lemonade, etc.

A & W Brand's Mission Statement

As a company, our objective is to increase the value of our shareholders' ownership in A & W Brands. Achieving that goal, and assuring future success, means ongoing dedication to our key business strategies: to balance product and marketing innovations with time-tested business techniques; to increase our sales in new and existing markets by developing innovative strategies for marketing, advertising and promotion; to work as partners with our bottlers in order to strengthen and improve our brands' market positions; to support a positive, productive environment for the people of A & W Brands who work in marketing, sales, finance, production, quality assurance and administration; to ensure that each trademark remains the single most outstanding brand in its category.

In a very different business, you will find Arkansas Freightways Corporation, a scheduled, for-hire, common and contract motor carrier transporting primarily less-than-truckload shipments of general commodities throughout the southcentral United States. From its headquarters in Harrison, Arkansas, Arkansas Freightways records revenues of around $200 million and an operating income of about $16 million.

This is what it says drives its business:

Arkansas Freightways Mission Statement

Business Principles:

A company's stated business principles provide the best idea of what a company is and where it is going. At AF, the following principles have been our guide since our inception:

Take Care of Our Customers

Take Care of Our People

Honor Our Commitments

Work Hard, Work Smart, Work Together

Have Fun

Corporate Strategy:

The company believes that growth is required to take care of the needs and requirements of our four main constituents:

Our Customers

Our People

Our Vendors

Our Investors

However, this growth has to be logical and kept under control for it to be successful in fulfilling these needs. Arkansas Freightways entered 1992 in a controlled growth mode once again to take advantage of the challenges and opportunities that it faced in the LTL industry. This is a dynamic industry which is constantly changing to keep up with the increased demands of a more customer-defined market since deregulation. This market presents many challenges that must be met to provide quality service. Arkansas Freightways' strategy for seizing these opportunities and successfully meeting these challenges is best stated in one word:

ATTACK!

NIPSCO Industries, Inc. (Northern Indiana Public Service Company) is in yet another industry. It has operating revenues approaching $2 billion and operating income around $300 million. Here is its mission statement:

NIPSCO Industries, Inc. Mission Statement

NIPSCO is an energy company committed to profitability based on fair values and competitive products in energy and energy-related services.

THE COMPANY is dedicated to rendering quality service and will strive to achieve customer satisfaction.

THE COMPANY will maximize productivity of its human and capital resources for the benefit of its customers, investors and employees.

THE COMPANY will provide efficient, reliable and modern energy capability to all customers and will support the growth, vitality and diversity of its markets.

THE COMPANY will also pursue other energy-related business ventures that offer a profit opportunity and that can better utilize its service organization and other resources.

THE COMPANY is committed to providing an environment for its employees that includes training and career development, compensation programs and work place facilities necessary to achieve job satisfaction and high productivity.

THE COMPANY will communicate actively with customers, investors, employees and the public, and will encourage responsible community leadership in its service area.

Campbell Soup Company, Inc., the Camden, New Jersey multi-billion dollar sales food products company condenses everything to two sentences: "All of Campbell's activities begin with our focus on consumers. Our goals: Maximize profitability and shareholder value by marketing consumer food products that lead in quality and value; and build and defend the first or second position in every category in which we compete."

As you probably know, Navistar International Corporation is the Chicago-based company that now manufactures and markets what was formerly International Harvester trucks and buses. Here is what it says about this topic:

Navistar International Corporation Mission Statement

Corporate Mission

Our primary enterprise objective is to increase the value of our shareowners' investment by managing our resources and serving customers better than and more efficiently than our competitors.

We will grow in markets where we can create enough advantage to earn a good return for our shareholders. We will deploy resources from markets where we cannot.

By achieving our objectives, we expect to reward our shareowners, whose continuing investment in the Company is vital, and to reward our employees, whose creativity and commitment to winning through teamwork is the key to our competitiveness.

As maddeningly vague as the Navistar Mission Statement is, (and you would suspect that the vagueness was on purpose) the Ben & Jerry's Statement of Mission is refreshingly specific. Ben & Jerry's Homemade, Inc. has headquarters in the tiny town of Waterbury, Vermont; it manufactures and markets super premium natural ice cream in pints and bulk packages, frozen yogurts and other ice cream novelties. It also franchises Ben & Jerry's ice cream scoop shops. Its net sales are around $100 million, operating income about $7 million and it has almost no long-term debt. Ben & Jerry's clearly is not a typical U. S. corporation (not yet, at least).

Ben & Jerry's Statement of Mission

Ben & Jerry's is dedicated to the creation and demonstration of a new corporate concept of linked prosperity. Our mission consists of three interrelated parts:

Product Mission

To make, distribute and sell the finest quality all-natural ice cream and related products in a wide variety of innovative flavors made from Vermont dairy products.

Social Mission

To operate the company in a way that actively recognizes the central role that business plays in the structure of society by initiating innovative ways to improve the quality of life of a broad community: local, national and international.

Economic Mission

To operate the company on a sound financial basis of profitable growth, increasing value for our shareholders and creating career opportunities and financial rewards for our employees.

Underlying the mission of Ben & Jerry's is the determination to seek new and creative ways of addressing all three parts, while holding a deep respect for individuals, inside and outside the company, and for the communities of which they are a part.

Central Reserve Life Corporation is a health insurance company with a home office in Strongsville, Ohio. CRL's total income grew from $36 million to $147 million in the decade from 1982 to 1991, while net income grew from $553,000 to $3,372,000. This company looks the future squarely in the face:

Central Reserve Life Corporation
Mission Statement

CRL's Future

CRL's short-range goal is to reach $250 million in premium. We plan to achieve that goal through an expanded team concept utilizing enhanced computer technology, combined with an excellent product mix featuring new "stand-alone" products to generate increased business. To begin this growth process, we have developed a five-year strategic plan which is now in place.

The talented and hard-working staff at CRL is preparing for this promising future by refining control systems and products. Two examples of this effort are the ALPHA OMEGA Renewal Option Program (which allows employers to select from three different renewal options to reduce their premium costs) and the Verification Application Program. These programs work together to assure that CRL attracts and retains high quality, preferred risk clients while minimizing claim expenses.

Products such as the Eagle Plan have taken hold and are now generating millions of dollars in new premiums. The Eagle Plan is unique in that it is designed specifically for individuals instead of employer groups and provides portability of insurance coverage. This product is proving to be extremely popular with a large and growing segment of the U. S. work force.

Since the small employer insurance market is complicated and demanding, many insurance companies are finding it difficult to compete, while many others are not capable of even entering the market. This gives CRL the edge. With our knowledge of the insurance industry and the expertise in our area, there is enormous growth potential.

Buffets, Inc., Eden Prairies, Minnesota, operates over 100 company-owned restaurants around the U. S. doing business as OLD COUNTRY BUFFET restaurants. They generate sales in excess of $200 million. It would be hard to find a clearer expression of 1) what business the company is in now,

2) what business the company intends to be in, and 3) how it expects to get there, than the one put forward by Buffets' management.

Buffets, Inc. Company Mission and Values

The primary mission of the Company is to provide superior financial results and growth for its shareholders by operating a high-quality buffet restaurant chain which appeals to value-oriented customers of all ages.

We will attempt to achieve our mission by adhering to the following principles:

Honesty and Integrity

Our word is good, our dealings direct and our payments timely. We value our reputation, and through our actions we strive to treat others as we would like to be treated.

Old-Fashioned Service

When it comes to our customers and service, we are old-fashioned. We take the time to care for our customers. We know them and what they like. We make them feel welcome. Eating at our restaurants is like coming home.

Exceptional Quality

To us, top quality means giving our customers *more* than they expect. Fresh and flavorful food to please every age and taste, a warm and friendly environment, cleanliness and care throughout-these are the ingredients that create loyal customers and goodwill ambassadors.

Top Value for Our Customers and for Our Shareholders

We seek to provide the highest quality dining experience at the lowest possible price for our customers. Similarly, we try to maximize shareholder value. We find there is direct correlation between providing customer value and achieving optimum shareholder value.

Controlled Growth

Our corporate health is based on well researched and controlled growth into geographic areas in which we are able to meet our business objectives.

Employees—Partners in Success

It is not surprising in a "people business" such as ours, that we place a high value on our employees. They *are* the company and the key to its success. We treat each other with respect and we encourage employee success through a commitment to training, open two-way communication, and by providing an environment in which individuals can achieve their full personal and career potential.

BSG builds and markets software products aimed at managing the performance of today's complex data processing systems. Its headquarters are in Waltham, Massachusetts, and its products are distributed world-wide. BSG's 1992 revenues were $25 million and its operating income was $8 million. However, BSG may not have thought very deeply about what mission statements are supposed to do. Here is what it says:

BSG's Mission Statement

BSG's investments in European subsidiaries, new products, and the BSG/IBM product development alliance are an important part of our strategy for improving revenues and revenue growth rates.

However, our primary mission is the achievement of orderly growth.

MISSION STATEMENTS FROM AROUND THE WORLD

Companies everywhere in the world have found it valuable to develop mission statements for their businesses. Here is a wide variety of examples:

Stena Line AB is headquartered in Gothenburg, Sweden and it is the world's largest company engaged in international ferry traffic. Its ships connect ports in Norway, Sweden, Germany, Denmark, France, United Kingdom and Ireland. It calls its mission statement "Objectives and Business Concept."

Stena Line AB's Mission Statement

Objectives

Stena Line's objective is to retain and strengthen its position as the world's leading ferry traffic company in international ferry traffic. This objective will be achieved by:

- operating an attractive route network, in which each route has the optimum geographical position, a high traffic frequency and enjoys market dominance.

- using modern, well-maintained and safe ships, adapted to the requirements of the travel and transport service concept.

- providing a broad range of products and services for well-defined market segments.

- offering a better and more customer-oriented service than our competitors in each main market.

- constantly striving to be more efficient than our competitors in every sphere of operations.

Business Concept

The Group's business concept is to be an international travel and transport service company, focusing on three customer categories: private travellers, companies and the travel industry. In this context, companies demand freight transport, as well as travel and conference facilities.

Canarc Resource Corporation is an international gold exploration and mining company headquartered in Vancouver, B. C., Canada. It has operations in Canada, Costa Rica, Venezuela, Guyana and Suriname. Notice in its mission statement how very specific it is about the company's goals and the near, medium and long-term strategies for reaching those goals.

Carnac Resource Corporation Mission Statement

Corporate Goals and Strategy

Canarc Resource Corp. is a growth-oriented, international gold exploration and mining company. Our focus on growth reflects the Company's primary goal of discovering and developing large gold deposits for sale or joint venture with major mining companies.

Because the gold business entails significant risks, management has devised a corporate strategy to minimize investor risk while maximizing shareholder returns as follows:

- Focus on discovering large, million-ounce-plus gold deposits such as Plaris-Taku. Not only does this optimize our upside potential, it increases the likelihood of attracting major mining companies to purchase or joint venture our gold discoveries.

- Add value to gold properties by concentrating on exploration discoveries rather than mine development. All of the directors, senior management and geological staff have direct experience in the discovery of mineral deposits and new gold reserves.

- Take a portfolio approach to exploration—several properties in several countries-so that the Company has multiple opportunities for a major gold discovery without being over-exposed to the political and economic risks of any one country.

- Seek out strong local partners in foreign countries—for instance, Dr. Rubin Lie Pauw Sam in Suriname. This strategy has expedited access to, and development of, Canarc's gold properties at reduced risk in these countries.

- Systematically reduce the portfolio as quickly and prudently as possible—evaluate the prospects without getting married to them—so as to focus our time and money on the best prospects.

- Our near-term goal at Polaris-Taku is to increase the mineral inventory of total contained gold beyond 1.4 million ounces so as to maximize the size of future mining and milling operations and projected cash flows prior to seeking a buyer or partner.

- Canarc's medium-term goal in South America is to discover one or more million-ounce-plus gold deposits suitable for mine development by American Barrick Resources Corporation or other major mining companies where Canarc would retain an interest in production.

- Canarc's long-term goal is to add production growth to our continued exploration growth, largely through the success of our own exploration efforts, while giving due consideration to acquisition opportunities as they arise.

Sappi Limited is a pulp and paper company with headquarters in Johannesburg, South Africa. It has sales of approximately US$2 billion in pulp, packaging papers and fine papers. This is its approach to a mission statement:

Sappi Limited Mission Statement

Making a world of difference . . .

As a prominent force in the international pulp and paper industry, Sappi has a responsibility to all its stakeholders—one that it readily assumes

We have the capability and the will to make a world of difference

For our customers, with research and technology that delivers competitive world-class products, and with service to meet their most demanding needs

For our employees by consistently providing opportunities for growth and development

For our shareholders by creating wealth through growth

For all the communities around us through programmes focused on developing self-sufficiency

For the environment by protecting and nurturing our natural resources

---

From Brussels, Belgium, Solvay S. A. sells about US$9 million worth of chemicals, plastics and pharmaceuticals around the world.

Solvay S.A.'s Mission Statement

Mission of the Solvay Group

To provide quality—and cost effective—chemicals, pharmaceuticals and related products and services, and in turn, to ensure:

- that company shareholders receive a satisfactory and growing level of dividend and stock value,

- that employees have the opportunity to develop their full potential,

- and that the quality of life of an increasing number of human beings is improved.

Strategy of the Solvay Group

- To be the first choice supplier for customers in a wide range of major industries.

- To concentrate on five sectors of activity: Alkalis, Peroxygens, Plastics, Processing and Health, and to be a world leader in selected areas where we have competitive advantage.

- To improve the quality and added value of our products and services through continuous and cost-effective innovation.

- To have a higher growth rate in the Americas and the Asia-Pacific region than in the whole of Europe to achieve better geographical balance.

- To recruit top-quality employees and with their participation create an organization that motivates and encourages them to realize their potential while rewarding them competitively.

- To delegate authority and responsibility as far as possible in order to create a lean, participative, and entrepreneurial organization that is highly responsive to the market.

- To conduct our business ethically and legally at all times and to be a responsible neighbour in the communities in which we operate.

- To earn profits that will ensure regular growth of dividends and stock value and provide the cashflow needed to implement our business strategies.

YOUR COMPANY'S MISSION STATEMENT

Marketing Planning Page 8-1 is intended to help you deal with the three elements that a good mission statement should address. Make a number of copies of the blank page because it is unlikely that you will be satisfied with your first attempts.

Marketing Planning Page 8-1

YOUR COMPANY'S MISSION STATEMENT

Definition of the business you are in now _____

_____

_____

_____

Definition of the business you want to be in _____

_____

_____

_____

Description of how you are going to get there _____

_____

_____

_____

Your mission statement _____

_____

_____

_____

_____

Marketing Planning Page 8-1

YOUR COMPANY'S MISSION STATEMENT *(continued)*

_____

_____

_____

_____

_____

_____

_____

_____

_____

_____

_____

_____

_____

_____

_____

_____

_____

_____

_____

_____

_____

_____

Now that you have a working mission statement, you have three more tasks to perform. Each is important and must be done in sequence.

1. Circulate your draft of the mission statement fairly widely among your managers. Ask for reaction and feedback, anonymously. Produce a final draft.

2. Communicate the final mission statement widely throughout the organization, the financial community, your customers and your suppliers.

3. Translate the key ideas and objectives of the mission statement into performance objectives that are directly related to the accomplishment of the goals specified in the mission statement. Make sure employees at every level have specific financial objectives in seeing that the objectives in the mission statement are accomplished.

Remember, Talk Is Cheap

In 1992, Matt Oechsli, a Greensboro, North Carolina management consultant, surveyed over 500 growing companies about their mission statements and how they are actually used. Here is what he found among management personnel and non-management personnel.

Percentage Who Said "Yes" About This Statement	Management Employees	Non-Management Employees
Does your company have a clear written mission statement?	97%	77%
Is that statement supported by management's actions?	54%	55%
Do all departments, branches, and divisions have specific and measurable goals?	54%	57%
Does every employee understand what is expected in terms of performance?	46%	38%
Are all employees held accountable for daily performance?	21%	22%

It is well worth studying Oechsli's results because of the three very important points that are illustrated here. 1) While management employees may be aware of the mission statement, it cannot be automatically assumed that all of the other employees in the company are aware of it. 2) If you are going to have a mission statement, then you must be serious about managing as if you were serious about the content of your mission statement. Anything less simply discredits the whole process. 3) If you are going to gain full contribution from all of your employees, then they *must understand what is expected of them*, and how and when it will be measured.

TWO COMPANIES THAT REALLY WORK THEIR MISSION STATEMENTS

If you are going to get real value from your mission statement, then it must become an integral part of the way you do business. Virtually every decision has to be referenced against it and in an explicit manner, not just silently. Two companies are renowned for the way in which they make their mission statements part of their daily management practices: General Electric and 3M.

At GE, they call their mission statement, "G. E. Management Values" and here is what CEO Jack Welch has to say about it:

> . . . But I like to think that the whole thing evolves around people and values. I think that the success of our company lies in the fact that a lot of people understand these values. They have joined the company knowing these were the values, and they work to implement them. *This is our life. This is how we behave.* (emphasis added) If someone cheats in our company, they are thrown out the first time. If somebody's boundary-or-turf oriented, they get a second chance, but they don't get a third. If they're not open, if they don't share ideas, that's bad behavior. *We're translating values into operational behavior.* (emphasis added) That's what is different.

At 3M, they call their mission statement:

3M Vision and Values

Vision:

 To be the most innovative enterprise and the preferred supplier.

Values:

 Satisfying our customers with superior quality and value.

 Providing investors with an attractive return through sustained, high-quality growth.

 Respecting our social and physical environment.

 Being a company that employees are proud to be a part of.

   It is worth noting that James C. Collins and Jerry I. Porras in their study of companies that had been successful for over fifty years found that their single most important characteristic was their *commitment to the company's vision*, regardless of what that vision was. You can pursue this topic further in their book, *Built to Last—Successful Habits of Visionary Companies*, (New York: HarperCollins Publisher, 1994. (ISBN 0-88730-671-3.)

   Marketing Planning Page 8-2 is designed to give you a chance to try revising your draft of a mission statement for your organization to ensure that it is a set of principles that you truly can live by day in and day out.

Marketing Planning Page 8-2

A MISSION STATEMENT FOR YOUR BUSINESS

_____

_____

_____

_____

_____

_____

_____

_____

_____

_____

What specific actions can you take to ensure that your employees really use the mission statement as a constant reference point in their decision making?

1) _____

_____

_____

2) _____

_____

_____

3) _____

_____

_____

Marketing Intelligence and Your Customers

OVERVIEW OF SECTION NINE: In Section Five, you learned how to find and use historical facts about your markets. While that is fine, the information was general and did not (usually) apply specifically to your customers or to their behavior. Now this is what you will want to develop. That is the job of primary (as opposed to secondary) research. But marketing research is a very specific activity conducted by experienced professionals. Section Nine will help you understand what is at stake in planning and executing primary research projects designed to help you understand your customers better. While Section Nine will not make you a professional market researcher, it will give you all of the information you need to manage the marketing research function.

Finally, Section Nine will demonstrate that your customers, when you get to know them well, are not all created equal and what you should do about that fact.

BASE ALL ACTIONS ON FACTS

In Section One, it was noted that Procter & Gamble's number two Business Principle is *"Base all actions on facts*—One fact is worth many judgments. Strive always to find the factual truth on a subject before acting. This applies to all fields of business: product, packaging, advertising, promotions, and expenditures."* In Section Two it was noted that an important criterion for the Baldrige Award was "Management by Fact." Here is the text supporting that criterion:

> A modern business management system needs to be built upon a framework of measurement, information, data and analysis. Measurements must derive from the company's strategy and encompass all key processes and the outputs and results of those processes. Facts and data needed for performance improvement and assessment are of many types, including: customer, product and service performance, operations, market, competitive comparisons, supplier, employee-related, and cost and financial. Analysis refers to extracting larger meaning from data to support evaluation and decision making at various levels within the company. Such analysis may entail using data to reveal information—such as trends, projections, and cause and effect—that might not be evident without analysis. Facts, data, and analysis support a variety of company purposes, such as planning, reviewing company performance, improving operations, and comparing company performance with competitors' or with "best practices" benchmarks.

So far in this book, you have learned to develop and use a wide variety of extremely useful facts. In Section Four you learned how to collect and organize company internal data to assess your company's strengths and weaknesses. Section Five showed you how to collect and organize external secondary data about your markets. And Section Six explained how to collect and analyze a wide variety of data about your competitors and your competitive position.

Section Seven demonstrated how business failures at Singer (with products) and at American Express (with services) flowed directly from a failure to understand their customers; now this Section will be devoted to techniques for gathering formal and informal intelligence about, and from, your customers and your potential customers. The August 16, 1995 issue of the *Los Angeles Times* carried a story and analysis entitled, "Can the Department Store Survive?" which included this particularly telling observation:

As the classic retailers have always done, Martinez (the Chairman and CEO of Sears) walked the stores. Sam Walton, the late founder of Wal-Mart, spent his life visiting stores. So did Stanley Marcus, founder of Neiman-Marcus.

But generations of Carter Hawley Hale managers did not visit the stores to talk to customers or employees, critics say. "They like to eat at the California Club," reports an executive who worked for them. So, he says, the business declined.

At this point in time, there really should be no lingering questions about the fact that truly successful businesses stay close to their customers.

"Walking the floor" is one way for managers to stay close to their customers. Listening to their complaints and comments is another way. Procter & Gamble prints a Customer Service Department telephone number on all of its products. For example: 1-800-957-2653 for BOLD Plus®, or 1-800-688-SOFT for Ultra DOWNY®, and managers are required to devote several hours every week listening to Procter & Gamble's customers talk about its products.

The warranty cards packed in with many products and services provide another good way to stay close to customers (as well as serve as an outstanding source for building a database, which we discuss later). Unfortunately, too many companies don't provide an incentive to return the cards and therefore miss out on a wonderful source of information about specific customers. And, beyond all comprehension, some companies fail to make their registration cards postage paid!

While these methods just described are all good and should be part of every company's strategy, they suffer one drawback in that they are all passive, i.e., the company has to wait for the customer to do something first to gather data. The active method of gathering data about and from customers is usually called marketing research and that is what we want to discuss now.

THE MARKETING RESEARCH PROCESS

All of the fact and information gathering that has been discussed so far is work that you can do on your own. But at some point, your information requirements may well call for the assistance of professional market researchers. Professional experience and skills are particularly valuable when you have to answer two kinds of questions about your customers: "why?" (qualitative research) and "how many?" (quantitative research).

In either case, there is a "process" to the work that must be done by the marketing manager and the marketing researcher which is a series of eight distinct steps that must be negotiated successfully to produce valid, usable information. Both the manager and the researcher bear responsibilities at each step, but their contribution varies from step to step.

The first step involves "Determining the Need for Information." This need can take either of two forms, a problem to be solved or an opportunity to be exploited. A problem to be solved could be in the nature of, "Sales seem to be weak in the Atlanta district. Is this actually true, and if it is, why are sales down in Atlanta?" An opportunity to be exploited could be in the form of, "Would our customers spend more money with us if we offered them home delivery?" This first step, identifying the need for usable information is primarily the responsibility of the marketing manager, but early discussions with the market researcher are often very helpful in framing the issue.

The next step is "Specifying the Research Objectives." The task here is to turn the need for information into a structure that marketing research can reliably measure and report on in a manner that will allow the marketing manager to take some specific action (or, perhaps not take action). For example, a research objective might be to compare year-to-year sales of all customers in the Atlanta district for the past three years and compare them with the Southeast Region and the U. S. total to determine if sales are, in fact, weak in Atlanta. If there does appear to be a problem, a sample of customers with declining sales might be interviewed to determine the reasons for the decline. Both the marketing manager and the marketing researcher bear responsibilities here.

The third step is "Determining the Source of the Data." The marketing researcher brings valuable insights and experience to this step. He or she can explain and compare the advantages and disadvantages of various data sources. For example, here are the possibilities for our Atlanta district sales problem, i.e., should the appropriate data be internal sales records for the Atlanta district, data purchased from a commercial data source such as the A. C. Nielsen Company, data gathered from the customers themselves, or could it come from government records?

The fourth step is closely related to the third because it involves "Deciding How to Collect the Data." Suppose it is determined that internal sales records for the Atlanta district would be the best source of data. Then you must decide whether to ask the accounting department to supply the data, or should it be the Southeast Regional Manager, or should it be the Atlanta district sales people, or should it be the warehouse that controls all of the shipments into the Atlanta district, etc. Usually the marketing researcher has the primary responsibility here.

The fifth step is "Planning the Research Project." At this stage, the marketing researcher should prepare a written proposal specifying his or her understanding of the problem or opportunity, what actionable data the marketing research is expected to produce, the source of the data, the method of collection, the types of analysis to be used, the reporting format, a timetable and a budget. The marketing manager should sign off on this proposal as evidence that both parties see the project in the same light.

In the sixth step, the marketing researcher goes ahead and "Collects the Data," and in the seventh step, the collected data are "Analyzed for Meaning" and a final report prepared. (It is not unusual for interim reports to be issued by the marketing researcher to keep the marketing manager abreast of developments.)

The final, eighth step in the Marketing Research Process involves presenting the results of the project. This could be in the form of a written report and/or in a meeting with other interested people, as well as other formats. This step needs to be taken with particular care. Many marketing researchers will want to report their results as, "66% of all respondents answered 'Yes' to Question 9, and that is accurate ± 3 percentage points at the 95% level of confidence." (Translation: You can be pretty sure that if you asked *every* customer, not just a sample, that somewhere between 63% and 69% would answer question nine "Yes.")

But most marketing managers want the answer in terms of "What does that mean for my business?" The marketing researcher must be able to translate 66% "yes" answers into some direction and meaning for the marketing manager without encroaching on the marketing manager's area of responsibility. While this sounds like a simple enough task, in real life it is often difficult.

While it is true that the process described above is useful for all kinds of information and fact gathering activities, it is absolutely crucial when professional marketing researchers are employed. Every step must be taken explicitly and in order to ensure that extremely valuable time and money are not wasted.

QUALITATIVE RESEARCH

When the important questions revolve around the "why" of customer behavior, the most likely tool to be used is qualitative research which is exploratory and seeks to discover in-depth, usually subjective, answers that are not usually measurable in hard and fast numbers. Determinant attributes are usually uncovered with qualitative research techniques. The Advertising Research Foundation presents the following definition of qualitative research:

> The intent of qualitative research is to gain insights concerning consumer attitudes, beliefs, motivations and behaviors. When creatively and perceptively analyzed and reported, qualitative research offers insights which go beyond the surface. The qualitative research approach provides "feel," "texture," a sense of intensity, and a degree of nuance. Qualitative research is usually reported discursively, often in the respondents' own words. Qualitative research typically uses a relatively small sample and relies on non-directive, semi-structured interviews.

Focus Group Interviews

The tools of qualitative research have been developed by psychologists and psychiatrists, and applied to business problems over the past forty years. They have included projective techniques like word association, analogies, projections, cartoon drawings, photo sorts, storytelling and in-depth one-on-one interviews. However, the one technique that has found the widest acceptance and has proved most useful is the "focus group interview."

In a focus group interview, a group of eight to twelve carefully selected people are assembled at some neutral location. For the next hour or two, the group is guided through a discussion of the topic of interest by a skilled moderator. Focus group interviews are usually video- and audio-recorded. The interview is also frequently observed through a one-way mirror by marketing researchers and marketing managers.

Three Examples

First: At one time, there was consideration being given to moving the Cotton Bowl and the adjoining Texas State Fair Grounds. A key question that developed during the evaluation stage of this project was what role did the Texas State Fair play in the lives of the people who attended it. A series of focus group interviews held in and around Dallas, Texas disclosed that the State Fair played an extremely important part in the lives of many people because the intense sights, smells, sounds, etc. served to act as a powerful emotional release mechanism.

Second: A series of focus group interviews examined how people judged the freshness of potato chips and all of the tactile sensations involved in eating snack foods. As it turns out, most people judge the freshness of potato chips by holding one between their teeth and breaking it in two by bending it with their fingers. A fresh potato chip produces a sharp snap. A stale chip simply bends and doesn't break.

Third: Focus group interviews were conducted to explore how the financial officers of smaller companies viewed the service and treatment that they received from their respective banks. It turned out that many of them were angry because they felt that the banks did not recognize them personally and were not aware that their companies were doing business with the bank. They felt their business with the bank was not valued at all.

Some Thoughts About Using Focus Group Interviews

The Discussion Guide: A carefully prepared Discussion Guide is essential to successfully using qualitative research methods. It represents the "path" that is to be covered in the research and its preparation ensures that no important topic is left out of the interview. This is particularly true if more than one Discussion Leader will be working on the research project. The marketing manager and the marketing researcher work out the Discussion Guide together. It usually begins with broad, general questions and progresses to more and more sharply defined questions. The snack food research mentioned earlier began with the general question, "How do you feel about the snack foods your family eats?" This produced a discussion of what constituted a snack food and it allowed the moderator to "naturally" focus the discussion on purchased snack foods like potato chips, cheese puffs, pretzels, etc.

The final questioning asked, "Well, how do you know that the potato chips you bought were fresh?" This led to demonstrations, using the products already introduced into the discussion, of how freshness was determined.

Exhibit 9-1 is an example of a discussion guide used in an actual qualitative research project designed to explore the reactions of salespeople in consumer electronics stores to a completely new product they would have to sell. Carefully study how it has been designed to produce actionable information.

Exhibit 9-1

A FOCUS GROUP DISCUSSION GUIDE

I. Introduction (10 minutes)

   —Purpose of focus groups

   —Speak up, one at a time, avoid bandwagon effect

   —I am tape recording sessions, colleagues in back

   —round robin introductions

II. Awareness of Direct-To-Home Television Programming (15 minutes)

   A. Are you familiar with any direct-to-home television programming? Does that phrase or concept mean anything to you?

   B. What do you know about it? What have you heard? (If mention of SKYPIX, What are they doing? Training? What do they like/not like? How is it being marketed? In-store materials used?) Have you, or anyone in your store, talked to any direct-to-home company? If so, which company? Have you, or anyone you know, been trained by any direct-to-home company? Which one? Please describe the training program.

   C. What brands of direct-to-home companies are you aware of?

III. Awareness of DirectTV? (5 minutes)

   Are you aware of DirecTV? What company is going to offer DirecTV? Describe everything you know or have heard about DirecTV.

IV. Reactions to DirecTV Concept (20 minutes)

   A. Show/Read concept. What is your reaction to this idea? What do you like/dislike about it? (Both from a consumer and sales point of view.)

   B. What kinds of people do you think will purchase this? TV junkies? Cable subscribers? Affluent folks? Down scale people? Entertainment freaks? Sports addicts? Non-cable owners? Videophiles? Etc. etc. How would you "size-up" the consumer who would be interested in DirecTV?

Exhibit 9-1

A FOCUS GROUP DISCUSSION GUIDE *(continued)*

V.   DirecTV Sales (25 minutes)

A. What kinds of sales aids would you need to help you sell this PRODUCT? This SERVICE? Anything else?

B. How willing/receptive do you think you will be to selling this PRODUCT? What about the SERVICE? Why? (Hardware will be $700; service $5 a month—commission based on what they sell on-the-spot)

C. Here are some ideas that DirecTV COULD provide you with to help sell. (Show exhibits one at a time) For each one. . .(is it appropriate for a retailer?)

—What is your reaction to it?

—Would you use it/display it? Why or why not?

—Any suggestions to improve this idea?

—Any suggestions for stuff that you would like to have that we haven't shown you? What?

—Would you/your store demonstrate DirecTV? What is necessary to be on the floor?

D. After you sell someone a large TV set or other video equipment, do you ever contact that person with information about sales, new products, etc.? Why/why not? (Is "keeping a dialog with customers" a reasonable thing to ask salespeople to do?)

VI. Incentive Programs for launching a new product/promoting established products (15 minutes)

A. Which manufacturers have most successfully instituted such programs? (Who has the best reputation for giving me what I need to sell their product?

B. How does your management feel about such programs? (Are there companies that give salespeople incentives directly? How do your managers feel about it?

VII. Training Programs (10 minutes)

Which manufacturers do the best job of training? What is done? Why is it so effective?

The Discussion Leader

The Discussion Leader is responsible for making all of the participants feel at ease in the unfamiliar situation, for making sure that every participant has repeated opportunities to express an opinion. He or she generally controls the small group dynamics, while all the time moving the group forward following the Discussion Guide. There is no agreement whatsoever among experts on exactly what qualifications a good moderator should have. It is crucial that the Discussion Leader maintain an air of impartiality and objectivity at all times. The marketing manager and the marketing researcher both have to be comfortable with the chosen discussion leader.

The Participants

The participants are obviously the customers, or potential customers, you wish to interview. Deciding exactly how to profile and qualify prospective participants is a joint decision between the marketing manager and the marketing researcher. Identifying prospective participants is usually done with a questionnaire that contains the questions designed to determine the qualifications of the prospective participant. The screening may be done on the telephone, or in person in some location such as a major shopping mall. Participants are paid for their time. Payments can range from $20–$25 per person to several hundreds of dollars since, for example, medical doctors will participate in focus group interviews but only for significant compensation.

It is always best if the participants do not know each other. Familiarity significantly reduces the willingness of participants to be open and frank with their opinions. Since qualitative research is usually exploratory and wide-ranging, it is very important not to inhibit the free flow of ideas. To illustrate that point, a nightmare situation for the Discussion Leader developed in a focus group interview conducted for the Texas State Fair project discussed earlier. The interview was one of several held in small, rural towns around Dallas to develop insights into any differences of perceptions of state fairs between urban and rural Texans. In this particular group, the town matriarch had been recruited as one of the participants. She answered every one of the Discussion Leader's questions first and the other participants were absolutely mute in deference to the matriarch's role in the town society. To make matters worse, the town matriarch answered the questions with what she believed to be "politically correct" answers, not the actual facts! Yes indeed, strangers make much better participants.

A Word or Two of Advice About Focus Group Research

Always conduct focus group research in multiples of three. It is amazing how often the first group leads you in one direction and the second leads you in a completely different direction. That means that if you only do one group, you never get to know about the second direction. But if you only do two, you never get to know which direction is most likely.

The other caution is to not overreach the abilities of focus group research; don't conduct three focus groups and decide that you know how all of your customers act, or think, or feel. This type of research can be very powerful in helping you understand "why," but it can tell you absolutely nothing about "how many." Use qualitative research to develop fresh insights, new ideas, understanding of why, but use quantitative research to count the numbers.

QUANTITATIVE RESEARCH

When the market intelligence you need involves questions about "how many," then you are most likely going to need quantitative research. (You can also ask those questions of customer databases, but that is a different topic. See Section Thirteen for a discussion of databases.) Most quantitative research is survey research, and a survey is a set of specific questions asked of a specific group of people.

Quantitative research has great power: if you correctly choose the specific people to question, you do not have to ask every person in the target group the questions you are interested in to be able to get reliable answers to questions about "how many." Surveys that allow you to do this are called *random* or *probability* surveys. In probability surveys every member of the target group has an *equal* chance of being interviewed. In such a case, the laws of mathematics allow you to say quite precise things about the results of your survey. The most important thing that they let you say is the margin of error in your survey results.

For example, suppose you conducted a survey of a random sample of some small proportion of your customers and discovered that 35% said they were interested in doing a certain activity. Your first question to yourself should be, "What would happen if I asked every single one of my customers about their interest in that activity? Would I find that 35% were interested, or would it be some other number, say 75%?" Since your sample was selected randomly, your 35% answer is an *unbiased estimate*. That means that your 35% is in fact an estimate of the true percentage you would have found if you had asked every single person, *but* it is possible for you to know the amount of error, in either direction (plus or minus), likely in that estimate. It allows you to draw conclusions such as, "If we had asked everyone, we would have gotten a proportion between 33% and 35% ninety-five times out of a hundred (the level of confidence)."

The level of confidence you can have in your survey results is a function of two factors. One is the size of the proportion. It is easier to be precise about very small proportions, i.e., 10% and very large proportion, i.e., 90%, than it is to be precise about mid-level proportions, i.e., 45%, 50%, 55%, etc. The second factor is the size of the sample. The more people you ask, the higher the confidence level in the answer. Actually, the two factors work together to determine the level of confidence.

A more detailed discussion of the mathematical laws of probability, proportionality and confidence levels is beyond our limitations here. However, if you would like to learn more about the subject, *Research for Marketing Decisions* by Paul E. Green and Donald S. Tull, Prentice-Hall, Inc., Englewood Cliffs, New Jersey, contains an excellent detailed presentation. However, you are most likely to be best served by obtaining the assistance of a professional market researcher to determine the desired sample size.

What the market researcher cannot specify is what level of confidence *you* require to make decisions based on the survey results. For example, is it sufficient to know that most people like your new product idea in order for you to decide to proceed with the project, or do you need a fairly precise estimate? Suppose you found that 65% of your customers favored your new idea. Would it make any difference to you if the true proportion were actually 75%, 83%, 91%? Or do you really have to know that the best estimate is 71% ± 2 % points?

The answer to that question is solely the province of the marketing manager. As you think about the answer, remember that (usually) more precision costs more money. And be very careful about non-random surveys like intercepting people in shopping malls. They can sound like scientific research, but they are never representative of anything except some of the people who happened to visit that particular shopping mall on that particular day of the interview.

About the Questions

If half of the value of quantitative research lies in carefully selecting the people you are going to talk to, the other half lies in carefully selecting the questions. Bad questions will give you bad answers. For example, for many years, one survey asked the question, "On an average day, how many glasses of beer do you drink?" There are huge sources of error in this question. Everyone who had to answer also had to decide some things for themselves. 1) Exactly what does an average day mean? 2) Would that be an average day in the summer or in the winter? 3) How big a glass are they asking about? Since there was no way for the interviewer to know how each of these three questions was being answered, the answers that were given were essentially useless. Or worse, completely misleading!

Writing questions and constructing questionnaires is part art, part science and part experience. It is one activity that really should be left to experienced professional market researchers. However, if you would like to study the subject on your own so as to be better able to evaluate questionnaires submitted to you for approval, consult Arlene Fink's book, *How to Ask Survey Questions* (Thousand Oaks, California: Sage Publications, 1995).

HOW TO FIND AND SELECT A PROFESSIONAL MARKETING RESEARCHER

The Yellow Pages of most local telephone books have a listing under *Marketing Research and Analysis* which will give you a starting place. A better place may be the American Marketing Association's 199X Yellow Pages and International Membership Directory. This annual publication lists hundreds of professional marketing research firms and consultants from around the world. Addresses, telephone and fax numbers, and contact person are all displayed. All of the listed organizations and individuals are cross listed geographically and by research specialty. You can obtain your current copy of this publication from the Publications Order Department, American Marketing Association, 250 South Wacker Drive, Suite 200, Chicago, IL 60606.

After you have located several marketing research professionals in your area, all with excellent credentials, you will have a second, more difficult task, and that is of selection. To help you with that job, we have asked Charles A. Walker to draw on his twenty-five years of experience in the marketing research industry, both as a buyer for J. Walter Thompson Co. and for Hunt-Wesson Foods, Inc. and as a supplier with his own firm, (C. A. Walker & Associates, Inc., 3800 Barham Boulevard, Los Angeles, CA 90068). Here are his ideas on what to look for when you are choosing a marketing research professional or group, what to expect and how to get the most value from your association.

HOW TO SELECT A MARKETING INTELLIGENCE PROFESSIONAL

If you consult a national directory of marketing research firms, you will find literally thousands from which to choose. Even if you consult a local yellow page directory, chances are you will find a long listing of marketing research companies and marketing research consultants. Companies will range from very large, multi-office organizations with hundreds of employees to a single consultant working out of a Small Office/Home Office (SOHO) with telephone, an answering machine, a fax and a computer. So the question is how do you go about selecting marketing intelligence professionals to work with from the large number and wide variety available?

The reality is that, for any particular project, there are many professionals who will do a good, effective and high quality job. My experience suggests that to select the best marketing intelligence professional for your requirements you should use a two-stage process. First, a screening process to make certain that the professionals have the best qualifications. The second stage is designed to find people who are comfortable working with you because you will be making important decisions based on their work.

First Stage: Screening Criteria

1. Experience in your industry or type of business. Although basic research principles apply no matter what type of product or industry you are researching, there are some definite advantages to selecting a company that is familiar with the industry you are in. By the same token,there are also some possible disadvantages to working with a company that has completed little, or no, research in your business area. Some advantages from selecting research professionals who know your industry include:

- They can save money. They have already gone through a trial and error process, and have probably learned the most efficient and effective ways to successfully complete the project. They will understand what works and what doesn't.

- They can design a more effective questionnaire. Professionals who frequently conduct research in an industry understand the best way to phrase questions, what questions to ask, and which questions not to ask, e.g., which ones will not produce actionable information. They will know and use the correct jargon for the industry.

- They can save time. Professionals who are familiar with an industry won't have to waste your time learning your business. They will understand the structure of your industry and will be able to recommend the best methodology to get the information you need efficiently.

- They can provide more insightful analysis. Unfortunately, many times when a marketing intelligence professional works in an industry for the first time, he or she may end up reporting as major findings that which is actually common knowledge in the business. People with a solid base of experience in an industry can more easily separate important new information from common knowledge.

2. Experience in a particular research technique. Some research companies specialize in particular techniques or applications, such as qualitative research or large mail surveys. If you have some idea of the type of research project that is appropriate for your marketing intelligence needs, looking for companies which specialize in that method, or that at least have a good base of experience in it, will be a good bet.

3. Size of the company and its resources. As mentioned earlier, marketing intelligence professional suppliers range from one-man shops to one with hundreds of employees working in multiple locations around the world. The size that is right for you will depend somewhat on the size of your project, the frequency with which you plan to do research, and your own personal preference.

A larger company will generally have in-house capabilities for most, or all, aspects of a study. This would include conducting the interviews, coding, data entry, tabulation of the results, analysis, reporting, etc. A smaller company will sub-contract parts of the project to other firms. For example, the interviewing will be done by a company which has a telephone interviewing facility, and the data tabulations by another company. In general, a company with internal resources will be better able to control costs and timing and quality than one that sub-contracts its work.

But even with larger companies you may want to verify where the work actually gets done. If you are working with a branch office of a large company, the branch may be sending part of your project to the home office which is handling hundreds of other studies. Although this is not necessarily undesirable, it can sometimes create problems in communications and timing.

4. The people with whom you will actually be working. Research companies have different organizational structures. For example, some have account executives who are responsible for obtaining projects, but the actual work is done by others in the office. These people whom you may not get to meet may be senior, experienced marketing intelligence professionals who prefer conducting the research rather than meeting with clients, or they may be junior-level trainees who work under the direction of the account executive. In other companies, the marketing intelligence professional you talk to initially is the person who actually works on the project from beginning to end, writing questionnaires, supervising fieldwork, specifying data tabulations and writing the final report.

Again, there is no one best way. They all can and do work. However, you should know, before you award a project, who will be doing the work, how it will be executed, and you should be comfortable with the proposed handling of your entire project.

5. What quality control measures will be used. In any particular project, there are many ways for problems to occur, even if all safeguards are being followed. However, there are certain standard practices that good research companies routinely employ to reduce the possibility of error. For example, do they pre-test the questionnaire to make sure that it is clear, easy to follow and administer, and that it flows in a logical order? The time to catch problems is in the pre-test stage, not after completing hundreds of interviews

Do they verify at least 15% of all interviews? There have been instances where interviewers, in their desire to meet quotas and schedules, might fabricate an interview. Or more commonly, a respondent may refuse to continue the interview after it has been partially completed and the interviewer has been known to fabricate the remainder of the interview. To protect against being misled by such occurrences, professional research companies assign a supervisor to re-contact about 15% of each interviewer's respondents to verify that they were actually interviewed and that the entire interview was completed. If any questions whatsoever are found, 100% of that interviewer's work is re-checked. You should make sure that any prospective market intelligence suppliers follow this procedure.

Other typical quality control measures include:

- A thorough briefing of the interviewers by a senior project leader to make absolutely certain that they understand the questionnaire, how questions should be asked, how to answer questions from respondents, and how to deal with unexpected events.

- An adequate number of supervisors who verify and check over completed questionnaires to make sure instructions have been followed and all questions that should have been asked were asked.

- A procedure for double checking the key punch entry of data to ensure that no answers are entered incorrectly.

- A thorough check of the print-out of the results by the project director to ensure that responses add up to 100%, the correct number of respondents are indicated for each question, etc.

Another good indicator of quality work is whether the prospective marketing intelligence supplier is a member of the Council of American Survey Research Organizations (CASRO). This trade association has formal guidelines and standards for the conduct of research organizations. To qualify for, and maintain, membership, a company must demonstrate that it follows the CASRO guidelines.

6. Who are the other clients of a proposed marketing intelligence supplier company? Will it provide references from these clients? The old saying that "you are known by the company you keep" is true for marketing intelligence companies as well. For instance, does the proposed supplier work with large, established, sophisticated buyers of marketing intelligence? If it does, then it most likely provides highly professional, reliable work. A large, sophisticated company has the resources and the personnel to set high standards and to ensure that they are met consistently. But the downside risk of working with professionals who have large company clients who fund many large scale projects is that your initial project may not get first class attention, or that it may be assigned to a junior, less experienced person.

Also verify that the client list you are shown is for current clients who are providing repeat business to the proposed supplier. Repeated assignments are an excellent indicator that the research company performs at a high level.

Final Screening Criteria

After you have finished the screening criteria described above, you will most likely still have a number of research supplier companies that will do a highly professional, on-time job for you and do it with similar costs. So the final decision criteria become the same ones you use with every professional you deal with, i.e., your dentist, your doctor, your accountant, your lawyer. Do you feel comfortable working with this person(s)? Can you communicate easily? Do you have a feeling of confidence and trust? There is no escaping the fact that mutual trust is a major factor in any professional relationship. You will have to have just such a relationship with your marketing intelligence professional if your relationship is to be successful.

The Crucial Document in Quantitative Research—The Research Project Proposal

You always want to have a written research project proposal when dealing with marketing research professionals. It will lessen the possibility of having spent your money and, more important, your time doing the wrong research. Each proposal should include a background section that specifies what the market research professional understands about the problem to be studied. It should also include a section on the methodology to be used to conduct the research. It should specify how the analysis will be conducted and how the results will be reported. Finally, the proposal should specify the budget required for the research and an exact timetable for each step of the project.

Research project proposals for qualitative research have to, of necessity, deal with the *process* of the research because the work is exploratory, i.e., nobody knows exactly what will be found. However, quantitative research project proposals should almost always be quite specific about the *outcome* of the research. The more specific and detailed the proposal, the fewer surprises you will encounter later. Exhibit 9-2 is an excellent example of how a research proposal for a quantitative research project for a very complex survey is constructed. Study it carefully to understand how every possible method to anticipate any event has been specified. It is the kind of proposal you want to get.

Exhibit 9-2

A PROPOSAL FOR CONDUCTING
A TRAVEL SURVEY OF COUNTY RESIDENTS

I.   INTRODUCTION

The Association of Governments is seeking a qualified consultant to conduct a household-based travel behavior survey in the Spring of 1995. The results of this survey will update from previous surveys conducted in 1966, 1977 and 1986.

The data generated is used for three main purposes: 1) to calibrate regional transportation and air quality model 2) to serve as a comprehensive data base for short-range transportation system management projects and, 3) to monitor trends in travel behavior in the region.

Conducting the survey requires a consultant who has technical expertise in sampling populations, and processing large scale surveys. The consultant should also exhibit strong organizational and logistical skills, along with common sense. It requires a company with a large support staff and the ability to meet deadlines and schedules.

C. A. Walker & Associates is a marketing research consultancy that meets these qualifications perfectly. Through the almost 25 years we have been in business, we have handled literally thousands of large scale, complex projects. Our staff of over 30 full-time and 100 part-time people is experienced and understands the importance of accuracy, timeliness and attention to detail.

II. TECHNICAL APPROACH—OVERVIEW

The following section outlines how we would approach each task outlined in Section II of the RFP (Request for Proposal). These tasks are related to the following overall procedures outlined below:

- Contact households by telephone through a random selection process
- Collect basic household demographic profiles from participating households and assign a travel day
- Re-contact on the day before travel as a reminder
- Contact the household on the assigned travel day to collect travel information by telephone

Exhibit 9-2 *(continued)*

While these activities sound deceivingly simple, the scale of the project and the necessity for absolutely accurate reporting make accomplishing these tasks very complex.

III. TECHNICAL APPROACH—DETAILS

A. *Develop and Produce Survey Questionnaire and Other Material*

C. A. Walker will meet with the ASSOCIATION project committee to develop a detailed outline of information required and how it needs to be reported. Obviously, we would want to examine closely the instrument used in past surveys, discuss the learning that has taken place, understand the problems and short-fall encountered last time.

Following this, we will produce a detailed outline of the survey instrument for review by the ASSOCIATION. Then, following any modifications to the content outline, we will lay out the questionnaire format which would represent the interviewer instructions, skip patterns, the way the data will be recorded, etc. Once reviewed and approved, we will program this questionnaire on our Computer Assisted Telephone Interviewing System (CATI). The use of a CATI technique will improve the accuracy of the interview, provide quicker turnaround time of results and provide a way to monitor the status of the project.

The use of CATI will also mean that incomplete surveys will be minimized. Households requiring callbacks will also be identified and callback times rescheduled.

B. *Determine Sample Size and Selection Procedures*

Based on the information in the RFP, we understand that a sample size of 2800 households is desired. (This would approximate the last survey which produced 2754 interviews.)

The sample size we are recommending is 2500 households, which we estimate will yield over 5,000 trip diaries (we assume all household members and visitors over age 16 will be required to fill out a trip diary).

However, this sample size may not be sufficient to represent certain population characteristics important to the transportation model. These would include, but not necessarily be limited to, household size, income, trips to downtown, and perhaps even area of residence.

Exhibit 9-2 *(continued)*

Using a stratified, random sample, we would then weight the total results so that the stratification variables are in proportion to their occurrence in the populations.

For purposes of this proposal, we are assuming we would need to recruit a total of 3000 households to yield an ending sample of 2500. This sample would be collected over approximately 4 months, with an even distribution of sample by month. Furthermore, we would split the sample into key geographic regions and sample evenly from these.

NUMBER OF HOUSEHOLDS PARTICIPATION BY MONTH AND AREA

Area	*Feb.*	*March*	*April*	*May*	*Total*
East	150	150	150	150	600
South	150	150	150	150	600
Central	150	150	150	150	600
North	150	150	150	150	600
Balance of County	150	150	150	150	600
TOTALS	750	750	750	750	3000

The total would then be weighted by area to put the area into proportion based on household counts. For example, if East contains 20% of the county households, East would be given a 20% weight in the total.

Selection of households to be included in the survey will be done using a random digit dialing technique. If the quotas by area are agreed to, then we will generate a random list of phone numbers using the pre-fix for the areas to be quota sampled.

This will ensure, to the maximum extent possible, that households with new and unlisted phone numbers are included in the study.

Once contacted, a C. A. Walker interviewer will ask to speak to an adult head of the household. The household head will be told that he or she was selected through a scientific random selection process to take part in a very important study that will assist the government of the COUNTY and provide improved traffic and road services to its citizens.

Exhibit 9-2 *(continued)*

It will be explained that the survey will require that person to keep a log detailing any activities/trips for one 24-hour period to be assigned. In return, a $5.00 donation will be made in that person's name to one of a pre-determined list of charities.

Cooperating households will be assigned a travel day approximately 10 days from the day recruited and basic household composition and demographic data will be obtained. The interviewer will enter into the CATI system the reminder call date, and callback date for receiving the information.

The interviewer will note the number of trip/activity diaries to be shipped and send the name and address of the recruited household to the Department Fulfillment at C. A. Walker's headquarters.

Then a confirmation and thank-you letter will be inserted into the packet along with the appropriate number of diaries. (Note: the diary will contain a list of the charities selected by the ASSOCIATION for which a donation will be sent. The respondent head of household will be asked to indicate which of these, if any, is the charity of choice. C. A. Walker will be responsible for tabulating the number of contributions for each charity and for sending out a letter in the respondent's name along with a check for $5.00.)

The confirmation letter with scheduled travel day, questionnaires for each household member and up to two visitors will be put into an envelope and mailed first class to the respondent.

C. *Conduct a Pretest*

30 households will take place in a pre-test of the survey instrument. These households will be randomly recruited to participate, using the same procedure outlined above.

The C. A. Walker project director for this project will monitor all interviews during the period. In addition to supervision of the callbacks and noting any areas of confusion, the project director will record whether the household successfully completed the task as required and if not, why not. The project director will also debrief the respondent following the interview to obtain respondent feedback on whether instructions were clear, if anything was hard to follow or understand, and what problems, if any, were experienced in recording the diary.

The results of this pre-test, including our recommendation for changes, will be provided to the ASSOCIATION in the form of a written report.

Exhibit 9-2 *(continued)*

D. *Conduct the Travel Survey*

Based on the interview schedule outlined previously, 750 households will need to be recruited to participate each month.

The recruiting for the travel survey will take place 7 days a week. While the majority of the recruiting will take place on weekday evenings from 4:00 PM to 9:00 PM, day time and weekend calls will also be made to ensure that all county households have an opportunity to be included.

If a household number is busy, the CATI system will automatically schedule another time for calls. Five attempts will be made to contact each household before another household is substituted; should substitution be necessary, selection will be by the same random process used to select the original number.

Once the household is recruited and assigned a travel day, the reminder call will automatically be scheduled in the CATI system. Each household's travel day will also be recorded and the callback to collect the data also scheduled. A control number will be assigned to track the status of that household throughout the survey.

Once all travel information is collected, the household will be coded "C" for complete. Again, our CATI system will be able to track the status of each household and schedules for callbacks. After a travel survey is completed by an interviewer, the supervisor will check it that same day, often within 5 minutes. Missing data or illogical responses will be noted and the status of the survey will change from "C" to "PC" (partial complete). An interviewer will be assigned to call back the household to complete the data or clarify any problems.

To ensure that all trips are reported, interviewers will review the diary record and ask about any long periods of time in the day unaccounted for by travel. Also, if the respondent reports a trip from home to work, work to the store, but not from the store to home, trained interviewers will probe to verify why the ending point is different from the beginning point for a particular day.

Quotas for specific subgroups will be tracked daily and reviewed daily by the superiors.

E. *Code and Correct the Survey*

As stated earlier, 100% of the surveys are checked by a supervisor. C. A. Walker & Associates maintains a very high supervisor-to-interviewer ratio

---

Exhibit 9-2 *(continued)*

---

of 10 to 1. A minimum of 20% of every interviewer's work is validated by a supervisor through use of a callback. If a problem is detected, then 100% of that interviewer's work is checked.

At the end of each day's interviewing, the results will be downloaded from the CATI system and dumped onto either an 8mm tape or 3.5" diskette. If desired, the completed interview file can be modemed to the ASSOCIA-TION each day. If the ASSOCIATION discovers missing data which prevents proper geocoding, this household record would be returned to C. A. Walker and an attempt will be made to collect the missing data. If unsuccessful, C. A. Walker will randomly select a replacement household.

F. *Expand the Survey*

Survey results will be weighted and balanced to reflect the household profile of households in the COUNTY area. The criteria for this weighting will be the 1990 Census data, for which updated and population estimates are available through the ASSOCIATION.

Possible expansion variables include households by size, ethnicity, income, vehicle, driving age population, household density, education and occupation.

G. *Document the Survey and Provide Final Report*

On Friday of each week, a status flash report will be provided to the ASSO-CIATION. It will show completed recruits vs. goal, completes vs. goal, participation rates, trip rate and status of key stratification quotas.

Within 4 weeks following completion of the last interview, C. A. Walker will provide to the technical committee 10 copies of a draft report for review and comments. Modifications and revisions will be made as requested and 10 copies of the final report supplied. Included in the report will be a summary, detailed findings and appendix documenting the survey methodology and procedures. In addition to 10 bound, hard copies, results will also be provided on diskette, in WordPerfect 5.1 or higher format.

IV. PROJECT ORGANIZATION AND MANAGEMENT

This part outlines the members of the project team and their qualifications and backgrounds.

THE FOCUS IS ON CUSTOMERS

All of this attention to market intelligence is based on the simple fact that the only way you can build your business is to build it with customers. And the more you know about your customers, the more likely you are to be successful in expanding your business. But all customers are not created equal and there are significant differences in both the costs and the profit potential of different types of customers.

There are two basic types of customers that illustrate this point. They are:

1. New customers that have never bought from you before.
2. Existing customers who are buying from you now.

Although the details vary from industry to industry, research has demonstrated that it costs five to twenty times more to get a NEW customer than to retain an EXISTING customer. Here is a made-up example:

Suppose you sell a product for $10.00 and you have a Net Profit Before Taxes of 15% (not at all unreasonable) so you make $1.50 on each sale before selling costs. Then suppose that it costs you $0.50 to keep an existing customer. If we use an easy number from the lower part of the range, we could say that, for this example, it costs ten times as much to get a new customer than it does to keep an existing customer (it costs $5.00 to get a new customer vs. $0.50 to keep an existing customer). But to put it in more practical terms, it means that you will have to get five new customers to reach the same profit position you would have reached from keeping just one existing customer. Since most companies operate in Mature Markets, taking customers directly from competitors is an extremely difficult task.

Note: It is probably much easier and less expensive to get new customers in Expanding Markets, and that is just one more reason that rapidly expanding markets are so attractive. Also, it probably is almost impossible to get new customers in Declining Markets (see Section Three).

Marketing Planning Page 9-1

NEW CUSTOMER COST ANALYSIS—BRAND A

Work out an estimate below of how these facts apply to a typical product or service in your business.

Typical Selling Price Per Unit: _____

Typical Net Profit Before Selling Costs: _____

Estimated Cost to Retain a Customer: _____

Estimated Cost to Attract a New Customer: _____

1. Number of New Customers required to equal the profitability of one existing customer: _____

2. Approximate Number of Existing Customers: _____

3. Ten percent of Existing Customers (assuming you wish to grow 10% annually): _____

4. Number of New Customers needed to grow at 10% annually. (1) × (3): ____

Difficulty of obtaining that many new customers next year:

Great difficulty   [ ]

Moderate difficulty   [ ]

Little difficulty   [ ]

Marketing Planning Page 9-2

NEW CUSTOMER COST ANALYSIS—BRAND B

Work out an estimate below of how these facts apply to a typical product or service in your business.

Typical Selling Price Per Unit: _____

Typical Net Profit Before Selling Costs: _____

Estimated Cost to Retain a Customer: _____

Estimated Cost to Attract a New Customer: _____

1. Number of New Customers required to equal the profitability of one existing customer: _____

2. Approximate Number of Existing Customers: _____

3. Ten percent of Existing Customers (assuming you wish to grow 10% annually): _____

4. Number of New Customers needed to grow at 10% annually. (1) × (3): _____

Difficulty of obtaining that many new customers next year:

Great difficulty   [ ]

Moderate difficulty   [ ]

Little difficulty   [ ]

Marketing Planning Page 9-3

NEW CUSTOMER COST ANALYSIS—BRAND C

Work out an estimate below of how these facts apply to a typical product or service in your business.

Typical Selling Price Per Unit: _____

Typical Net Profit Before Selling Costs: _____

Estimated Cost to Retain a Customer: _____

Estimated Cost to Attract a New Customer: _____

1. Number of New Customers required to equal the profitability of one existing customer: _____

2. Approximate Number of Existing Customers: _____

3. Ten percent of Existing Customers (assuming you wish to grow 10% annually): _____

4. Number of New Customers needed to grow at 10% annually. (1) × (3): _____

Difficulty of obtaining that many new customers next year:

Great difficulty   [ ]

Moderate difficulty   [ ]

Little difficulty   [ ]

Marketing Planning Page 9-4

NEW CUSTOMER COST ANALYSIS—BRAND D

Work out an estimate below of how these facts apply to a typical product or service in your business.

Typical Selling Price Per Unit: _____

Typical Net Profit Before Selling Costs: _____

Estimated Cost to Retain a Customer: _____

Estimated Cost to Attract a New Customer: _____

1. Number of New Customers required to equal the profitability of one existing customer: _____

2. Approximate Number of Existing Customers: _____

3. Ten percent of Existing Customers (assuming you wish to grow 10% annually): _____

4. Number of New Customers needed to grow at 10% annually. (1) × (3): ____

Difficulty of obtaining that many new customers next year:

Great difficulty   [ ]

Moderate difficulty   [ ]

Little difficulty   [ ]

While you can never stop attempting to attract new customers, because you will always need new ones to replace those who die, go out of business, no longer need your kind of products or services, etc., the most profitable marketing plans and strategy will allocate the promotion budget in proportion to the profit potential of different types of customers.

THE 80/20 PRINCIPLE

Vilfredo Pareto was an Italian economist and sociologist who lived from 1848 to 1923. Pareto was particularly interested in applying the mathematics of economics to the study of sociology. His research led him to observe that in human events 20% of the events resulted in 80% of the outcomes. While Pareto is generally forgotten today, his observation is widely noted as the 80/20 principle. For example, the top 20% of all U. S. households now have about 80% of all of the country's wealth.

What is of particular interest to business people is how often a version of Pareto's 80/20 principle shows up in their operations. Twenty percent of all of your products produce eighty percent of your profits. Twenty percent of your accounts produce eighty percent of your sales volume. Twenty percent of your products produce eighty percent of your returns. And so on.

The key words here are "a version of." While day-to-day life is seldom as neatly organized as 80/20, it is, almost always, organized so that a small group produces the majority of the results (which, of course, was Pareto's observation in the first place). For example, a recent study[*] of the U. S. supermarket industry found that the top 20% of customers provided 64% of total sales. They found that the top 30% of the customers produced 77% of total sales (while the bottom 20% of all customers produced only 1% of total sales).

[*]To get your own copy of this excellent piece of work, write to:

CCRRC STUDY
P. O. Drawer 1734
Atlanta, GA 30301

and request a copy of:

"Measured Marketing—A Tool to Shape Food Store Strategy"

The important point here is that "heavy users" constitute a relatively small group of existing customers and yet as a group account for a majority of sales and profits. Let's apply these ideas to our earlier example.

Selling Price per Unit: $10.00

Net Profit Before Selling Costs: $1.50

Heavy Users account for 80% of sales

Light Users account for 20% of sales

Potential Users account for 0% of sales, of course

Therefore, in a typical purchase cycle:

A Heavy User buys four times as much as a Light User, or $40.00

A Light User therefore buys $10.00

A Potential User buys, of course $ 0.00

Now suppose a new customer costs ten times as much as keeping an existing customer. Let's say it costs $.50 to keep and existing customer. Therefore new customers cost $5.00 to aquire. Here are the economics of this example:

Customer Type	Gross Sales	Profit Before Selling Costs	Cost to Sell One Customer	Net Profit
Heavy User	$40.00	$6.00	$.50	$5.50
Light User	$10.00	$1.50	$.50	$1.00
Potential User	$10.00	$1.50	$5.00	($3.50)

Now make some reasonable estimates about your business and use Marketing Planning Pages 9-5 through 9-8 to display your results.

Marketing Planning Page 9-5

PROFITABILITY BY CUSTOMER TYPE—BRAND A

Customer Type	Gross Sales	Profit Before Selling Costs	Cost to Sell One Customer	Net Profit
Heavy User (_%)	$_____	$_____	$_____	$_____
Light User (_%)	$_____	$_____	$_____	$_____
Potential Users	$_____	$_____	$_____	$_____

Marketing Planning Page 9-6

PROFITABILITY BY CUSTOMER TYPE—BRAND B

Customer Type	Gross Sales	Profit Before Selling Costs	Cost to Sell One Customer	Net Profit
Heavy User (_%)	$_____	$_____	$_____	$_____
Light User (_%)	$_____	$_____	$_____	$_____
Potential Users	$_____	$_____	$_____	$_____

Marketing Planning Page 9-7

PROFITABILITY BY CUSTOMER TYPE—BRAND C

Customer Type	Gross Sales	Profit Before Selling Costs	Cost to Sell One Customer	Net Profit
Heavy User (_%)	$_____	$_____	$_____	$_____
Light User (_%)	$_____	$_____	$_____	$_____
Potential Users	$_____	$_____	$_____	$_____

Marketing Planning Page 9-8

PROFITABILITY BY CUSTOMER TYPE—BRAND D

Customer Type	*Gross Sales*	*Profit Before Selling Costs*	*Cost to Sell One Customer*	*Net Profit*
Heavy User (_%)	$_____	$_____	$_____	$_____
Light User (_%)	$_____	$_____	$_____	$_____
Potential Users	$_____	$_____	$_____	$_____

HEAVY USERS

Make a table like the ones above for each different product or service you sell that has a separate promotion budget (and that includes time spent on sales calls). The numbers in each of those tables should weigh heavily in how you allocate your promotion expenditures.

There are three different ways in which you can increase your business, and your profits, by treating your Heavy Users in special ways. They all involve encouraging them to change their behavior in your favor.

1. You can encourage them to buy more from you at each purchasing occasion. American Express Travel Related Services packages airline tickets, hotel accommodations, automobile rentals, sightseeing trips, etc. into a single purchase to capture more of each customer's travel purchases.

2. You can encourage them to buy from you more frequently. The Vons Grocery Company's Value Plus Club encourages such behavior because members get additional discounts on items they buy in Vons supermarkets, so the more shopping trips, the greater the potential savings.

3. You can encourage them to stay with you longer. Many businesses lose 20%, or more, of their customers every year. Each customer that you can retain is one new customer you won't have to acquire. American Airlines' (as well as many others) Frequent Flyer Program does exactly this since you have to pile up travel on American Airlines to earn free travel awards.

FREQUENCY MARKETING PROGRAMS

While Heavy Users and Frequent Customers may not be exactly the same, many companies are organizing their most important customer programs around the idea of "frequency marketing." That is a strategy designed to identify, maintain and increase the value of your best customers through specific long-term programs to strengthen the relationship between you and your customers. In fact, you may find it useful to ask for a free subscription to *Colloquy*©, *The Quarterly Frequency Marketing Newsletter*, which is published by Frequency Marketing, Inc. in Cincinnati, Ohio. Contact Rick Barlow (publisher of the newsletter and president of FMI) at (800) 543-4653 to sign up for your free subscription to a very interesting and useful source of ideas. Here are some brief examples of companies that have adopted frequency marketing programs:

Farm Fresh is a fifty-nine-store supermarket chain headquartered in Norfolk, Virginia. Their most important customers get Gold Cards. When a shopper enters a Farm Fresh store, he or she "swipes" the Gold Card through a kiosk containing a computer. The shopper's accumulated shopping history is instantly reviewed and a high speed printer produces a personalized shopping list with up to 25 special deals for that *specific* customer!

Starbuck's Coffee Shops issue frequent buyer cards that give the owner the 10th cup of coffee free. When the card is used up, the customer fills in the name and address spaces on the back of the card and is entered in a drawing for a free meal at a local restaurant.

AT&T has a number of frequency marketing programs aimed at specific target markets under the overall "AT&T True Rewards"™ program. "Moving Ahead" is aimed at recent college graduates. "Reach Out World Savings" is aimed at people who frequently call overseas. Business customers are targeted with "Maximum Advantage."

Federal Express encourages small business customers to increase their use of FedEx shipping services with its "Express Plan." For $25 a year, businesses can join the plan and earn 100 Award Points with every $25 of qualified shipments with FedEx. Members can redeem the points for business products and services such as management books, pagers, fax machines, personal computers, etc.

Arby's Inc. fast food restaurant chain encourages its customers to eat at Arby's more often through its Club Arby program. Customers complete a free enrollment form with personal information and food preferences. Then they present their cards at the cash register to earn points for the purchase of other Arby foods. In its testing of this program, Arby's found that an average customer eats at one of its restaurants 1.8 times per month. Club members average 3.0 visits a month.

Waldenbooks is the second largest chain of bookstores in the United States and it has had a frequency program since 1990. Four million people have joined "Waldenbooks Preferred Reader" program. They pay a $5.00 membership fee and get a 10% discount on books, a 5% rebate on other items, check approval, toll free ordering and other services. After the first year of operation, 35% of the Waldenbook's revenue originated with its Preferred Readers.

ORGANIZING WHAT YOU KNOW
ABOUT YOUR CUSTOMERS

In Section Five, you started to think about the things that define your served market, who your best customers are, what your competitive advantage is, and the same ideas for your major competitors. Now it is time to be specific about what you know about your customers, and more important, what you don't know. Following this procedure will identify your needs for improved market intelligence. Marketing Planning Pages 9-9 through 9-12 are designed to help you organize what you know, and don't know, about your customers.

ANOTHER IDEA: A CUSTOMER ADVISORY BOARD

A company that is really interested in keeping close to its customers should find some way to allow its customers to openly discuss their problems directly with the company's managers on a regular basis. One way to accomplish this is to create an XYZ Customer Advisory Board. Select ten or twelve customers (usually heavy users) to serve as an advisory board. Hold one or two meetings a year. Change a third of the members every year so that a completely new board is created every three years. Hold the meetings away from the company premises. Prepare and circulate an agenda in advance. Allow members to contribute items to the agenda in advance.

Pay the members a modest, but not trivial, amount for their time. (Remember that these people will become great public relations spokespeople for your company.) Conduct the meetings with every bit of professionalism that you would use in a meeting with your R&D people, or the sales force, etc. Don't allow the meeting to simply become a "feel good" session. Work on real problems and search for real solutions. Don't hide information from your Customer Advisory Board and don't pull any punches.

A number of industrial companies accomplish the same thing by holding annual (or more often) seminars with their customers to get guidance for their own development direction. Honeywell, Inc., the Minneapolis, Minnesota industrial controls products company, holds customer advisory meetings for direction in developing its products. The AYCO Company, L. P., an Irvine, California financial management company, holds annual seminars to discuss the financial services that it provides to its corporate customers, and to identify emerging customer problems. Use Marketing Planning Page 9-13 to identify a tentative group of members of your first customer advisory board.

Marketing Planning Page 9-9

CUSTOMER PROFILE—BRAND A

DETERMINANT ATTRIBUTES FOR THIS MARKET ARE: _____

_____

_____

_____

_____

OUR CUSTOMER PROFILE IS: (Demographics, SIC Codes, etc. for numerical quantities): _____

_____

_____

_____

_____

TOTAL ANNUAL SALES ACCOUNTED FOR BY:

    TOP 10% OF ALL YOUR CUSTOMERS: _____

    NEXT 10% OF ALL YOUR CUSTOMERS:_____

    NEXT 10% OF ALL YOUR CUSTOMERS:_____

    NEXT 10% OF ALL YOUR CUSTOMERS:_____

    TOTAL SALES ACCOUNTED FOR BY TOP 40%: _____

DESCRIBE A PROGRAM YOU COULD BEGIN TO IMPROVE YOUR RELA-TIONS WITH YOUR MOST IMPORTANT CUSTOMERS (Or improve a program you have in place now.) _____

_____

_____

_____

_____

Marketing Planning Page 9-10

Customer Profile — Brand B

DETERMINANT ATTRIBUTES FOR THIS MARKET ARE: _____

_____

_____

_____

_____

OUR CUSTOMER PROFILE IS: (Demographics, SIC Codes, etc. for numerical quantities): _____

_____

_____

_____

_____

TOTAL ANNUAL SALES ACCOUNTED FOR BY:

    TOP 10% OF ALL YOUR CUSTOMERS: _____

    NEXT 10% OF ALL YOUR CUSTOMERS:_____

    NEXT 10% OF ALL YOUR CUSTOMERS:_____

    NEXT 10% OF ALL YOUR CUSTOMERS:_____

    TOTAL SALES ACCOUNTED FOR BY TOP 40%: _____

DESCRIBE A PROGRAM YOU COULD BEGIN TO IMPROVE YOUR RELATIONS WITH YOUR MOST IMPORTANT CUSTOMERS (Or improve a program you have in place now.) _____

_____

_____

_____

_____

Marketing Planning Page 9-11

CUSTOMER PROFILE — BRAND C

DETERMINANT ATTRIBUTES FOR THIS MARKET ARE: _____

_____

_____

_____

_____

OUR CUSTOMER PROFILE IS: (Demographics, SIC Codes, etc. for numerical quantities): _____

_____

_____ _____

_____

_____

TOTAL ANNUAL SALES ACCOUNTED FOR BY:

    TOP 10% OF ALL YOUR CUSTOMERS: _____

    NEXT 10% OF ALL YOUR CUSTOMERS:_____

    NEXT 10% OF ALL YOUR CUSTOMERS:_____

    NEXT 10% OF ALL YOUR CUSTOMERS:_____

    TOTAL SALES ACCOUNTED FOR BY TOP 40%: _____

DESCRIBE A PROGRAM YOU COULD BEGIN TO IMPROVE YOUR RELA-
TIONS WITH YOUR MOST IMPORTANT CUSTOMERS (Or improve a program you have in place now.) _____

_____

_____

_____

_____

Marketing Planning Page 9-12

CUSTOMER PROFILE — BRAND D

DETERMINANT ATTRIBUTES FOR THIS MARKET ARE: _____

_____

_____

_____

_____

OUR CUSTOMER PROFILE IS: (Demographics, SIC Codes, etc. for numerical quantities): _____

_____

_____

_____

_____

TOTAL ANNUAL SALES ACCOUNTED FOR BY:

    TOP 10% OF ALL YOUR CUSTOMERS: _____

    NEXT 10% OF ALL YOUR CUSTOMERS:_____

    NEXT 10% OF ALL YOUR CUSTOMERS:_____

    NEXT 10% OF ALL YOUR CUSTOMERS:_____

    TOTAL SALES ACCOUNTED FOR BY TOP 40%: _____

DESCRIBE A PROGRAM YOU COULD BEGIN TO IMPROVE YOUR RELATIONS WITH YOUR MOST IMPORTANT CUSTOMERS (Or improve a program you have in place now.) _____

_____

_____

_____

_____

Marketing Planning Page 9-13

PROSPECTIVE MEMBERS OF YOUR CUSTOMER ADVISORY BOARD

Sales Force Planning and Management

OVERVIEW OF SECTION TEN: Your salespeople are among the most expensive employees in your company when you calculate all of their costs. Therefore, it is very important that you direct your sales force to the most profitable accounts. Section Ten shows you how to do that job.

In addition, one of the most difficult jobs that managers are faced with is sales forecasting. Section Ten shows you a number of ways to do this job with the least amount of pain and the maximum likelihood of accuracy.

HOW TO GET THE MOST
OUT OF YOUR SALES FORCE

The Sales and Marketing Executives Association's slogan is "Nothing happens until somebody sells something." That is true for your business as well. But in many companies, the coordination and integration of sales force management and planning is one of the weakest aspects of the business.

217

Success in this area today depends on two things: 1) deploying the sales force against the highest sales potential areas. This can be accomplished by combining the work on category and brand development indices from Section Five and the sales forecasting methods described later in this Section, and 2) developing a special relationship between your salespeople and your best customers (described in Section Nine). For over thirty years, thoughtful sales managers have recognized the importance of having problem-solving, relationship-building salespeople. Unfortunately, too many companies have set very high unit sales quotas and have demanded that the sales force "slam the boxes," as they used to say at Xerox.

Today, rapidly changing distribution methods (described and discussed in Section Thirteen) demand that salespeople become partners with their customers. This shifting situation is finally reducing the largest problem in professional selling, that of divided loyalty between the salesperson's customers and his/her company. More and more businesses are coming to understand that their customers' best interests are their own best interests.

The clearest evidence of this change in how the sales function is being accomplished is that a number of companies now include measures of customer satisfaction as well as sales results in regular personnel evaluations. IBM has studied this customer-conscious approach to sales and has discovered that every percentage point increase in customer satisfaction scores means an additional $500 million in sales over the next five years (and every decreased percentage point means a $500 million loss in business). IBM has taken this work very seriously and now as much as 45% of an IBM salesperson's compensation is based on customer satisfaction.

This, in turn, means that you will have to invest in training your salespeople in new ways to deal with customers. For example, Hallmark salespeople now have laptop computers that let each one analyze the mix of Hallmark greeting cards sold at individual stores, with direct assistance from Hallmark headquarters, in order to create a merchandising package tailored to best develop the potential of each individual store customer. Now stores sell more Hallmark cards and everyone wins.

Compaq Computer has instituted a similar program with its sales force by giving every salesperson a fully equipped computer with access to comprehensive headquarters databases that provide complete and up-to-date information on every client and every product. Compaq even closed all of its sales offices and salespeople now work out of their homes. In the first two years of this program, Compaq reduced its sales force by a third and doubled its sales volume. Relationship selling really does produce results!

Leading edge companies are finally realizing that a complete reliance on quotas and commissions to reward the sales force produces extremely counter-productive results in many parts of the company. For example, quarterly quotas frequently force salespeople to jam enough orders into the final weeks of the quarter to meet their quotas. This "abnormal" situation reverberates throughout the company as shipping is strained, inventories are depleted and production is erratic.

When David Mahoney was Chairman of Norton Simon Industries in the 1960s, he demanded a 20% increase in sales every quarter. To meet this quota, the sales department advanced so many orders into the current quarter that it was frequently two or three or four weeks into the next quarter before the company received *any new orders!*

It is easy to see how sales planning can become uncoordinated and disconnected from the rest of the company's operations. It is difficult to imagine anything more customer-unfriendly than the behavior described above. Nevertheless, the most important job for sales managers will remain motivating his/her salespeople over time. But the tools to accomplish this job will be more varied and interesting than ever before.

FOCUSING THE SALES FORCE ON YOUR MOST IMPORTANT CUSTOMERS

If you focus the activities of your sales force on your most important customers, you will have provided yourself with one of the best defenses possible against the poor management practices described above. The first thing to do is to review the category/brand development indices you constructed in Section Five. Then combine these markets into your existing sales territories (or construct new sales territories to reflect real market potentials for your products and/or services). Next, review the sales history for the last year of each account you sell to in each territory. Rank these accounts from largest to smallest and run a cumulative total alongside of the ranking list.

Now review the call reports from your sales force and estimate what percentage of its selling effort was directed to each of these accounts. If your sales force is deployed in the optimum manner, 80% of its efforts will be directed to the top 20% of your customers (again, the important point is not the exact numbers, it is the approximation that is important). Marketing Planning Pages 10-1 through 10-4 are designed to help you with this task. If you have more than four sales territories (quite likely), make additional copies.

Marketing Planning Page 10-1

CUSTOMER IMPORTANCE VS. SALES FORCE EFFORT ANALYSIS

Territory One: _____   FY 199 _____

Customer Name	Total Sales	Gross Profits	Cume %	Hours of Sales Time On This Account	% of Annual Sales Time	Cume %
_____	_____	_____	_____	_____	_____	_____
_____	_____	_____	_____	_____	_____	_____
_____	_____	_____	_____	_____	_____	_____
_____	_____	_____	_____	_____	_____	_____
_____	_____	_____	_____	_____	_____	_____
_____	_____	_____	_____	_____	_____	_____
_____	_____	_____	_____	_____	_____	_____
_____	_____	_____	_____	_____	_____	_____
_____	_____	_____	_____	_____	_____	_____
_____	_____	_____	_____	_____	_____	_____
_____	_____	_____	_____	_____	_____	_____
_____	_____	_____	_____	_____	_____	_____
_____	_____	_____	_____	_____	_____	_____
_____	_____	_____	_____	_____	_____	_____
_____	_____	_____	_____	_____	_____	_____
_____	_____	_____	_____	_____	_____	_____
_____	_____	_____	_____	_____	_____	_____
_____	_____	_____	_____	_____	_____	_____
_____	_____	_____	_____	_____	_____	_____
_____	_____	_____	_____	_____	_____	_____

Marketing Planning Page 10-2

Customer Importance vs. Sales Force Effort Analysis

Territory Two: _____   FY 199 _____

Customer Name	Total Sales	Gross Profits	Cume %	Hours of Sales Time On This Account	% of Annual Sales Time	Cume %
____	____	____	____	____	____	____
____	____	____	____	____	____	____
____	____	____	____	____	____	____
____	____	____	____	____	____	____
____	____	____	____	____	____	____
____	____	____	____	____	____	____
____	____	____	____	____	____	____
____	____	____	____	____	____	____
____	____	____	____	____	____	____
____	____	____	____	____	____	____
____	____	____	____	____	____	____
____	____	____	____	____	____	____
____	____	____	____	____	____	____
____	____	____	____	____	____	____
____	____	____	____	____	____	____
____	____	____	____	____	____	____
____	____	____	____	____	____	____
____	____	____	____	____	____	____
____	____	____	____	____	____	____
____	____	____	____	____	____	____

Marketing Planning Page 10-3

CUSTOMER IMPORTANCE VS. SALES FORCE EFFORT ANALYSIS

Territory Three: _____   FY 199 _____

Customer Name	Total Sales	Gross Profits	Cume %	Hours of Sales Time On This Account	% of Annual Sales Time	Cume %
_____	_____	_____	_____	_____	_____	_____
_____	_____	_____	_____	_____	_____	_____
_____	_____	_____	_____	_____	_____	_____
_____	_____	_____	_____	_____	_____	_____
_____	_____	_____	_____	_____	_____	_____
_____	_____	_____	_____	_____	_____	_____
_____	_____	_____	_____	_____	_____	_____
_____	_____	_____	_____	_____	_____	_____
_____	_____	_____	_____	_____	_____	_____
_____	_____	_____	_____	_____	_____	_____
_____	_____	_____	_____	_____	_____	_____
_____	_____	_____	_____	_____	_____	_____
_____	_____	_____	_____	_____	_____	_____
_____	_____	_____	_____	_____	_____	_____
_____	_____	_____	_____	_____	_____	_____
_____	_____	_____	_____	_____	_____	_____
_____	_____	_____	_____	_____	_____	_____
_____	_____	_____	_____	_____	_____	_____
_____	_____	_____	_____	_____	_____	_____

Marketing Planning Page 10-4

CUSTOMER IMPORTANCE VS. SALES FORCE EFFORT ANALYSIS

Territory Four: _____   FY 199 _____

Customer Name	Total Sales	Gross Profits	Cume %	Hours of Sales Time On This Account	% of Annual Sales Time	Cume %
___	___	___	___	___	___	___
___	___	___	___	___	___	___
___	___	___	___	___	___	___
___	___	___	___	___	___	___
___	___	___	___	___	___	___
___	___	___	___	___	___	___
___	___	___	___	___	___	___
___	___	___	___	___	___	___
___	___	___	___	___	___	___
___	___	___	___	___	___	___
___	___	___	___	___	___	___
___	___	___	___	___	___	___
___	___	___	___	___	___	___
___	___	___	___	___	___	___
___	___	___	___	___	___	___
___	___	___	___	___	___	___
___	___	___	___	___	___	___
___	___	___	___	___	___	___
___	___	___	___	___	___	___
___	___	___	___	___	___	___

SALES FORECASTING

The well-known management consultant, Peter Drucker, has observed that businesses can survive for long periods of time without profits, but not at all without cash. And that is exactly correct. Therefore, an extremely important part of your planning revolves around your sales activities because sales are most likely your sole on-going source of cash into the company.

That, in turn, brings up the subject of sales forecasting, what it is, how to do it and how to use it. Generally speaking, you will want to forecast sales for the next three years out on an annual basis and one year out on a quarterly and monthly basis.

Forecasting: How to Organize Your Best Guesses About the Future

So far we have been dealing primarily with the past, with history. We have looked at ways to understand your markets, to understand how they have grown, how your competition has developed, what your strengths and weaknesses are, how the world around you is changing, what directions you would like your company to take. Now you have a chance to pull all this information and insight together and begin to think about what it all means for the future.

Now it is time to use all of that information to take a glimpse at the future, to try to figure out what is *most likely* to happen in the future. This is the job for forecasting.

WHAT IS FORECASTING? It is very important to understand exactly what most forecasting in planning and strategy involves. Most usable forecasting simply involves extending the immediate past into the immediate future. Generally speaking, the past is the best guide to what will happen in the future. Several hundred years ago, William Shakespeare made the point quite eloquently when he said, "Past is prologue."

There are real reasons that this is so. As you know, most companies operate in mature markets, and these markets have well-developed structures that reward people for behaving in certain ways and punish others for not behaving in certain ways. As you also know from studying the Product Life Cycle, these market structures are very powerful forces. They interact to ensure that tomorrow will be more like today than like anything else.

In actual fact, a great deal of life is like that. The U. S. Weather Service, and every local TV weather reporter, would rather that you did not know that the *best single* forecast of the weather tomorrow is the weather today.

WHAT FORECASTING IS NOT! It is equally important to understand clearly what forecasting does not include. Forecasting IS NOT a prediction about what WILL HAPPEN in the future! Forecasting is simply a description of what could happen if nothing changed as the future unfolded. The problem is that things almost always DO CHANGE. The one lesson we have learned in the past twenty years is that it is impossible to forecast (predict) the future with any accuracy at all.

On the other hand, we have also learned that it is absolutely necessary for businesses to create "numerical scenarios" (which is what forecasts are) of the future, because without them there is no possibility of measuring progress toward the future and controlling the present. This then creates the dilemma of forecasting. You have to do it, but it is virtually impossible to do it with any real degree of accuracy.

You should always remember that there are some people who have not learned this lesson, and still believe that they can forecast/predict the future with accuracy. They are usually called economists. Here are two thoughts to put such claims in perspective. Robert Reich, the U. S. Secretary of Labor, has observed that, "Economic forecasts were invented to make astrology look good." And Joan Robinson, the noted British economist, has observed that, "The only reason to study economics is to protect yourself from economic forecasts."

TWO VERY LARGE DANGERS IN FORECASTING There are two very serious problems that can seriously damage forecasts of the future based on past performance. The only way to avoid these problems is to understand their causes and constantly guard against them.

THE DATA PROBLEM If you forecast the future using the wrong data, you will get wrong forecasts of the future every time! Doing this is almost always the result of careless, inaccurate definitions of the real markets for your products and services. Here is a story about not understanding markets that is both timeless and awesome in its simplicity. Remember that the total market is almost always the *wrong* market!

About 1967, a representative from JETRO (the Japan External Trade Organization) approached an executive of the Los Angeles consulting firm, Economics Associates, Inc., for advice about a business problem that he had been assigned by Tokyo headquarters. It seems that Mitsubishi had five hundred farm tractors parked in a storage lot adjacent to the American River near Sacramento, California. The tractors were evenly divided between 12hp and 20hp sizes. They were painted blue and white, the colors of Mitsubishi's American partner, the McCulloch Corporation, with McCulloch's name and trademark prominently displayed. The problem was that the tractors had been there in storage for two years and not one had been sold.

Mitsubishi had turned to JETRO for help in understanding why its tractors were not selling. After all, the tractors were identical to the tractors that Mitsubishi sold very successfully at home. In turn, the JETRO representative in Los Angeles wanted the consultants to prepare a proposal to tell Mitsubishi what it should do to resolve its problem. As a starting point, the JETRO representative presented the consultants with the market study that Mitsubishi had relied on for its business planning. The central piece of evidence was a U.S. Department of Commerce report on total tractor sales in the United States since 1945. Sales were growing rapidly and the graphical representation moved sharply up to the right hand side of the graph. The JETRO representative in Los Angeles was just as confused as the Mitsubishi managers in Japan.

It took the consultants only a few hours to uncover the basic problem. The U. S. market for tractors is segmented into three distinctively different markets, identified by horsepower size, and each one is driven by a separate market logic. One market segment comprised small riding tractors, under 10hp, that wealthy Americans drive around their suburban yards to mow grass, rake leaves, etc. This segment was growing rapidly.

Another segment included big tractors, over 50hp, that pull the huge gang planters, combines and harvesters that America's growing corporate farms use to increase productivity and profitability dramatically. This segment was also growing rapidly as American agriculture transformed itself from small family farms to huge corporate farms.

The third segment included tractors from 10hp to 49hp, the size of tractors appropriate for the American family farms that were disappearing at lightening pace. Not surprisingly, the sales in this market segment were dropping at a rapid clip.

The consultants pointed out to the JETRO representative that the sizes of the tractors that were well suited for the small Japanese farms were very poorly suited for the American market, and the information was duly relayed back to Japan. Mitsubishi then loaded up the tractors and brought them back to Japan for repainting and new insignia.

The best protection against this kind of expensive mistake is to truly understand who your customers are and why they use your products and/or services. This is just one more reason why you must define your markets as carefully and accurately as you can. In this example, the U. S. Department of Agriculture, not the Department of Commerce, keeps records of tractor sales by exactly these three engine sizes. If the original Mitsubishi researchers had simply pushed their search for data a little harder, they would almost surely have found the Department of Agriculture data. They would have avoided the entire expensive and embarrassing episode. This might be a good time to return to Section Two and review the material about how to work with a business librarian to find the data you need.

Discontinuities

Peter Drucker, the noted management consultant, calls the other forecasting problem "discontinuities," and that is a good name because it clearly describes what is happening. Discontinuities are those times when there is a sharp, sudden and *permanent* shift in the forces that are driving the market. When this occurs, the past gives you little guidance about the future (by definition). In fact, relying on the past for guidance through a discontinuity can be extremely dangerous.

The difficulty for managers who develop plans and strategy is that discontinuities are very difficult to distinguish from "disruptions." Disruptions are sharp, sudden but *temporary* shifts in the forces that drive the market. The crucial words here are *permanent* and *temporary*. A temporary disruption means that eventually everything will return to pretty much normal. A permanent discontinuity, however, means things never will return to "normal." Here is an example that was played out for everyone to see.

In the early 1970s, the Arab-Israeli War led to the formation of OPEC. In turn, OPEC members created a huge run-up in the price of crude oil. The world's oil companies went from paying the host country $3 to $5 a barrel to paying $25 or more. Just about every industry in the world was affected by this sharp, sudden change in the cost of a vital raw material.

Nowhere was the focus of this forecasting problem more sharply defined than at the Ford Motor Company. Ford's pricing policy was basically set by the weight of the cars it manufactured. Big, heavy cars meant big profits for Ford, and, as Henry Ford was fond of saying, "Mini-cars, mini-profits." The problem was that big, heavy cars did not get very good gas mileage and with gasoline prices quadrupling, the economics of automobile ownership also changed sharply. In addition, there was simply the problem of getting enough gasoline to operate a big car. As a result, large car sales dropped dramatically after the OPEC price increases.

Henry Ford and Lee Iacocca looked at exactly the same data and reached completely contrary interpretations. Henry "read" the events as a disruption and he was convinced that Americans' love for big cars would eventually bring things back to "normal." Lee saw it as a discontinuity and argued forcefully that the Ford Motor Company needed a crash program to develop a line of smaller, high-mileage automobiles. Eventually, Henry grew tired of Lee's nagging and fired him. As you know, Lee was right. A discontinuity had occurred and nothing would ever be the same in the automobile business.

It took the Ford Motor Company five more years and losses of over $2 billion (not just declining profits, bottom line red ink) and a change of leadership to develop a strategy to deal with the effects of the discontinuity. Interestingly, General Motors recognized exactly what had happened (in truth, so did most of the rest of the world's managers), and began an immediate crash program to develop a line of small cars. Unfortunately, GM's execution was very poor and it ended up worse off than Ford.

AN IMPORTANT ASIDE Both Ford and GM tried to execute their product strategies worldwide without giving consideration to individual markets. In Australia, this turned out to be a disaster for GM and a coup for Ford. When GM headquarters in Detroit forced the small car models on its Australian subsidiary, GM Holden, GM's market share fell dramatically. At the same time, Ford allowed its Australian subsidiary to continue making large cars and Ford seemed to pick up every share point that GM lost. The reason was quite simple. The extremely long distances in Australia and the large families meant that Australians had to have large cars no matter what the cost.

Remember: Think globally, act locally. And don't aggregate markets.

If you find yourself confronting the discontinuity/disruption problem, you must first recognize that time is both your enemy and your ally. The more time you wait to develop new, appropriate strategy, the greater lead that your competitors can secure. But the more time you wait, the more likely it will be that you find the right interpretation. Begin by writing out the answers to the following four questions. Have your top managers do the same thing. Circulate the results. Work out an agreement on the best set of combined answers.

1. Exactly what information will we need to decide whether the current situation is a discontinuity or a disruption?

2. How much information will we need to decide whether the current situation is a discontinuity?

3. How long can we wait to make a decision?

4. What are the consequences of being wrong, no matter which way we decide?

How Long A Period To Forecast Many companies find a three-year planning horizon is the most useful. However, there is no just right number. If your business is growing rapidly, or is in an extremely volatile market, you may find that a shorter period is more useful. The real answer is to experiment to find what works best for your business.

What To Forecast Prepare forecasts for individual products and/or services. Each product is serving a different market, growing at different rates with different competitors, etc. Do not aggregate products. Remember the Japanese tractor story.

The first thing you want to forecast is total industry/market sales. Then you can forecast your market share and calculate your expected sales levels, or you can forecast your sales and calculate your market share. Whichever is easier.

Forecasting Techniques The most useful forecasting techniques are really quite simple to understand and to use. There are two very important reasons to use simple forecasting techniques and to not use sophisticated mathematical computer programs.

Sophisticated computer-based forecasting models rely on reams of data and countless formulas. In creating forecasts in this way, the real data are "hidden" from the end user. Remember that the primary end users of the forecasts are the managers who will execute the plans and strategy. Whenever the end users (who are very seldom high powered mathematicians or computer programmers) can't "see" what went on in the forecasting process, they become very distrustful of the forecasts and are unlikely to actually use them. Or, in an even worse case, they only pretend to use them! Your goal is for all of the end users to be able "to look over your shoulder" and see exactly how each forecast was made.

The second reason to use simple methods is that the forecasts they produce are every bit as good as the forecasts produced by sophisticated computer-based models. But the simple methods have two enormous advantages: they are faster and cheaper.

FORECASTING TOOLS: You will need just three tools to prepare your forecasts. One is some simple graph paper. The second is a long, thin, flexible ruler that can be made either of metal or plastic. The third is some kind of writing instrument. This method is usually called "free hand smoothing."

The first thing to do is to plot the historical data that you are trying to forecast on a piece of graph paper. Here is a set of examples for you to work with in practicing forecasting. Table 10-1 shows recent trends in U. S. per capita consumption of commercial beverages.

Table 10-1

U.S. PER CAPITA CONSUMPTION OF VARIOUS BEVERAGES

(in gallons)

Beverage	1987	1988	1989	1990	1991
Soft drinks	44.1	46.0	46.6	47.5	47.3
Milk	25.8	25.9	26.9	26.9	26.6
Coffee	26.8	25.4	26.6	26.3	26.6
Beer	23.8	23.7	23.4	24.1	23.2
Bottled Water	6.4	7.2	8.1	8.8	8.8
Tea	7.0	7.0	6.9	7.1	7.0
Juices	6.7	7.1	6.8	6.2	6.4
Powdered Drinks	5.4	5.2	4.8	5.3	5.6
Wine	2.4	2.2	2.1	2.1	1.9
Distilled Spirits	1.6	1.5	1.5	1.5	1.4

As a practice exercise, take a piece of graph paper and plot these data. Then your task is to take a thin flexible ruler and a pencil or pen, and draw a line that you think extends the basic trend line for each of these beverage categories. As you undertake this task, bear this in mind: Beverage companies think in terms of "share of the belly". By that they mean that human beings can only drink so much liquid before getting a "full belly." Therefore, if people are consuming more of one class of beverage, they must be consuming less of something else.

The only significant beverage not included in the table above is tap water.

FORECASTING WITH PERCENTAGE CHANGE As you have now discovered, there is a lot of room for judgment when you are forecasting using free hand smoothing. A useful way to double check your forecasts is to do the same job using other methods. To use the Percentage Change method, you calculate the average annual change in the data and simply extend that annual average out into the future. Here is what it looks like for the soft drink data:

Table 10-2

U.S. PER CAPITA CONSUMPTION OF SOFT DRINKS

Year	Per Capita Consumption (in gallons)	Annual % Change
1987	44.1	n. a.
1988	46.0	+4.3%
1989	46.6	+1.3%
1990	47.5	+1.9%
1991	47.3	-0.5%

The average annual percentage change in U. S. per capita soft drink consumption is 1.75%. To forecast future changes in per capita soft drink consumption, you construct a table like 10-3.

Table 10-3

FORECASTED PER CAPITA SOFT DRINK CONSUMPTION

Year	Per Capita Consumption (in gallons)	Annual % Change
1992	48.1	+1.175%
1993	49.0	+1.175%
1994	49.8	+1.175%
1995	50.7	+1.175%
1996	51.6	+1.175%

Chain Forecasting

While companies in the soft drink business are undoubtedly encouraged by the fact that we have just forecasted solid, if modest, growth in per capita consumption through the mid 1990s, the number they really need to base their planning and strategy on is the number of gallons of soft drinks that will be consumed. To get that number, we need to forecast U. S. population growth.

We can do that using the percentage change method also. In 1980, the population of the United States was 228,487,100, and in 1991 it was 253,629,100 This is a growth of +11%, or an average of +1% a year. That produces a population growth forecast like the one shown in Table 10-4.

Table 10-4

FORECAST OF U.S. POPULATION GROWTH

Year	U. S. Population (000)	Annual % Change
1992	256,165.4	+1.0%
1993	258,727.0	+1.0%
1994	261,314.3	+1.0%
1995	263,927.5	+1.0%
1996	266,566.7	+1.0%

Now you can combine the two forecasts into a chain forecast like this:

Forecast Per Capita   *Forecast Size of*   *Total Market*
Soft Drink   ×   *U. S. Population*   =   *for Soft Drinks*
Consumption   *in the U. S.*

And your forecast for 1996 looks like this:

51.6 gallons × *266,566,700* = *13,755,000,000 gallons of soft drinks*

CHAIN FORECASTS IN INDUSTRIAL MARKETS Sometimes historical data in industrial markets can be very difficult to obtain and/or contain serious discrepancies and/or not apply exactly to your markets. In this case, chain forecasts can be quite useful in approximating the forecasts you need.

Suppose that you manufacture special plate glass for high-rise office buildings and you want to forecast the demand for your products. The trouble that you encounter is that the available industry data includes glass for residential construction and factory construction as well as for office buildings. As you know, the factors that drive demand for office buildings are quite different from those driving residential or factory construction. Here is what you can do to get around this problem.

Government agencies keep very accurate records of the number and value of permits issued for new construction. You need to select a sample of projects where you have supplied the glass and look up when the permits were originally issued so you can calculate the average amount of time between issuing the permit and ordering the glass. Then you calculate the percentage of the value of the project accounted for by the type of glass you supply.

Finally, go to several major banks in the geographic areas where you do business and ask for their forecasts of new office construction. This is one activity that banks are always forecasting because it is an important market for their loans.

Your chain forecast looks like this:

Bank Forecast of   *Percent of Value of*   *Size of the Market*
Value of New Office   ×   *New Office Construction*   =   *for Office*
Building Construction   *Devoted to Window Glass*   *Building Glass*[*]

---

*Adjusted for lag time between permit and ordering, if necessary.

Linear Regression

What you have been doing is attempting to fit a line, straight or curved, to a set of data points and then to extend that line into the future. It is possible to create a line mathematically that actually *best fits* the data points. This line minimizes, in relation to all other possible lines, the vertical deviations of the data points from that line. This process is called the least-squares method of linear regression and the general formula is:

$$y = a + bx$$

The values for *a* and *b* are found by solving these two equations:

$$b = \frac{n(xy) - (xy)}{n(x2) - (x)2}$$

$$a = \overline{y} - \overline{b(x)}$$

where:

    n = *the number of observations (data points)*

    x = *the independent variable (time in years in our example)*

    y = *the dependent variable (whatever you are forecasting)*

    a = *the point where the line crosses the y axis when x is at 0*

    b = *the slope of the line (how fast it is changing)*

$$\overline{y} = \frac{y}{n}$$

$$\overline{x} = \frac{x}{n}$$

Here is how you would use this formula to forecast the U. S. per capita consumption of soft drinks. The first step requires a work table like this;

x^{**}	y	xy	y^2	x^2
-2(1987)	44.1	-88.2	1944.8	4
-1(1988)	46.0	-46.0	2116.0	1
0(1989)	46.6	0	2171.6	0
+1(1990)	47.5	47.5	2256.3	1
+2(1991)	47.3	94.6	2237.3	4
0	231.5	7.9	10,726.0	10

**Note: If you index the years, (i. e., 1987 = -2, 1988 = -1, 1989 = 0, 1990 = +1, and 1991 = +2) the solution is considerably simplified. The idea is to index the time series part of your data so that the total of the x values is equal to zero.

$$n = 5$$

$$\overline{y} = \frac{231.5}{5} = 46.3$$

$$\overline{x} = 0$$

$$a = 46.3 - 0.79(0)$$

$$b = \frac{5(7.9) - 0(231.5)}{5(10) - (0)^2} = \frac{39.5}{50.0} = 0.79$$

Therefore:

$$y = a + bx$$
$$y = 46.3 + (.079 \times 7^{**}) = 46.3 + 5.53 = 51.83$$

**Note: 1996 has been indexed as 7. 1995 would be indexed as +6 and so on.

Finally, you will probably have noticed that your forecasts, the percentage change method and the regression analysis all produced slightly different forecasts of U. S. per capita soft drink consumption. Study why these differences were produced and why the differences are inherent in the techniques. It will be a useful exercise when you begin making forecasts for your own business.

What to Do if You Have No Historical Data to Extend

There are some conditions where there may be no data to use for your forecasts. Here are four possibilities that can create such a situation:

- Your industry is very new.
- There is no sales history.
- The government, or industry, is secretive, or uncooperative, and will not make data available. It can happen.
- Data is simply missing. You are most likely to encounter this problem in international markets.

Judgmental Forecasting Methods

These methods make use of expert opinion to fill in the numbers for the future using best judgment. There are three separate sets of expert opinion available to you.

- Your own managers have experience in the business and have demonstrated good judgment.
- Your own salespeople are close to the source of your business, your customers.
- Your customers are most likely going through the same exercise you are and will have the best ideas about how much of your products and/or services they are likely to buy.

Judgmental methods have some distinct advantages. For instance:

- The data are relatively easy to obtain. You just have to ask for it.
- They are easy to use. Just add up what you have been told.
- The data are relatively inexpensive to obtain.
- They include human evaluations.

But they also have some major drawbacks, such as these three, that can cause you serious problems if you do not control for the problems:

- They are not rigorous. That means that every individual forecaster will be using different internal reference points for basing their forecasts.
- They can be political. Careers can be seen as rising or falling based on optimistic, or pessimistic, forecasts. Salespeople can maneuver in anticipation of sales quotas.
- Customers can use the forecasts for opening rounds in upcoming negotiations.
- They can be unstable over time. As people change, as attitudes change, from year to year, inconsistencies may arise.

*Note: If you want to see a real life example of what happens when the sales force "sand bags" its forecasts to make quotas easy to reach, look at the production and shipping problems that Apple Computer encountered in 1994 and 1995 when it did not have sufficient products to ship during the crucial Christmas selling period.

There are three things that you can do, if you have to use judgmental forecasts, to minimize all of these shortcomings.

First, create formal written forecasting forms. Organize the answers that you are asking for in a way that is easy for the forecaster to provide, not necessarily so they will be easy for you to use. One major brewery, for many years, asked forecasters to answer this question, "On a typical day, how many glasses of beer do you think an average beer drinker will consume?" You can almost see the wheels turn in the head of whoever wrote that question. He had calculated how many glasses of beer there are in a 42-gallon-barrel of beer and he could translate whatever data he received directly into production directions for the brewery.

But his data were useless because every forecaster had a different "typical day" in mind, a different idea of what made an "average" beer drinker, and some forecasters included drinking directly from cans or bottles, while others did not.

Second, get your forecasts in the smallest increments possible. That means do not ask the Northeast Regional Manager to forecast for his or her market area. Instead, ask his or her salespeople to make the forecasts for their own territories, and ask them for customer-by-customer forecasts. You can add it all up later and in doing so, you will be able to "see" everything that went into the forecasts.

Third, on each forecasting form, make a provision so that next year you can show the forecaster his or her forecast for this year and the actual numbers for this year. Try and help your forecasters get better and better at the job.

The Next Step: Forecasting Your Market Share

You now have a reasonable forecast of the total market growth for each of your products for the next three years based on growth trends for the past five years (or based on best judgment). Now you need to examine the recent history of your share of market. Then forecast changes in your share of market for the next three years.

Next, use all of the data you have accumulated to forecast your sales for the next three years using three different methods: Graphically, Percentage of Change and Share of Market. Marketing Planning Pages 10-5 through 10-8 are designed to help you organize your data to accomplish this task. Finally, examine all three forecasts and make a judgment forecast in the space provided.

Breaking Down Annual Forecasts into Quarterly and Monthly Forecasts

Virtually every business has some sort of seasonal pattern to its sales, so the next job is to break down the annual forecasts into quarterly and monthly forecasts. The first step is to take the last four or five years' annual sales data and break it down into quarterly sales. Then calculate the percentage of the total year's sales accounted for by each quarter. Examine the pattern of quarterly data and calculate an average percentage for each quarter, or select a typical percentage for each quarter. Multiply the total forecast by the quarterly percentage to calculate the sales level to expect each quarter.

Then take each quarter's forecasted sales and divide by three (months) to forecast the monthly sales for the next year. Last, since your planned promotional, pricing, etc. activities will have an impact on one or more month's sales in the upcoming year, adjust the monthly figure to reflect your planned activities. Marketing Planning Pages 10-9 through 10-12 will help you with this work.

Marketing Planning Page 10-5

Sales Forecast—Brand A

Year	Industry Historical Sales	Your Historical Sales	Your Market Share	Year to Year Change in Market Share
199X	_____	_____	_____ %	_____ %
199X	_____	_____	_____ %	_____ %
199X	_____	_____	_____ %	_____ %
199X	_____	_____	_____ %	_____ %
199X	_____	_____	_____ %	_____ %

FORECAST COMPANY SALES—THREE METHODS

Year	Forecast Industry Sales	Graph Method	Percentage of Change Method	Share of Market Method	[Forecast Share of Market]
199X	_____	_____	_____	_____	[_____ %]
199X	_____	_____	_____	_____	[_____ %]
199X	_____	_____	_____	_____	[_____ %]

YOUR SALES—BEST JUDGMENT COMBINATION FORECAST

199X	_____
199X	_____
199X	_____

Marketing Planning Page 10-6

SALES FORECAST — BRAND B

Year	Industry Historical Sales	Your Historical Sales	Your Market Share	Year to Year Change in Market Share
199X	_____	_____	_____%	_____%
199X	_____	_____	_____%	_____%
199X	_____	_____	_____%	_____%
199X	_____	_____	_____%	_____%
199X	_____	_____	_____%	_____%

FORECAST COMPANY SALES—THREE METHODS

Year	Forecast Industry Sales	Graph Method	Percentage of Change Method	Share of Market Method	[Forecast Share of Market]
199X	_____	_____	_____	_____	[_____%]
199X	_____	_____	_____	_____	[_____%]
199X	_____	_____	_____	_____	[_____%]

YOUR SALES—BEST JUDGMENT COMBINATION FORECAST

199X	_____
199X	_____
199X	_____

Marketing Planning Page 10-7

SALES FORECAST—BRAND C

Year	Industry Historical Sales	Your Historical Sales	Your Market Share	Year to Year Change in Market Share
199X	_____	_____	_____ %	_____ %
199X	_____	_____	_____ %	_____ %
199X	_____	_____	_____ %	_____ %
199X	_____	_____	_____ %	_____ %
199X	_____	_____	_____ %	_____ %

FORECAST COMPANY SALES—THREE METHODS

Year	Forecast Industry Sales	Graph Method	Percentage of Change Method	Share of Market Method	[Forecast Share of Market]
199X	_____	_____	_____	_____	[_____ %]
199X	_____	_____	_____	_____	[_____ %]
199X	_____	_____	_____	_____	[_____ %]

YOUR SALES—BEST JUDGMENT COMBINATION FORECAST

199X	_____
199X	_____
199X	_____

Marketing Planning Page 10-8

SALES FORECAST — BRAND D

Year	Industry Historical Sales	Your Historical Sales	Your Market Share	Year to Year Change in Market Share
199X	_____	_____	_____%	_____%
199X	_____	_____	_____%	_____%
199X	_____	_____	_____%	_____%
199X	_____	_____	_____%	_____%
199X	_____	_____	_____%	_____%

FORECAST COMPANY SALES—THREE METHODS

Year	Forecast Industry Sales	Graph Method	Percentage of Change Method	Share of Market Method	[Forecast Share of Market]
199X	_____	_____	_____	_____	[_____%]
199X	_____	_____	_____	_____	[_____%]
199X	_____	_____	_____	_____	[_____%]

YOUR SALES—BEST JUDGMENT COMBINATION FORECAST

199X	_____
199X	_____
199X	_____

Marketing Planning Page 10-9

Quarterly and Monthly Sales Forecasts—Brand A

Total Past Sales	1st Qtr	% of the Year	2nd Qtr	% of the Year	3rd Qtr	% of the Year	4th Qtr	% of the Year
199X	____	____%	____	____%	____	____%	____	____%
199X	____	____%	____	____%	____	____%	____	____%
199X	____	____%	____	____%	____	____%	____	____%
199X	____	____%	____	____%	____	____%	____	____%
199X	____	____%	____	____%	____	____%	____	____%

Average/Typical Sales by Quarter:

1st Qtr ____%   2nd Qtr ____%   3rd Qtr ____%   4th Qtr ____% : 100%

Next Year's Quarterly Sales Forecast:

1st Qtr _____   2nd Qtr _____   3rd Qtr _____   4th Qtr _____

MONTHLY ADJUSTMENT TO FORECAST SALES

Month	Forecast Monthly Sales	Adjusted Monthly Sales	Reason for Adjustment
January	_____	_____	_____
February	_____	_____	_____
March	_____	_____	_____
April	_____	_____	_____
May	_____	_____	_____
June	_____	_____	_____
July	_____	_____	_____
August	_____	_____	_____
September	_____	_____	_____
October	_____	_____	_____
November	_____	_____	_____
December	_____	_____	_____

Marketing Planning Page 10-10

QUARTERLY AND MONTHLY SALES FORECASTS — BRAND B

Total Past Sales	1st Qtr	% of the Year	2nd Qtr	% of the Year	3rd Qtr	% of the Year	4th Qtr	% of the Year
199X	____	____%	____	____%	____	____%	____	____%
199X	____	____%	____	____%	____	____%	____	____%
199X	____	____%	____	____%	____	____%	____	____%
199X	____	____%	____	____%	____	____%	____	____%
199X	____	____%	____	____%	____	____%	____	____%

Average/Typical Sales by Quarter:

1st Qtr _____%   2nd Qtr _____%   3rd Qtr _____%   4th Qtr _____% : 100%

Next Year's Quarterly Sales Forecast:

1st Qtr _____   2nd Qtr _____   3rd Qtr _____   4th Qtr _____

MONTHLY ADJUSTMENT TO FORECAST SALES

Month	Forecast Monthly Sales	Adjusted Monthly Sales	Reason for Adjustment
January	_____	_____	_____
February	_____	_____	_____
March	_____	_____	_____
April	_____	_____	_____
May	_____	_____	_____
June	_____	_____	_____
July	_____	_____	_____
August	_____	_____	_____
September	_____	_____	_____
October	_____	_____	_____
November	_____	_____	_____
December	_____	_____	_____

Marketing Planning Page 10-11

QUARTERLY AND MONTHLY SALES FORECASTS—BRAND C

Total Past Sales	1st Qtr	% of the Year	2nd Qtr	% of the Year	3rd Qtr	% of the Year	4th Qtr	% of the Year
199X	____	____%	____	____%	____	____%	____	____%
199X	____	____%	____	____%	____	____%	____	____%
199X	____	____%	____	____%	____	____%	____	____%
199X	____	____%	____	____%	____	____%	____	____%
199X	____	____%	____	____%	____	____%	____	____%

Average/Typical Sales by Quarter:

1st Qtr _____% 2nd Qtr _____% 3rd Qtr _____% 4th Qtr _____% : 100%

Next Year's Quarterly Sales Forecast:

1st Qtr _____ 2nd Qtr _____ 3rd Qtr _____ 4th Qtr _____

MONTHLY ADJUSTMENT TO FORECAST SALES

Month	Forecast Monthly Sales	Adjusted Monthly Sales	Reason for Adjustment
January	_____	_____	_____
February	_____	_____	_____
March	_____	_____	_____
April	_____	_____	_____
May	_____	_____	_____
June	_____	_____	_____
July	_____	_____	_____
August	_____	_____	_____
September	_____	_____	_____
October	_____	_____	_____
November	_____	_____	_____
December	_____	_____	_____

Marketing Planning Page 10-12

QUARTERLY AND MONTHLY SALES FORECASTS — BRAND D

Total Past Sales	1st Qtr	% of the Year	2nd Qtr	% of the Year	3rd Qtr	% of the Year	4th Qtr	% of the Year
199X	____	____%	____	____%	____	____%	____	____%
199X	____	____%	____	____%	____	____%	____	____%
199X	____	____%	____	____%	____	____%	____	____%
199X	____	____%	____	____%	____	____%	____	____%
199X	____	____%	____	____%	____	____%	____	____%

Average/Typical Sales by Quarter:

1st Qtr _____%   2nd Qtr _____%   3rd Qtr _____%   4th Qtr _____% : 100%

Next Year's Quarterly Sales Forecast:

1st Qtr _____   2nd Qtr _____   3rd Qtr _____   4th Qtr _____

MONTHLY ADJUSTMENT TO FORECAST SALES

Month	Forecast Monthly Sales	Adjusted Monthly Sales	Reason for Adjustment
January	_____	_____	_____
February	_____	_____	_____
March	_____	_____	_____
April	_____	_____	_____
May	_____	_____	_____
June	_____	_____	_____
July	_____	_____	_____
August	_____	_____	_____
September	_____	_____	_____
October	_____	_____	_____
November	_____	_____	_____
December	_____	_____	_____

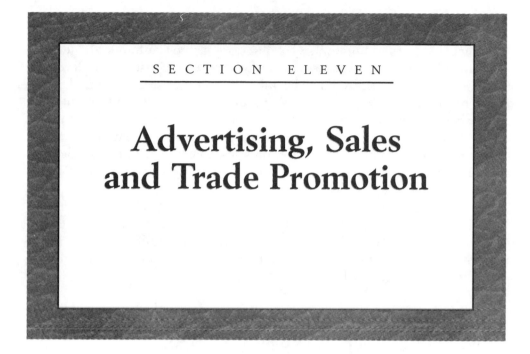

Advertising, Sales and Trade Promotion

OVERVIEW OF SECTION ELEVEN: Without a doubt, you can waste money faster on unproductive advertising, sales promotion and trade promotion than in any other part of your business. Section Eleven shows you exactly how to avoid losing those hard-earned funds and how to maximize the return you get from your advertising, sales promotion and trade promotion budgets.

IMPERSONAL COMMUNICATION WITH YOUR CUSTOMERS

Your sales force is the way you communicate with your customers directly. Advertising, sales promotion and trade promotion are the ways you communicate with them indirectly. In these ways you can waste a rather large amount of money rather rapidly. A well developed, sharply focused marketing strategy and plan is your best insurance against wasting your time and money.

In the middle of the 19th century, John Wanamaker, the developer of the modern department store, is thought to have said, "Half of the money I spend on advertising is wasted. I just don't know which half." He could just as well have included sales promotion in his observation. Now, a hundred and fifty years after John Wanamaker made his pithy observation, evidence is developing that he was pretty close to right. John Philip Jones recently completed a major research effort aimed at measuring the effectiveness of advertising for established brands. He studied 111,140 purchases of eighty different brands in twelve different product categories for a full year. He found that in about half of the cases, advertising had no effect on sales whatsoever. For more details, see Chapter Three of his book, *When Ads Work* (New York: Lexington Books, 1995.) (ISBN 0-02-916662-4)

When you consider that something over $300 BILLION were spent on local and national advertising and sales promotion in 1995, that is an enormous amount of waste! This section is designed to minimize your contribution to the waste side of the ledger and to maximize your contribution to the effective results side.

IMPORTANT TRENDS IN ADVERTISING AND SALES PROMOTION

Any planning of budgets for advertising and sales promotion must recognize some very powerful trends that have swept through marketing in the United States in the past decade. But first, a few explanations are in order. Advertising can be directed toward consumers, other businesses, professional people, wholesalers, retailers, and stock market analysts, to name some of its targets. Advertising has demonstrated that it can do two jobs, but only these two jobs: transmit information and sometimes change attitudes. But don't ask it to do any more. You will just be wasting your money.

Sales promotion can be directed towards all of the same targets as advertising. The basic job that sales promotion can do is change behavior among specific groups of people for specific periods of time. It is divided into two basic categories. Consumer promotion is aimed directly at consumers and trade promotion is aimed primarily at retailers (with the expectation that it will finally affect consumers).

Now, about the trends in advertising and sales promotion spending. In 1984, 37% of all marketing dollars were spent on trade promotion, 35% on advertising and 25% on consumer promotion. By 1994, about 25% of a much larger amount of dollars was spent on advertising and about 26% on consumer promotion, with the remaining 49% spent on trade promotion.

The effect of these changes has been profound. The dollars spent on advertising have shown a significant reduction which has produced a major recession in the advertising agency business. The growth in consumer promotion, while not a major increase in proportion, has grown mightily because the total expenditure has grown roughly threefold since 1984. You have seen the evidence of this growth in your mail box, among other places. In 1995, approximately 320 BILLION coupons were distributed in the United States. That works out to be over three thousand coupons for every one of the 96 million U. S. households!

Two different factors appear to be driving these changes. The shift away from advertising and toward consumer promotion seems to be primarily driven by a search for more effective marketing tools. It is as if advertisers have collectively come to share John Wanamaker's insight and, since they also can't tell which half is wasted, have decided to reduce the waste by reducing the amount spent. The shift to consumer promotion at least gives companies a tool that produces sales results they can see and measure.

The massive diversion of dollars into trade promotion is being driven by quite a different factor. It is easiest to see in the grocery business, but it is occurring to some degree in almost every sector of the retail trade. Here is a rudely condensed version of what has happened. Ever since World War II ended, the relationship between grocery manufacturers and grocery chains has been highly adversarial. Companies like Procter & Gamble used the strength of their large market shares of popular consumer products and their massive advertising budgets to force retailers to take the actions the manufacturers wanted. While such actions were not necessarily negative to retailers, they harbored deep resentment about their loss of control in their own stores. Many other companies copied P & G's style of trade relations.

But as the 1970s developed, retailers found that manufacturers were presenting them with thousands and thousands of new products every year. Since each new product that found a place on the shelf required the removal of an existing product, retailers realized that they had considerable leverage against manufacturers. Without really thinking through their role in the distribution system, retailers rushed to charge manufacturers for access to the space on their shelves. Manufacturers responded, however reluctantly, by shifting marketing funds out of advertising and directly into the coffers of the retailers.

All of this activity really intensified the adversarial relations between the manufacturers and the retailers. Each side went to extraordinary lengths to outwit the other. Forward buying and diversion are good examples. To ensure their shelf space, manufacturers turned increasingly to short-term price reductions (which is basically what trade promotion is all about). Retailers began to "forward buy" very large quantities of products which were on "deal," i.e., short-term price reductions. These quantities would be substantial enough to supply the retailer long after the short-term promotion ended and the retail price went back to normal. In this way, retailers significantly lowered their cost of goods purchased for some period of time.

When a manufacturer conducted a deal in only a few markets in which a retailer operator did business, the retailer would buy large quantities of "deal" merchandise in those markets where the short-term promotional price was in effect, and ship the extra product to their markets where the deal was not in effect, thus creating "diversion." It is thought that some retailers made *all* of their profits in some years completely from forward buying and diverting. In other words, the focus of some retailers has shifted from selling to buying! At the same time, manufacturing schedules and inventory management have become nightmares for manufacturers.

FUTURE PROSPECTS FOR THESE TRENDS

There is some compelling evidence that the trend toward ever-increasing amounts invested in trade promotion is coming to an end. Interestingly enough, this anti-trend is being led by the notorious Procter & Gamble, Inc. which has now instituted a program of Every Day Low Prices (EDLP) in which it has lowered the price, to the retailer, of many of its products. The company says that it can lower prices because it has sharply reduced the amounts that it spends on promotion, trade and consumer. But some retailers are beginning to complain that EDLP is boring their customers and that they need the excitement of high/low pricing to keep their stores interesting. Section Thirteen examines the new developments in distribution that have the ability to heal the wounds between manufacturers and retailers in the food business. However, the downward trend in advertising expenditure and the upward trend in consumer promotion show no sign of changing direction. It appears that most advertisers still don't know which half of their advertising isn't working.

A LITTLE PERSPECTIVE

While the trends described above are indeed important, they need to be kept in perspective. Perhaps one way to do that is to remember that Leslie Wexner built The Limited, Inc. into an over $7 billion company without advertising, or consumer promotion or trade promotion. But he takes very good care of his frequent customers. (See Section Nine.)

ADVERTISING

There are two significant ways to waste money in advertising. One is to fail to understand exactly who your customers are; you then spend money on media that do not efficiently or effectively reach your customers. The other way to waste money is to say the wrong things to your customers. Each of these problems will be discussed in turn.

Knowing Your Customers: Part One

Every advertising medium delivers a certain number of customers, and potential customers, for your products and/or services. And every advertising medium delivers a very large set of non-customers for your products and/or services. Since you will be paying for the entire audience of the advertising medium (customers, potential customers and non-customers), you will get the most benefit from spending your advertising dollars in media that contain the largest proportion of customers and potential customers.

In turn, this means that you must know a great deal about who your customers and your potential customers are, and you must know a great deal about the audience delivered by each possible advertising medium. You can begin by reviewing Sections Five and Nine where you began to write down what you know about your customers. Now you need to organize what you know (and to highlight what you don't know) in a format that allows you to easily analyze what various advertising mediums you might consider. Marketing Planning Pages 11-1 through 11-4 show a demographic customer profile analysis that is fairly widely used in the advertising media business. Begin by filling out the data section on your own customers. Then ask each advertising medium sales representative for matching data about the audience for that particular medium. If he or she cannot provide all, or most of, these data, you have just discovered a major caution signal.

Marketing Planning Page 11-1

DEMOGRAPHIC PROFILE—CUSTOMERS OF BRAND A

Customer Profile—Brand A _____

Definition of Heavy User _____

Definition of Light User _____

Media Comparison for _____

Item	Your Customers %	Total Audience #	Total Audience %	Heavy Users #	Heavy Users %	Light Users #	Light Users %	Non-Users #	Non-Users %
Total Adults	____	____	____	____	____	____	____	____	____
Males	____	____	____	____	____	____	____	____	____
Females	____	____	____	____	____	____	____	____	____
18–24	____	____	____	____	____	____	____	____	____
25–34	____	____	____	____	____	____	____	____	____
35–44	____	____	____	____	____	____	____	____	____
45–54	____	____	____	____	____	____	____	____	____
55–64	____	____	____	____	____	____	____	____	____
65+	____	____	____	____	____	____	____	____	____
Graduated College	____	____	____	____	____	____	____	____	____
Attended College	____	____	____	____	____	____	____	____	____
Graduated High School	____	____	____	____	____	____	____	____	____
Did Not Graduate High School	____	____	____	____	____	____	____	____	____

Marketing Planning Page 11-1

Demographic Profile — Customers of Brand A *(continued)*

Item	Your Customers %	Total Audience #	%	Heavy Users #	%	Light Users #	%	Non-Users #	%
Employed Males	____	____	____	____	____	____	____	____	____
Employed Females	____	____	____	____	____	____	____	____	____
Employed Full-Time	____	____	____	____	____	____	____	____	____
Employed Part-Time	____	____	____	____	____	____	____	____	____
Not Employed	____	____	____	____	____	____	____	____	____
Professional/ Manager	____	____	____	____	____	____	____	____	____
Technical/ Clerical/ Sales	____	____	____	____	____	____	____	____	____
Precision/ Craft	____	____	____	____	____	____	____	____	____
Other Employed	____	____	____	____	____	____	____	____	____
Single	____	____	____	____	____	____	____	____	____
Married	____	____	____	____	____	____	____	____	____
Divorced/ Separated/ Widowed	____	____	____	____	____	____	____	____	____
Parents	____	____	____	____	____	____	____	____	____
White	____	____	____	____	____	____	____	____	____
Black	____	____	____	____	____	____	____	____	____
Other	____	____	____	____	____	____	____	____	____

Marketing Planning Page 11-1

DEMOGRAPHIC PROFILE—CUSTOMERS OF BRAND A *(continued)*

Household Income	Your Customers %	Total Audience #	%	Heavy Users #	%	Light Users #	%	Non-Users #	%
+$75k	_____	_____	_____	_____	_____	_____	_____	_____	_____
+$60k	_____	_____	_____	_____	_____	_____	_____	_____	_____
+$50k	_____	_____	_____	_____	_____	_____	_____	_____	_____
+$40k	_____	_____	_____	_____	_____	_____	_____	_____	_____
+$30k	_____	_____	_____	_____	_____	_____	_____	_____	_____
+$20k	_____	_____	_____	_____	_____	_____	_____	_____	_____
+10k	_____	_____	_____	_____	_____	_____	_____	_____	_____
Under $10, 000	_____	_____	_____	_____	_____	_____	_____	_____	_____
1 person household	_____	_____	_____	_____	_____	_____	_____	_____	_____
2 people	_____	_____	_____	_____	_____	_____	_____	_____	_____
3 or 4 people	_____	_____	_____	_____	_____	_____	_____	_____	_____
5 or more people	_____	_____	_____	_____	_____	_____	_____	_____	_____
No child in the household	_____	_____	_____	_____	_____	_____	_____	_____	_____
Residence Owned	%	#	%	#	%	#	%	#	%
Value: +$70k	_____	_____	_____	_____	_____	_____	_____	_____	_____
Value: >$70k	_____	_____	_____	_____	_____	_____	_____	_____	_____

Marketing Planning Page 11-2

DEMOGRAPHIC PROFILE—CUSTOMERS OF BRAND B

Customer Profile—Brand B _____

Definition of Heavy User _____

Definition of Light User _____

Media Comparison for _____

Item	Your Customers %	Total Audience #	Total Audience %	Heavy Users #	Heavy Users %	Light Users #	Light Users %	Non-Users #	Non-Users %
Total Adults	____	____	____	____	____	____	____	____	____
Males	____	____	____	____	____	____	____	____	____
Females	____	____	____	____	____	____	____	____	____
18–24	____	____	____	____	____	____	____	____	____
25–34	____	____	____	____	____	____	____	____	____
35–44	____	____	____	____	____	____	____	____	____
45–54	____	____	____	____	____	____	____	____	____
55–64	____	____	____	____	____	____	____	____	____
65+	____	____	____	____	____	____	____	____	____
Graduated College	____	____	____	____	____	____	____	____	____
Attended College	____	____	____	____	____	____	____	____	____
Graduated High School	____	____	____	____	____	____	____	____	____
Did Not Graduate High School	____	____	____	____	____	____	____	____	____

Marketing Planning Page 11-2

DEMOGRAPHIC PROFILE — CUSTOMERS OF BRAND B *(continued)*

Item	Your Customers %	Total Audience #	Total Audience %	Heavy Users #	Heavy Users %	Light Users #	Light Users %	Non-Users #	Non-Users %
Employed Males	___	___	___	___	___	___	___	___	___
Employed Females	___	___	___	___	___	___	___	___	___
Employed Full-Time	___	___	___	___	___	___	___	___	___
Employed Part-Time	___	___	___	___	___	___	___	___	___
Not Employed	___	___	___	___	___	___	___	___	___
Professional/ Manager	___	___	___	___	___	___	___	___	___
Technical/ Clerical/ Sales	___	___	___	___	___	___	___	___	___
Precision/ Craft	___	___	___	___	___	___	___	___	___
Other Employed	___	___	___	___	___	___	___	___	___
Single	___	___	___	___	___	___	___	___	___
Married	___	___	___	___	___	___	___	___	___
Divorced/ Separated/ Widowed	___	___	___	___	___	___	___	___	___
Parents	___	___	___	___	___	___	___	___	___
White	___	___	___	___	___	___	___	___	___
Black	___	___	___	___	___	___	___	___	___
Other	___	___	___	___	___	___	___	___	___

Marketing Planning Page 11-2

DEMOGRAPHIC PROFILE—CUSTOMERS OF BRAND B *(continued)*

Household Income	Your Customers %	Total Audience #	%	Heavy Users #	%	Light Users #	%	Non-Users #	%
+$75k	____	____	____	____	____	____	____	____	____
+$60k	____	____	____	____	____	____	____	____	____
+$50k	____	____	____	____	____	____	____	____	____
+$40k	____	____	____	____	____	____	____	____	____
+$30k	____	____	____	____	____	____	____	____	____
+$20k	____	____	____	____	____	____	____	____	____
+10k	____	____	____	____	____	____	____	____	____
Under $10,000	____	____	____	____	____	____	____	____	____
1 person household	____	____	____	____	____	____	____	____	____
2 people	____	____	____	____	____	____	____	____	____
3 or 4 people	____	____	____	____	____	____	____	____	____
5 or more people	____	____	____	____	____	____	____	____	____
No child in the household	____	____	____	____	____	____	____	____	____

Residence Owned	%	#	%	#	%	#	%	#	%
Value: +$70k	____	____	____	____	____	____	____	____	____
Value: >$70k	____	____	____	____	____	____	____	____	____

Marketing Planning Page 11-3

DEMOGRAPHIC PROFILE—CUSTOMERS OF BRAND C

Customer Profile—Brand C _____

Definition of Heavy User _____

Definition of Light User _____

Media Comparison for _____

Item	Your Customers %	Total Audience #	Total Audience %	Heavy Users #	Heavy Users %	Light Users #	Light Users %	Non-Users #	Non-Users %
Total Adults	____	____	____	____	____	____	____	____	____
Males	____	____	____	____	____	____	____	____	____
Females	____	____	____	____	____	____	____	____	____
18–24	____	____	____	____	____	____	____	____	____
25–34	____	____	____	____	____	____	____	____	____
35–44	____	____	____	____	____	____	____	____	____
45–54	____	____	____	____	____	____	____	____	____
55–64	____	____	____	____	____	____	____	____	____
65+	____	____	____	____	____	____	____	____	____
Graduated College	____	____	____	____	____	____	____	____	____
Attended College	____	____	____	____	____	____	____	____	____
Graduated High School	____	____	____	____	____	____	____	____	____
Did Not Graduate High School	____	____	____	____	____	____	____	____	____

Marketing Planning Page 11-3

DEMOGRAPHIC PROFILE — CUSTOMERS OF BRAND C *(continued)*

Item	Your Customers %	Total Audience #	%	Heavy Users #	%	Light Users #	%	Non-Users #	%
Employed Males	____	____	____	____	____	____	____	____	____
Employed Females	____	____	____	____	____	____	____	____	____
Employed Full-Time	____	____	____	____	____	____	____	____	____
Employed Part-Time	____	____	____	____	____	____	____	____	____
Not Employed	____	____	____	____	____	____	____	____	____
Professional/ Manager	____	____	____	____	____	____	____	____	____
Technical/ Clerical/ Sales	____	____	____	____	____	____	____	____	____
Precision/ Craft	____	____	____	____	____	____	____	____	____
Other Employed	____	____	____	____	____	____	____	____	____
Single	____	____	____	____	____	____	____	____	____
Married	____	____	____	____	____	____	____	____	____
Divorced/ Separated/ Widowed	____	____	____	____	____	____	____	____	____
Parents	____	____	____	____	____	____	____	____	____
White	____	____	____	____	____	____	____	____	____
Black	____	____	____	____	____	____	____	____	____
Other	____	____	____	____	____	____	____	____	____

Marketing Planning Page 11-3

DEMOGRAPHIC PROFILE—CUSTOMERS OF BRAND C *(continued)*

Household Income	*Your Customers* %	*Total Audience* #	%	*Heavy Users* #	%	*Light Users* #	%	*Non-Users* #	%
+$75k	____	____	____	____	____	____	____	____	____
+$60k	____	____	____	____	____	____	____	____	____
+$50k	____	____	____	____	____	____	____	____	____
+$40k	____	____	____	____	____	____	____	____	____
+$30k	____	____	____	____	____	____	____	____	____
+$20k	____	____	____	____	____	____	____	____	____
+10k	____	____	____	____	____	____	____	____	____
Under $10, 000	____	____	____	____	____	____	____	____	____
1 person household	____	____	____	____	____	____	____	____	____
2 people	____	____	____	____	____	____	____	____	____
3 or 4 people	____	____	____	____	____	____	____	____	____
5 or more people	____	____	____	____	____	____	____	____	____
No child in the household	____	____	____	____	____	____	____	____	____
Residence Owned	%	#	%	#	%	#	%	#	%
Value: +$70k	____	____	____	____	____	____	____	____	____
Value: >$70k	____	____	____	____	____	____	____	____	____

Marketing Planning Page 11-4

DEMOGRAPHIC PROFILE—CUSTOMERS OF BRAND D

Customer Profile—Brand D _____

Definition of Heavy User _____

Definition of Light User _____

Media Comparison for _____

Item	Your Customers %	Total Audience #	Total Audience %	Heavy Users #	Heavy Users %	Light Users #	Light Users %	Non-Users #	Non-Users %
Total Adults	___	___	___	___	___	___	___	___	___
Males	___	___	___	___	___	___	___	___	___
Females	___	___	___	___	___	___	___	___	___
18–24	___	___	___	___	___	___	___	___	___
25–34	___	___	___	___	___	___	___	___	___
35–44	___	___	___	___	___	___	___	___	___
45–54	___	___	___	___	___	___	___	___	___
55–64	___	___	___	___	___	___	___	___	___
65+	___	___	___	___	___	___	___	___	___
Graduated College	___	___	___	___	___	___	___	___	___
Attended College	___	___	___	___	___	___	___	___	___
Graduated High School	___	___	___	___	___	___	___	___	___
Did Not Graduate High School	___	___	___	___	___	___	___	___	___

Marketing Planning Page 11-4

DEMOGRAPHIC PROFILE—CUSTOMERS OF BRAND D *(continued)*

Item	Your Customers %	Total Audience #	%	Heavy Users #	%	Light Users #	%	Non-Users #	%
Employed Males	___	___	___	___	___	___	___	___	___
Employed Females	___	___	___	___	___	___	___	___	___
Employed Full-Time	___	___	___	___	___	___	___	___	___
Employed Part-Time	___	___	___	___	___	___	___	___	___
Not Employed	___	___	___	___	___	___	___	___	___
Professional/ Manager	___	___	___	___	___	___	___	___	___
Technical/ Clerical/ Sales	___	___	___	___	___	___	___	___	___
Precision/ Craft	___	___	___	___	___	___	___	___	___
Other Employed	___	___	___	___	___	___	___	___	___
Single	___	___	___	___	___	___	___	___	___
Married	___	___	___	___	___	___	___	___	___
Divorced/ Separated/ Widowed	___	___	___	___	___	___	___	___	___
Parents	___	___	___	___	___	___	___	___	___
White	___	___	___	___	___	___	___	___	___
Black	___	___	___	___	___	___	___	___	___
Other	___	___	___	___	___	___	___	___	___

Marketing Planning Page 11-4

DEMOGRAPHIC PROFILE—CUSTOMERS OF BRAND D *(continued)*

	Your Customers		Total Audience	Heavy Users		Light Users		Non-Users	
Household Income	%	#	%	#	%	#	%	#	%
+$75k	____	____	____	____	____	____	____	____	____
+$60k	____	____	____	____	____	____	____	____	____
+$50k	____	____	____	____	____	____	____	____	____
+$40k	____	____	____	____	____	____	____	____	____
+$30k	____	____	____	____	____	____	____	____	____
+$20k	____	____	____	____	____	____	____	____	____
+10k	____	____	____	____	____	____	____	____	____
Under $10,000	____	____	____	____	____	____	____	____	____
1 person household	____	____	____	____	____	____	____	____	____
2 people	____	____	____	____	____	____	____	____	____
3 or 4 people	____	____	____	____	____	____	____	____	____
5 or more people	____	____	____	____	____	____	____	____	____
No child in the household	____	____	____	____	____	____	____	____	____
Residence Owned	%	#	%	#	%	#	%	#	%
Value: +$70k	____	____	____	____	____	____	____	____	____
Value: >$70k	____	____	____	____	____	____	____	____	____

Knowing Your Customers: Part Two

Your advertising can only work for you if your customers can buy your products and/or services. Any dollar spent talking to a customer who cannot physically buy your product is a wasted dollar. Period. End of discussion. And yet as obvious as that fact is, many advertisers simply ignore the importance of distribution when they do their media planning. So part one of Knowing Your Customers is knowing who they are and part two is knowing where they live (or perhaps where they work). Begin by returning to Section Five and reviewing the work you did to develop Brand and Category Development Indices. That will tell you a great deal about where your customers and your potential customers live.

Knowing where your customers live is extremely important for retailers who serve their customers out of physical store locations. Every retail store has some specific piece of geography surrounding the store location that accounts for 60% to 70% of the store's business. That particular piece of geography is called the store's "trading area." The objective of every retailer is to spend as much of his/her advertising budget inside of the trading areas possible. For an in-depth treatment of advertising for retail stores and trading areas, see *How to Develop a Successful Advertising Plan* (Lincolnwood, IL: NTC Business Books, 1993) (ISBN 0-8442-3526-1)

CHARACTERISTICS OF MEDIA

In addition to evaluating individual mediums in terms of their ability to deliver customers and potential customers in their audiences, the different media have inherent characteristics themselves that may be useful (or they may prove to be limitations) in your marketing planning and strategy. Here are the major characteristics of the major media.

Newspapers—Advantages

- Geographic selectivity. There are over 11,000 newspapers published in the U. S. Just over 1,700 of them are daily papers; the rest are semi-weekly or weekly. Every newspaper is focused on some particular piece of geography so combinations of newspapers give you the opportunity to cover almost any conceivable geographic configuration. (Note: *The Wall Street Journal*, *USA Today* and the *Christian Science Monitor* are exceptions. They attempt to be national newspapers. Whether they are is open to question.) In addition, many large newspapers offer the advertiser the opportunity to buy only limited, selected parts of their total circulations.

- Wide reach. In the United States, about 60 million households subscribe to a daily newspaper while a top-rated TV program reaches about 20 million households in a week.
- Readers' immediate interest. People frequently turn to newspapers to read the advertising as well as the news and editorial content.
- Short lead time. Newspapers will generally accept advertising material 24 to 48 hours ahead of publication so late breaking events, or sales, can be communicated readily.

Newspapers—Disadvantages

- Wasted circulation. This is the other side of the coin for wide reach. Newspapers will reach many households that are not customers or potential customers and you will have to pay for those households as well.
- Short life span. This is the opposite side of the immediate interest coin. Who ever reads two-day-old newspapers?
- Relatively poor reproduction. If making your product really look good is important, you will find that difficult to do in newspapers. The paper is porous, the presses run at high speeds and the ink spreads. But improvements are continually being made.

Magazines—Advantages

- Audience selectivity. There are over 1,200 magazines directed to consumers and farm families published in the U. S. There are also another 3,600 business and professional magazines published. (The number constantly changes because magazines are continually being started and others are being folded as reader and advertiser interest waxes and wanes.) Successful magazines have done a very good job of selecting specific audience interests and then servicing those interests. So if you sell ski boots, SKI magazine will deliver a very high proportion of its readers with interests in buying ski boots.
- Best quality reproduction: High quality coated papers and expensive inks and special presses allow magazines to reproduce the highest quality levels. So if it is important for your product to look good, magazines can make that happen.

- High levels of reader interest. Readers have made special efforts to buy, or subscribe to, specific magazines and they have paid a fairly high price to do so, which is good evidence that they are really interested in the magazine's subject material, and perhaps in your advertising as well.

- Long physical life. People save magazines and return to them multiple times. Magazines are frequently given to other people after the original reader finishes. These "pass along" readers can double the size of the circulation of the magazine without costing you extra.

Magazines—Disadvantages

- Long lead times. Magazines require your advertising material two to three months in advance of when the reader will actually see it.

- Limited geographic coverage. When the total audience of a special interest magazine is distributed among the various geographical markets, the number of readers in any one market frequently becomes very small. Thus it becomes difficult to use magazines to support local dealers.

- High costs. Magazines tend to be high-cost media because of their high production and distribution costs. However, on a per-customer basis, they may become much more economical. Use Marketing Planning Pages 11-1 to 11-4 to compare the costs of reaching heavy users of your products or services.

Television—Advantages

- Reach large audiences fast. Ninety-nine percent of all U. S. households have at least one TV set (+97 million households). While any one program may only reach 15 to 20 million households, it is fairly easy to assemble programs across all four networks that can raise that number to 60 million or more.

- Demonstration. If you have a product or service that really benefits from demonstration, TV has to be a major consideration. Nothing else comes close.

- Flexibility. It is possible to buy advertising time during any hour of the day, any day of the week and in any market in the country. It is solely your decision.

Television—Disadvantages

- Costs. It is not unusual to spend $200,000, or more, just to get one 30-second TV commercial on film. Then it can cost up to $300,000 to buy 30 seconds of time on a popular network TV program so you can show your expensive commercial. Costs in television tend to be breathtaking.

- Lack of selectivity. As with newspapers, when you reach a lot of people all at once, you also reach a lot of people you don't want to reach. That simply adds to the costs of reaching the people you really want to reach.

Radio—Advantages

- Costs. Radio is inexpensive. A good 60-second radio commercial can be produced for $5,000 or less. And 60 seconds of air time to run your commercial will cost only a few hundred dollars.

- Selectivity. Radio has survived the intense competition from television by becoming very selective in developing the audiences it delivers to advertisers. You can reach farmers with weather reports and bankers with classical music.

Radio—Disadvantages

- Can be difficult to buy. There are almost 10,000 commercial radio stations in the U. S., compared with 1,700 daily newspapers, 1,200 consumer magazines and 1,100 commercial TV stations. To build a substantial audience, you will have to deal with a lot of them.

- Sound only. All other media give the customer something to see. That puts a very heavy burden on the creative people who develop your radio advertising.

Outdoor—Advantage

- Flexibility. One can buy one location or you can buy thousands. You can buy them for a few weeks or for years. You can buy them anywhere in the country. And outdoor tends to be inexpensive compared with other media.

Outdoor—Disadvantage

- Verification. There is no way to determine who sees your outdoor advertising. There is no practical way to verify that you actually got outdoor advertising in all of the locations you paid for and for the length of time you paid for.

Direct Mail—Advantage

- Control. The overwhelming advantage of direct mail is that you control everything. You control exactly who receives it. You control exactly what it says. You control when it is received (within limits). And best of all, you can test every single element of the advertising before you commit to a full-scale program.

Direct Mail—Disadvantage

- Cost. If you look only at the raw numbers, direct mail advertising can cost from $500 to $1,000, or more, to reach 1,000 people. Compare that to $15 to $20 to reach 1,000 people on TV. However, when you examine actual response rates, the difference diminishes dramatically. See Section Thirteen for a discussion of the impact technology has had on using direct mail.

Cable TV—Advantage

- Cost. A 30-second TV slot on a cable TV channel in the Los Angeles Metropolitan Area can cost as little as $16, or as high as $65. Some cable TV companies will even produce your TV commercials for you free of charge.

Cable TV—Disadvantage

- A major mystery. It is impossible to tell who the audience for your TV commercial will be and, in fact, whether anybody at all will see it. Cable TV is one medium that requires carefully controlled testing to figure out how it will work for you.

USING MEDIA

Marketing Planning Pages 11-5 through 11-11 are designed to help you organize your thoughts about how to use media in advertising your products and/or services to your customers and/or potential customers.

Marketing Planning Page 11-5

How We Could Use Newspapers in Our Advertising Strategy

Marketing Planning Page 11-6

HOW WE COULD USE MAGAZINES
IN OUR ADVERTISING STRATEGY

_____

_____

_____

_____

_____

_____

_____

_____

_____

_____

_____

_____

_____

_____

_____

_____

_____

_____

_____

_____

_____

Marketing Planning Page 11-7

How We Could Use Television in Our Advertising Strategy

_____

_____

_____

_____

_____

_____

_____

_____

_____

_____

_____

_____

_____

_____

_____

_____

_____

_____

_____

_____

_____

_____

_____

Marketing Planning Page 11-8

How We Could Use Radio in Our Advertising Strategy

_____

_____

_____

_____

_____

_____

_____

_____

_____

_____

_____

_____

_____

_____

_____

_____

_____

_____

_____

_____

_____

_____

Marketing Planning Page 11-9
How We Could Use the Outdoors in Our Advertising Strategy

_____

_____

_____

_____

_____

_____

_____

_____

_____

_____

_____

_____

_____

_____

_____

_____

_____

_____

_____

_____

_____

_____

_____

Marketing Planning Page 11-10

HOW WE COULD USE DIRECT MAIL
IN OUR ADVERTISING STRATEGY

Marketing Planning Page 11-11

How We Could Use Cable TV
in Our Advertising Strategy

WHAT TO SAY TO YOUR CUSTOMERS

While it is, indeed, important to know who your customers are and why they buy from you, the fact of life is that there are severe limitations on the amount of money you can save in your advertising budget from matching your customers with the most efficient and effective media. Just because it is difficult does not mean you should ever stop trying to wring savings out of your media schedule.

However, the real control over your advertising expenditures comes from having a well thought-out, clearly written CREATIVE STRATEGY for each product and/or service that you sell. The problem you encounter in real life marketing management is that when advertising is being created, it is incredibly easy for the focus of the work to shift from selling your product or service to creating award-winning advertising for the agency. A rough guess might be that 80% of the waste in advertising stems directly from creating advertising for this purpose.

Note: For a more complete description of the problem and its causes, see: *How to Develop a Successful Advertising Plan* (Lincolnwood, IL: NTC Business Books, 1993) (ISBN 0-8442-3526-1)

Your absolutely best protection is to develop a Creative Strategy Statement for each product and service you sell. This statement is essentially an extension and elaboration of a brand's marketing strategy into the brand's advertising and creative area. It picks up from a creative standpoint where the marketing strategy stops and indicates basic, agreed-upon, long-term selling strategy to reach your customers.

A CREATIVE STRATEGY SPECIFIES:

1. The total net impression which advertising is expected to leave with a specific target group.

2. Other *basic* decisions which will shape and direct the content and form of the advertising.

Thus, the Creative Strategy Statement describes the basis upon which a product or service is to be distinguished from competitive products; how the product or service is to be positioned in the minds of the target group; how it will be given a distinct identity of its own.

It is used as a guide in the development of advertising and as a benchmark for evaluating advertising.

The Creative Strategy Statement should be thought of as long-term strategy since one of the purposes of this Statement is to give continuity to the advertising effort over a long period of time. Basic creative strategy is ordinarily changed only when:

1. there is a fundamental change in the character of the market, or

2. there is a fundamental change in the character of the product or service, or

3. there is a major competitive threat, or

4. there is demonstrated failure of the existing strategy to achieve its objectives.

Since the Creative Strategy Statement is a logical extension of the marketing plans, marketing strategy and objectives of the brand, the marketing group and the advertising agency account group are responsible for the initiation and development of a new or revised statement.

Every Creative Strategy Statement should include the specific, basic selling idea(s), or the basic concept(s) which the product or service's advertising is designed to establish in the minds of the customers and, as a direct result, provide the motivation to purchase your brand in preference to that of the competition.

The following ideas will ordinarily appear in a Creative Strategy Statement, but not all of them need appear in every statement.

1. A concise statement of the principal *benefit* offered by the product or service. This represents the basic reason customers are expected to purchase your product or service in preference to that of a competitor. *It is important to note that this part of the statement is NOT an analysis of all possible benefits, but represents a decision as to which of these benefits is to be emphasized in the advertising.*

2. A statement of the principal *characteristic* of the product or service which makes it possible to claim this benefit, i.e., the *reason why* this benefit exists and has meaning to the target group. For example: an ingredient like "ibuprofen," or a process like "packed with no preservatives," or a quality standard like, "made with only the most expensive leather." Procter & Gamble calls this point the "Permission to Buy." For example, Charmin tissues' principal benefit is softness. Is there anyone in the U. S. who is unaware of this fact? An illustration of the long-term nature of

the Creative Strategy Statement. Mr. Whipple shows the customer how to test for the softness and thus gives him or her a way to develop a personal permission to buy.

Stated another way, these ideas identify the points of product or service *superiority or distinctiveness* which bear directly on the benefit claimed.

3. A statement of the *character or personality* which is to be built for the product or service and which will be reflected in the mood, tone, atmosphere, etc. of the advertising long-term. In practice, this is usually a list of adjectives that are quite useful in creating advertising from year to year, advertising agency to advertising agency, marketing manager to marketing manager, print to broadcast, etc., that has the same look. A list that contained "modern, smooth, primary colors, sharp corners, bright, reflective" would produce advertising that would be quite different from a list that contained words like "old-fashioned, warm, earth tones, soft, slightly rough, rounded, friendly."

4. A statement of what the *product or service is, or what it is used for* when the answers to these questions are not obvious. Is it a main meal, or a snack? Is it a finished product, or an ingredient? Is it a time-saving service, or does it save money? In short, it answers the question "where does this product or service fit into the customer's experience?"

The real value of the Creative Strategy Statement lies in the fact that it assures that your advertising is *a direct outgrowth of your basic marketing strategy and nothing else.* As a long-term document, it provides continuity-of-impression in a brand's advertising that, over a period of time, helps the brand to come to stand for something specific in the minds of customers. It helps a brand achieve distinction in a competitive market.

HOW TO USE A CREATIVE STRATEGY STATEMENT

All of the analysis and thought about your marketing strategy that this guide has asked you to do so far will be extremely helpful in writing a Creative Strategy Statement for each of your brands. In particular, your understanding of your customers, your competitors and your products or services will help you make the best decision about the basic benefit that will differentiate you from your competitors and put you into the strongest competitive position for the long-term.

When you and your advertising agency have agreed upon a written Creative Strategy Statement, you can give it assignments such as, "Develop some new, fresh, captivating, different ways to communicate our basic benefit." Since the advertising agency understands completely what the basic benefit is, it has the best possible direction in which to proceed. When the agency brings you its best ideas about how to communicate the basic benefit, you have a standard for measuring its work, i.e., "Does this particular piece of advertising say (basic benefit) to our customers?" If it does, you okay it. If it doesn't, you send the agency back to try again.

In case there is a serious disagreement between you and the agency about whether the proposed advertisement communicates the basic benefit, it can be settled easily with some small-scale research. The agency simply prepares some reasonably finished version of the advertisement in question and it is shown to, say 100, customers with a single question asked, "What does this ad say to you about this product (service)?" If a majority plays back the basic benefit, you okay the ad. Otherwise, it goes back for more work. In either case, everyone involved knows exactly how the decision was made and that is incredibly important in an on-going relationship with your advertising agency.

Note: The communications test described above is the only piece of advertising research worth spending your money on. None of the rest will give you any reliable direction for action.

Here Is an Example of a Creative Strategy Statement in Use

William Grant & Sons, Inc., import Glenfiddich brand single malt scotch whiskey for distribution in the United States. Single malt whiskeys are premium priced and premium quality. This company knows a great deal about its customers whose primary characteristics are these:

- Male
- 25 to 49 years old
- Incomes of $40,000 or more
- Enjoy challenges and new experiences
- Constantly searching for premium products and experiences
- Believe that they can tell the quality of a scotch whiskey by its "smoothness."

Since the major competitive product's advertising (The Glenlivet, a Jos. Seagram, Inc. brand) focused on communicating a feeling of Scotland, William Grant & Sons decided that it had a real opportunity to establish its brand as the "smooth scotch." Accordingly, its Creative Strategy identified its principal benefit as "smoothness" and asked its agency, Chiat/Day Advertising, Inc. to create advertising that communicated that benefit.

This advertising campaign increased Glenfiddich's market share and, even more important, increased its sales in a declining market. The campaign is still running five years later.

Marketing Planning Pages 11-12 through 11-15 are designed to help you develop Creative Strategy Statements for some of your brands.

Note: If you have the slightest doubt about the importance of a Creative Strategy Statement in developing advertising, do the following exercise for yourself. Take a pad of writing paper and a pencil or pen, and settle down in front of your TV for a couple of hours. Every time a commercial comes on, write down the name of the sponsor and then write down the basic benefit that the product or service is supposed to offer its customers, if you can. Write down the commercials with a basic benefit on one side of the page and those without on the other side. You will rapidly see one side of your page getting longer and longer. Finally, ask yourself this question, "What in the world did the companies that spent their money on commercials with no benefit think that they were doing?" Then make your own estimate of how much money spent on advertising is wasted.

The most widely read trade publication in the advertising business is *Advertising Age*. You can subscribe by writing to Crain Communications, Inc., 965 East Jefferson, Detroit, MI 48207.

Marketing Planning Page 11-12

CREATIVE STRATEGY STATEMENT—BRAND A

Basic Benefit: _____

_____

_____

_____

_____

_____

Reason Why this Benefit is Possible: _____

_____

_____

_____

_____

_____

Character or Personality of this Product or Service: _____

_____

_____

_____

_____

_____

How to Use this Brand: _____

_____

_____

_____

Marketing Planning Page 11-13

CREATIVE STRATEGY STATEMENT — BRAND B

Basic Benefit: _____

_____

_____

_____

_____

_____

Reason Why this Benefit is Possible: _____

_____

_____

_____

_____

_____

Character or Personality of this Product or Service: _____

_____

_____

_____

_____

_____

How to Use this Brand: _____

_____

_____

_____

Marketing Planning Page 11-14
CREATIVE STRATEGY STATEMENT—BRAND C

Basic Benefit: _____

_____

_____

_____

_____

_____

Reason Why this Benefit is Possible: _____

_____

_____

_____

_____

_____

Character or Personality of this Product or Service: _____

_____

_____

_____

_____

_____

How to Use this Brand: _____

_____

_____

_____

Marketing Planning Page 11-15

CREATIVE STRATEGY STATEMENT — BRAND D

Basic Benefit: _____

_____

_____

_____

_____

_____

Reason Why this Benefit is Possible: _____

_____

_____

_____

_____

_____

Character or Personality of this Product or Service: _____

_____

_____

_____

_____

_____

How to Use this Brand: _____

_____

_____

_____

SALES PROMOTION

The best working definition of sales promotion is "those activities which you undertake to cause certain other people to change their behavior in specific ways during specific periods of time." *Promo* magazine's Source Book '96 says this is how money was spent on sales promotion in 1994.

Type of Promotion	*Gross Revenue (in $ millions)*
Premium incentives	$20,000
Point of Purchase displays	16,979
Couponing	6,995
Advertising specialties	6,880
Promotional licensing	4,900
Sponsored events	4,250
Specialty printing	3,000
Promotion fulfillment	2,180
Interactive/telepromotions	1,750
Research	857
Promotion agencies	833
In-store marketing	829
Product sampling	704
	$70,156

It is clear that a lot of money is being spent to get specific people to change their behavior in specific ways during specific time periods. And the money spent on sales promotion works best when it is highly coordinated with your advertising.

For some very good evidence that this is true, see John Philip Jones, *When Ads Work*, Chapter 5, "Advertising Versus Promotions—or Advertising Plus Promotions" (New York: Lexington Books, 1995) (ISBN 0-02-916662-4).

This simple sounding, but difficult to actually accomplish activity, coordinating your advertising with your sales promotion, has even been given the somewhat pompous sounding name of Integrated Marketing Communications. The main reason that this coordination is so important is clearly demonstrated by the 1995 Consumer Buying Habits Study conducted for the Point-of-Purchase Advertising Institute. The study found that 74% of all brand purchase decisions are made *in the store* by people shopping at mass merchandisers, and 70% are made *in the store* by people shopping in supermarkets. Although these were the only two types of retailers surveyed, it is not a big stretch of the imagination to realize that similar percentages are true for other types of stores.

The point is that a lot can happen to your customers between the time they see your advertising and the time that they make their purchases. Sales promotion generally lets you influence their behavior as close to the actual purchase as you can get. In other words, advertising and sales promotion working together let you control more of the purchasing decisions made by your customers (which also makes your customers more resistant to competitors' enticements).

Types of Sales Promotion

There is a wide variety of types of sales promotions and each one has some particular advantages and is best at encouraging certain kinds of behavior.

Sampling The best way to induce a behavior change is to put an actual sample of your product or service in the hands of a prospective customer. It may be a package of Hershey's Hugs that comes in the mail, or it may be a paper cup of Diet Pepsi that is handed out in a supermarket, or it may be a swatch of fabric that the customer takes home to see if the color goes with the furniture. Sampling also includes things like a test ride in the new Camry at your local Toyota dealer, a trial subscription to *Premiere* magazine, a small package of Armor All Car Wash shrink-wrapped onto a full-size package of Armor All Protectant, or the first night free at a hotel.

Sampling is particularly effective when the product has some attribute that cannot be described very well in advertising, i.e., a fragrance, a texture, a flavor, etc. Sampling is also particularly effective in converting potential customers into actual customers, e.g., ten free hours on America Online. Sampling is frequently used with industrial products and services. One of the most imaginative sample offers occurred when Lee Clow (now President of Chiat/Day Advertising, Inc.) offered to work for Jay Chiat (founder of Chiat/Day Advertising, Inc.) for a month without pay, as a way to get a job at Chiat/Day.

An interesting "not quite a sample" is the use of video tapes to "sample" products and services. Nordic Trak uses them to sell its exercise equipment. Monsanto, Inc. uses them to sell its Class A Foam for fighting wildfires.

Morningstar, Inc. uses them to sell its mutual fund evaluation services. Smith's Food & Drug Centers use video tapes to introduce its super stores to prospective customers in the store's trading area. Hannover Fairs USA uses them to sell participation in the world's largest trade fairs in Hannover, FRG. The National Sporting Goods Association uses videos to boost attendance at its World Expo trade shows. Infiniti used them to introduce its luxury automobiles to U. S. motorists.

A Big Word of Caution!!

Do not use samples of your product or service unless it is truly first class. You are asking your prospective customer to compare your product or service with what he or she currently prefers and is using. A big improvement will be expected. Make sure you deliver it. Here is an example of how to do it right. Berol, Ltd. developed a new permanent marker that won't dry out even if the cap is left off for as long as two weeks. It calls them the Berol Multi-Purpose Markers. A mailing went to 50,000 stationery buyers around the country. Each package contained a cover letter, a six-page brochure and a Berol Multi-Purpose Marker—without the cap. (Sales went up 25%.)

COUPONS Coupons are certificates, usually paper that can be used by your customers to get a reduced price, a refund, or a free package. They are issued by a particular store(s) and are only good at that store(s). The intention is to build up store traffic and, hopefully, additional purchases. They are also issued by manufacturers and those coupons are good at just about any store carrying the product. Manufacturer-issued coupons can have several purposes, such as to attract new customers, reward existing customers, fend off a competitor's offer, etc.

Coupons are widely used. Approximately 85% of all U. S. households report that they use coupons regularly. Coupons are also used with industrial products and services. The most widely used method of distributing coupons is free standing inserts (FSI), those preprinted sets of coupons that usually are delivered in your Sunday newspaper. Something over 80% of all coupons are distributed this way. Direct mail is the next most popular method (around 10%). Coupons are also distributed by hand-outs, in-the-page in magazines, door-to-door delivery, in and on-packages, in-the-page newspapers, and the rapidly growing method of electronic print-out coupons issued at the check-out counter.

A significant problem with almost all coupon programs is estimating the redemption rate accurately so you can budget accordingly. Redemption rates can range from some small fraction of a percentage point to ten percent or more. And that is a very large swing in your financial planning. Remember to put a time limit on your coupon offer. Otherwise the accounting department may want you to carry the promotion on the books as a liability for a very, very long time.

PRICE-OFFS   In this technique, the manufacturer produces some amount of the product with some new price, or a price reduction, printed on the label of the package. This limited quantity of the specially marked merchandise is then sold to retailers at a reduced price reflecting the new label price. What is happening is that the manufacturer has forced the retailer to offer a price reduction.

Manufacturers usually prefer to accomplish short-term price reductions through the use of trade promotions, i.e., lower price deals for limited periods of time. The idea behind trade promotions is that the retailers will buy extra amounts of the product "on deal," lower the price in the store, sell all of the product quickly, recover their cash and make an extra profit.

Price-offs require two inventories, regular merchandise and deal merchandise, both for the manufacturer and for the retailer. Some retailers see price-offs as manufacturers interfering with the retailer's business.

IN, ON AND NEAR PACKS   In these kinds of promotions, premiums are offered for the purchase of merchandise. The world's best known in-pack is the toy in a box of Cracker Jacks, which has been a feature of that product since 1912. But in-packs are also as modern as the plastic measuring spoon that Stern's Garden Products packs in its plant fertilizer products.

An on-pack is fastened in some way to the original product being sold. You may well have received a new Colgate toothbrush when you purchased a tube of Colgate toothpaste. A modern high-tech version can be found in all of the personal computers that come loaded with many types of software. The Macintosh that this book is written on came loaded with Claris Works®, Quicken®, American Heritage Dictionary®, Click Art, Mario Teaches Typing™, and two games. Another version involves selling the product in a special package. The NFL player-decorated drinking cups that McDonalds dispenses with soft drinks are an example.

Both in-pack and on-pack premiums create two inventory problems. A near-pack premium is one that is placed somewhere near the product being sold; the customer is supposed to find it, and the retailer is supposed to manage its inventory. The retailer Computer City places boxes of floppy disks near the cash registers. Customers are given free floppies in proportion to the amount of their purchases.

Aside from the inventory problems, the major difficulty with pack premiums is finding good value items that are associated with the product. A ball point pen with a bar of soap doesn't make much sense, but a special scrubbing sponge with that bar of soap does.

When coupons are distributed by packing them in or on-back and are redeemable for the next purchase of the same brand, they are called "bounce back" coupons. When such coupons are redeemable for some other product (usually a different one of your company, but not necessarily), they are called "cross ruff" coupons.

FREE-IN-THE-MAIL PREMIUMS In this type of promotion, you offer to mail a premium free of charge (or for a small handling fee) to every customer who sends you specific evidence that he or she has actually purchased the products or services. Such "proof-of-purchases" can be for single item purchases, multiple purchases, or purchases accumulated over time. Both consumer and industrial products and services companies have used these premiums with great success.

They avoid the double inventory problem and the pilferage problems that can plague in-, on- and near-packs. In addition, there is really no top limit on the size of the premium because it can be sized directly to the profits from the purchases.

Airline frequent flyer programs are undoubtedly the most elegant of the free-in-the-mail programs. The proof-of-purchase is your airline tickets. The airlines do the accounting for you. The reward is obviously closely associated with the way you earn proofs-of-purchase in the first place. And the size of the biggest award can be very large indeed. American Airlines will give you a first-class, round trip ticket from New York to Tokyo, which has a value today of over $8,500, for free if you can show enough American Airlines frequent flyer miles.

Free-in-the-mail premiums almost always have lower redemption rates than those that the customer can acquire directly.

Here is an example of an interesting variation on a free-in-the-mail program. First of all Pepsi-Cola distributed coupons good for a free "Reebok

Basketball" (with a purchase of any Reebok product) in several million specially marked multi-unit packages. But the coupons had to be redeemed at a Sears store to get the $15 value basketball. The basketballs were given at the store immediately with the purchase instead of by mail later. One major advantage of this well thought out promotion is that Pepsi and Sears provided most of the money to advertise the promotion.

SELF-LIQUIDATING PREMIUMS One way to avoid the store inventory problems associated with near-pack premiums is to require the customer to send some amount of money to pay for all, or some large part, of the cost of the premium, plus handling costs. You buy the premium item in a large quantity and offer it to your customers at a price lower than the normal retail price.

One of the advantages of self-liquidating premiums is that you can work with very high value merchandise to give your promotion some real excitement among your sales force, your customers, and the trade. Indeed, the trend in self-liquidating premiums lately has been to higher-priced merchandise. The biggest disadvantage is that self-liquidating premiums usually have very low redemption rates (1% is typical) so you must plan your promotion very carefully. Limited testing is highly advisable here before you order a zillion custommade units with your name and logo all over them. The surplus merchandise may be very hard to sell.

BONUS PACKS The idea here is to put extra product in your customers' hands. For example, an extra bar of soap is often sold wrapped together with three or four other bars of the same size. Or a special package allows the manufacturer to sell an extra quantity of the product at the regular price. A "baker's dozen" was the original bonus pack, thirteen buns for the price of twelve.

A big advantage of a bonus pack is that the customer can literally see the extra value being offered. Bonus packs can also encourage stocking up.

However, bonus packs also require a separate inventory and frequently separate packaging. In addition, you must make certain that the new package will fit on the store shelves and that retailers can't pull your package apart and sell the individual units at their regular price.

One way to solve these problems is to simply have a "One free with One," or a 1¢ sale (buy one and get the second for a penny). This solves all of the problems of dual inventories, extra packaging, etc.

CONTESTS AND SWEEPSTAKES The first point to make clear here is that contests and sweepstakes are legally different. Winning a contest must be based solely on chance, but winners of contests must have displayed some sort of skill (written a poem, answered questions, etc.). Anybody must be eligible to enter a sweepstakes, but it is possible to limit entrants into a contest to those who have actually purchased a product or service. So it should come as no surprise that ten times as many consumers will enter a sweepstakes compared with a contest.

Both contests and sweepstakes are exception methods to build excitement among target groups. Because of the legal differences described above, sweepstakes are most often aimed at consumers, while contests target your sales force and/or your distributors.

Sweepstakes and contests for consumers have lost a lot of appeal lately because of some major snafus in the execution of several in the late 1980s and early 1990s.

For example, the beverage company that was supposed to have printed prize awards on the bottom of the beverage cans, except that it never did. The food products company that printed millions of winning tickets instead of the hundreds that it had budgeted for. Or the employee who stole the winning numbers and distributed them to his relatives. All of these events generated a lot of bad publicity for their sponsors in the U. S.

Among sales forces and distributors, sales contests continue to be an outstanding incentive. The three most desired prizes are money, time-off and travel, with all other prizes far less motivating.

Planning Your Sales Promotion Programs

Sales promotion programs tend to be brief, and require a lot of activity during the period to be successful, so really thorough planning is mandatory. Marketing Planning Pages 11-16 through 11-19 are designed to help you organize your planning for sales promotion programs. Each section is discussed below.

Objectives: Remember that sales promotion programs are designed to create behavioral changes so objectives must specify what behavior you want to change, for what period, and by whom. "Increase September/October sales by 25%" is NOT a suitable objective.

Timing: The exact dates by which you are planning to effect a behavioral change must be clearly specified and communicated to everyone involved.

Resources required: Every sales promotion program discussed above required some special equipment, supplies, packaging, printing, etc. You must identify all of those materials in advance and make absolutely certain that they will be where you need them when you need them. There is little that is as wasteful as the point of purchase display material arriving at the store two weeks after the promotional period has ended.

Individual responsibilities: Sales promotion programs are non-routine, one-of-a-kind activities that are not automatically part of everyone's regular job description, so it is very important for you to identify exactly who will have to help you execute your programs, what you expect them to do, and when they are expected to do it.

Critical Deadlines Sales promotion programs usually consist of a number of separate activities that all converge at some point in time, and then lead to a short period of intense activity. If the deadlines are not identified and met, the whole program is in danger.

Budget required: Since sales promotion programs have their greatest value in NOT BEING repetitive, budgeting is always on a "first time" basis. Be sure to include all of the expenses.

Goal to be achieved: You must specify exactly what behavioral change levels constitute success for your program. For example, "Eight hundred dealer presentations will be made and 50% of them will result in minimum order quantities and 30% of them will result in full-line stocking orders. That will produce a minimum of 65,000 cases of new business."

Method of evaluation: Exactly how will you measure the results of the program? Once again, sales promotion activities tend to be one-of-a-kind which means you usually have to plan a one-of-a-kind evaluation procedure. If you don't plan to evaluate the results of your programs, you will never be able to improve them.

Finally, ALWAYS remember to make certain your sales promotion programs are consistent with and support your Creative Strategy Statement for the brand.

Marketing Planning Page 11-16

SALES PROMOTION PROGRAM—BRAND A—FY 19___

Objective(s):_____

_____

_____

Timing: _____

_____

Resources Required: _____

_____

_____

Critical deadlines: _____

_____

_____

Budget:_____

_____

_____

Program Goal(s):_____

_____

_____

Method of evaluation:_____

_____

_____

How does this program support the Creative Strategy for this brand? _____

_____

Marketing Planning Page 11-17

SALES PROMOTION PROGRAM—BRAND B—FY 19___

Objective(s):_____

_____

_____

Timing: _____

_____

Resources Required: _____

_____

_____

Critical deadlines: _____

_____

_____

Budget:_____

_____

_____

Program Goal(s):_____

_____

_____

Method of evaluation:_____

_____

_____

How does this program support the Creative Strategy for this brand? _____

_____

Marketing Planning Page 11-18

Sales Promotion Program — Brand C — FY 19___

Objective(s): _____

_____

_____

Timing: _____

_____

Resources Required: _____

_____

_____

Critical deadlines: _____

_____

_____

Budget: _____

_____

_____

Program Goal(s): _____

_____

_____

Method of evaluation: _____

_____

_____

How does this program support the Creative Strategy for this brand? _____

_____

Marketing Planning Page 11-19

SALES PROMOTION PROGRAM — BRAND D — FY 19___

Objective(s):_____

_____

_____

Timing: _____

_____

Resources Required: _____

_____

_____

Critical deadlines: _____

_____

_____

Budget:_____

_____

_____

Program Goal(s):_____

_____

_____

Method of evaluation:_____

_____

_____

How does this program support the Creative Strategy for this brand? _____

_____

TRADE PROMOTION

In the discussion at the beginning of this section, it was noted that about half of the marketing budget is spent on trade promotions as opposed to consumer promotions. Trade promotions are always temporary price reductions designed to encourage the trade to buy a larger than usual quantity. They most often take one of two forms. The simplest form is a simple price reduction for some specific period of time. For example: deduct 25% from the invoice on all merchandise ordered between October 1st and November 15th.

The other form is free goods. For example: one case free with every three cases ordered between October 1st and November 15th. As you can see, the financial implications are the same for both of these offers. The supplier will ship four cases and get paid for three cases. The free goods offer is frequently preferred by the retailers/wholesalers because it really seems like something for nothing. However, when manufacturers want to use some fractional discount, free goods gets to be a clumsy way to execute a temporary price reduction, e.g., seven cases free with every hundred cases ordered.

Sometimes the manufacturer will try to tie the discounted price to some activity that the retailer is supposed to conduct, i.e., run a local advertisement about the lowered price, a special end-aisle display, etc. The manufacturer then attempts to require the retailer to prove that the desired action was taken, i.e., supply a tearsheet from the local newspaper, submit a photograph, etc. These proof-of-performance requirements are always difficult to police on the manufacturer's part and are also a potential source of considerable irritation between the manufacturer and the retailer. The message here is that clean trade promotions are ALWAYS preferable to complicated ones.

But unless you have also organized some additional promotional programs to help the distributor/retailer "sell through" the additional merchandise that was purchased on your successful trade promotion, all you have really done is to transfer some inventory from your warehouse to the distributor/retailer's warehouse. And that really doesn't do much good for anyone.

Selecting an Advertising/Promotion Agency to Work With

Section Nine explored in depth how to select a marketing information specialist to work with. Choice of an advertising and/or promotion agency is just as important, but the rules are somewhat different.

A bit of waffling is required here. The nature of the advertising agency and/or promotion agency is undergoing rapid experimentation and change as these organizations attempt to learn how best to deal with the re-structuring of the business described earlier in the section. The emerging roles of technology (explored in Section Thirteen) add even more uncertainty to this process.

Basically, this is what is happening. Many advertising agencies are responding to the shift of marketing budgets out of advertising and into promotion by attempting to offer expert services and advice in that area as well as in advertising. The problem they encounter is that the billing practices in promotion work are quite different from those in traditional advertising, and the agencies are having difficulty making money in promotion. Furthermore, a large number of businesses have opened in recent years specifically to provide companies with expertise in promotion activities. These new promotion agencies seldom have the qualifications (or interest?) for acting as the client's advertising agency. Eventually, it will all get sorted out. You can expect that some organizations will specialize exclusively in advertising, some exclusively in promotion and a few will succeed in both areas. But the really interesting organizations will master the challenges of technology discussed in Section Thirteen and will create a whole new kind of marketing service organization.

In any case, for the moment, you may have to select one or the other type of organization to work with and what follows are some of the best ideas about how to go about that job, and to live happily with the agency you select.

- Make sure you have a very clear understanding of exactly what you expect from your agency. Just to get a fresh perspective, or generate some new ideas is not good enough.

- Make sure that the agency handles other accounts about the size of yours. Big accounts do best in big agencies and little accounts do best in little agencies. While there are occasionally exceptions to this rule, you take big risks with your business if you try to be one of them.

- Make sure that the organization is local. In spite of all the incredible advances in communications (see Section Thirteen), this is an incredibly personal business activity. Nothing in the cyberworld beats sitting around a table and kicking ideas around, or floating a partially-thought-through notion over drinks after work. Those are things that simply cannot be done successfully over a telephone wire, no matter what it is connected to.

- Make sure that the people who make the presentation to win your business are the ones who will work on your business. In many agencies there is quite a large gap between the talents of the people working in their new business function and the people assigned to work on the account once it is signed. Part of the reason is economics and that leads to the next point.

- Make sure you are prepared to pay the agency enough to allow it a reasonable profit. Its payment should be coming from your profits. If you pay your agency on a second-class, hard bargaining basis, don't be surprised when it assigns second-class people to your business, and don't be surprised when you get only second-class ideas.

- Make sure that you give the agency a "test" assignment that is real enough and large enough to serve as a real test of its talents. Don't hesitate to pay for the work either.

- Make sure that you have established clear criteria about what is understood to be successful performance on its part, and . . .

- Make sure that you hold regularly scheduled review meetings to evaluate and discuss the agency's performance.

For a more detailed discussion of selecting and living with an agency, consult "How To Choose A Promotion Agency," *Promo* Magazine's Source book '96, p. 42–3; and "Selecting an Advertising Agency," *How to Develop a Successful Advertising Plan*, NTC Business Books, p. 235–42.

You should also give serious consideration to subscribing to *Promo* Magazine, 50 Washington Street, 8th Floor, Norwalk, CT 06854. In addition to the magazine's excellent coverage of the entire promotion business, it also offers a number of excellent additional services online and by fax. You can subscribe by telephoning (800) 345-8112.

SECTION TWELVE

All Competition Is Now Global

OVERVIEW OF SECTION TWELVE: No matter what business you are in now, you can be absolutely certain that somewhere in the world there is a new competitor planning to take away your business. Your best chances lie in building an overseas business in your new competitor's backyard. Section Twelve will show you exactly how to do that job. It will also show you how to get the most out of trade shows and exhibits, the best competitive tool for small and medium size businesses building an international business for the first time. And if you already have an international business, Section Twelve will show you how to become a stronger competitor.

GLOBAL COMPETITION IS NOW
A FACT OF LIFE FOR EVERY BUSINESS

Everywhere you turn, the numbers on international trade are huge and growing rapidly. Here are a few examples:

- The value of U. S. exports and imports in 1994 was $1,177 *billion*

- U. S. exports and imports represent 23% of *all* U. S. economic activity in 1994

- U. S. exports and imports are expected to reach $1.2 *trillion* by the year 2000

- In fact, roughly one-third of *all* U. S. economic growth in this decade has been driven by exports

- In 1995, 61% of all U. S. exports were manufactured goods, 27% were services, 7% mineral fuels and 5% farm products

- In 1995, U. S. companies did 6,634 deals (acquisitions, mergers, alliances, etc.) worth $302 million, an increase of 313% over 1985.

- The U. S. Commerce Department estimates that approximately 105,000 U. S. companies export

- And it is not just a big company activity. In 1990, only 19% of Inc. magazine's top 500 companies had foreign sales. But in 1994 almost half (46%) had foreign sales

All of these numbers mean just two things to you. The export side means that there is probably a substantial opportunity for you to grow your business with sales to foreign customers. The import side means that out there somewhere there is a foreign company getting ready to take away your customers. You ignore international business at your peril.

A VERY BRIEF HISTORY OF WORLD TRADE

At this point, it may be useful to take a quick look at the development of world trade as a way of understanding what is happening today. Without a doubt, the first and most colorful world traders were the Polo brothers, Niccolo and Maffeo, who traveled the fabled Silk Route from Venice to China in 1260–69. (Their exploits were later made famous by Niccolo's son, Marco, in the book, *The Travels of Marco Polo*). From that time on until the early 1930s world trade among nations increased fairly regularly. And most of the world grew richer for it.

But as the unemployment caused by the Great Depression rolled round the world, some governments came to look on imports as jobs that were lost at home and turned to methods of restricting them. The most egregious actions were taken by the U. S. Congress when it passed the Smoot-Hawley

Act of 1930, which effectively raised the tariffs on all goods imported into the United States to 60%, and virtually terminated them. Other nations responded in like kind and, as a result, world trade ground to a halt, the depression worsened, and unemployment increased.

At the conclusion of World War II, the developed nations of the world agreed to never let that happen again and they formed an organization known as the General Agreement on Trade and Tariffs (GATT). GATT basically was a lengthy conference, attended by all members, with the objective of bargaining down tariffs (and other trade restrictions) one product or service at time. It had three basic principles: 1) Every member had to treat every other member the same way. So if France had a 20% tariff on wine imported from the United States, it had to levy an identical tariff on wine imported from Spain, Italy, etc. 2) All other forms of trade restraint beyond tariffs were discouraged. This meant that non-tariff barriers were to be eliminated. Some hilarious examples of non-tariff barriers were erected by the Japanese government in the 1980s when it banned the import of ski equipment on the grounds that Japanese snow was different and banned beef imports on the grounds that Japanese stomachs were different. 3) All forms of export subsidies were to be discouraged. For instance, the U. S. Government makes direct payments to wine makers to assist them in their international marketing efforts.

Measured by one standard, GATT has been wildly successful. Under GATT's aegis, average tariffs among member nations are now in the 2–4% range. However, on the three principles mentioned above, there is still a great deal of work to do.

As the final round of the GATT talks concluded in 1994, the original GATT was disbanded and a new organization, the World Trade Organization (WTO) was formed to continue GATT's work and to provide a forum for settling international disputes among its members. One hundred and five nations are members of the WTO at this time.

One Other Development of Importance

So many of the issues confronting the WTO are so politically explosive in individual countries that governments are hedging their bets and forming regional trade associations with the same aims as the WTO. The North American Free Trade Association (NAFTA) is one example. The European Community (EC) is another. MERCOSUR in South America and ASEAN in southeast Asia are others.

Where Does It All Stand Now?

The old, thoroughly discredited "protect our jobs" notion is still alive and well in every country. Ross Perot made it an issue in the 1992 U. S. elections and Pat Buchanan did the same thing in the 1996 elections. It is particularly troublesome in France. But on balance, most governments seem to understand that the growth that is going to finance their budgets relies heavily on increased trade and, as a result, they are protective of, and supportive of their exporters. U. S. Government assistance for your international business activities will be discussed shortly.

HOW TO BUILD YOUR INTERNATIONAL BUSINESS

Building your international business is much like building your domestic business. You need to thoroughly understand your products and/or services, your strengths and weaknesses, your customers, your competitors and your environment, everything that has been discussed so far in this book. However, there are some distinct differences when you begin to do business outside of your national boundaries and it is important that you understand them. When you do, you can make sensible decisions to make them work to your advantage.

Sources of Information

As noted, all plans should be based on information and facts. Here are some additional sources of information about international markets that you will find useful.

United Nations. The UN is a major source of worldwide information useful to businesses. Begin by writing to the UN Industrial Development Organization, P. O. Box 707, A-1011 Vienna, AUSTRIA.

Organization for Economic Cooperation and Development (OECD). The twenty-four most developed countries in the world are members and supporters of this organization that has as one of its primary tasks the gathering and disseminating of economic information about member countries. The OECD Publications and Information Center is at 2001 L Street N. W., Suite 700, Washington, DC 20036, and the telephone number is (202)785-6323. Ask to be placed on the mailing list for OECD Recent Publications.

The U. S. Government collects and publishes a wide variety of useful information about international markets and international business. It is available from the United States Government Printing Office, Superintendent of Documents, Washington, DC 20402, and the telephone number is (202) 512-1800. Order *A Basic Guide to Exporting*. It will help greatly with the paperwork and regulations involved in shipping overseas. Also, ask to be placed on the mailing list both for the publication *United States Government Information for Business* and for *Import/Export Publications*.

U.S. Department of Commerce. The Department of Commerce at (800 USA-TRADE) maintains a comprehensive source of information on all federal government export assistance programs. It also now has a home page on the Internet. You can find it at [http://www.ustr.gov/index.html] and what is important here is that this site is linked with other trade-related Internet locations. Be sure to investigate its Gold Key Service which is custom tailored for U. S. firms planning on visiting a new country. It includes market research, assistance with country strategy, orientation briefings, introductions to potential partners, interpreters and follow-up planning.

International Trade Administration. The U. S. Department of Commerce also operates the ITA to provide on-site assistance to exporters.

The Economist Intelligence Unit publishes a number of very current, very detailed economic studies of various countries and various markets. Its address is The Economist Intelligence Unit, The Economist Building, 111 West 57th Street, New York, NY 10019 at telephone number (212) 554-0600. Ask for lists of its current reports. Many are available on CD-ROM.

Trade Communications, Inc., 733 15th Street NW, Suite 1100, Washington, DC 20005 maintains a very helpful source of international business information on the Internet. The URL is [http://www.experttoday.com].

There are also some very important magazines and journals that you should be reading to keep up with developments around the world. Foremost among them is the *Economist*, located at the address given for the Economist Intelligence Unit above.

Business America—The Magazine of International Trade is published by the U. S. Department of Commerce and you can get a subscription at the U. S. Government Printing Office address given above.

International Business—Your Passport to the Global Marketplace is published by American International Publishing Corp., 500 Mamaroneck Avenue, Suite 314, Harrison, NY 10528. Call Subscriber Service at (800) 274-8187.

Export Today is published by Trade Communications, Inc. (address given above); you can subscribe by calling (800) 824-9785.

The OECD Observer is published by the OECD and subscriptions are available at the OECD address shown above.

Global Finance is published by the Global Finance Joint Venture, 11 West 19 Street, 2nd Floor, New York, NY 10011, telephone number (212) 337-5900.

The accounting firm, Price Waterhouse, publishes an absolutely excellent series of manuals entitled *Doing Business in Spain*, *Doing Business in Denmark*, *Doing Business in Mexico*, etc. Contact your local Price Waterhouse office to obtain these for the countries of interest to you.

Trade Shows and Exhibits

Your single, best source of information about markets, competitors, distributors, etc. will always be international trade shows and exhibits. There are literally thousands held around the world every year. Schedules are published by the United Nations and the U. S. Department of Commerce and you can obtain copies at the addresses shown above. In addition, Bill Communications, Inc., 633 Third Avenue, New York, NY 10164 publishes an annual *Directory of International Conventions and Exhibits Schedule*.

Business America regularly publishes a schedule of *International Trade Exhibitions* as part of each issue. The important point is that the trade shows listed there are sponsored by, or approved by, the U. S. Department of Commerce. Frequently, you can participate in the larger U. S. Department of Commerce-sponsored exhibit for a very low cost.

GETTING THE MOST OUT OF YOUR TRADE SHOW BUDGET A well-managed trade show budget can be one of the most effective and efficient ways you can spend your promotional dollars. But a poorly managed one can be a black hole into which you pour money and never see any results. There are several reasons for this. One is that the planning horizon for most trade shows is a decade, or more. That means you may be making commitments and allocating funds years in advance. Another reason is that all of the show activity takes place in a very short period of time and often seems frenetic and out of control. It is not.

There are nine straightforward steps to successfully managing your trade show budget and activities. They are:

1. *Set Objectives.* Decide *exactly what you expect to accomplish.* To meet some people, see what is going on, etc. is not satisfactory. To obtain pricing information on five major competitors is an objective. To find three potential distributors in the United Kingdom is an objective. To show your product line to 1,000 potential customers in Japan is an objective. To obtain the names of 500 good prospects in Australia is an objective.

2. *Select Shows.* Use the descriptions of the shows provided in the directories listed above to identify the shows that seem to be of interest to you. Write to each show manager or contact person, and ask for a "show packet." Whatever form this takes, it should tell you how many people attend the show, what their job titles are, where they are from, who the exhibitors are, and the details for participating in the show. If a show manager doesn't have this information, cross that show off your list. Examine all of the materials and make some judgments about how closely each show will come to satisfying your objectives. List the shows in rank order from best to worst.

3. *Develop Budgets and Schedules.* Use the master list from Step 2 to lay out a schedule for the next two years for the shows that you judge to be the most interesting. (Don't worry that your number one show is eighteen months from now and that show number six is in four months.) Then develop a quarterly budget for each of the next eight quarters to cover your trade show schedule, either as an attendee or a participant.

4. *Plan For Personnel and Training.* Trade shows take place in a very compressed time frame and you simply cannot leave it to the people involved to figure out what to do when the show starts. List the tasks to be done and assign specific personnel to each one. Then make sure that they know how to do their jobs. For example, trade show selling is quite different from what business-to-business sales people usually encounter. You need to show them how to best use a limited amount of time with a potential customer in a crowded, noisy environment. Make sure you plan to rotate the people working the show every four hours. Trade show selling is very fatiguing and you don't want tired, cranky salespeople talking to your customers.

5. *Attract Customers to Your Booth Before the Show Starts.* If you are participating in a trade show as an exhibitor, you will spend a sizable chunk of money in a very few days. There is no way around this. Therefore, you must make every effort to gain the maximum value from your participation. One of the key things to do is attract customers, current and potential, to your show booth *before* the show begins. Write to them in advance and tell them about your presence at the show and give them a map, directions, whatever, to your location. Trade shows can be very crowded and confusing. Also give them some specific reason to visit your booth and announce their presence. Offer a free pen and pencil set, a chance to enter a drawing for a trip around the world, etc. whatever your budget can afford.

6. *Screen Prospects.* At a well-attended trade show, the aisles will be full of people "walking the show." Some of them will be curious about what you have to offer in your booth. Some may become customers someday. Some never will be. The point is that you need some system to greet these folks, answer all of their questions, give them literature if appropriate, and be pleasant with them because someday they may be customers. But you want to do all that at the entrance to your booth. You want to make certain that the space *inside* your booth is available for serious prospects and customers. You can either train your own people, or you can engage a service to provide you with people trained to do exactly this kind of job. The show manager can provide you with a list of such services.

7. *Build Up Your Mailing List.* A trade show is a great way to build your mailing list. You will meet a lot of new people at a trade show and you need a system to make sure that their names, addresses, titles, company names, etc. are recorded easily and accurately. You also want to have a system to make sure that the requests of every visitor to your booth are recorded and can be acted upon. Here is one example of a good system to accomplish both goals: at some shows, the identification badges of the attendees are embossed plastic cards exactly like the credit cards in your pockets. Each exhibitor has an imprinting machine and a stack of pre-printed forms. The request (for literature by number, a salesperson to visit, etc.) is noted on the form. Then the form and the visitor's badge are run through the imprinter. The visitor gets a copy and the company retains the others. If the show you are interested in does not have a show-wide system in place, you will have to develop your own.

8. *Follow Up.* You need a system to make certain that all the promises that were made during the show actually get done. The right literature gets sent out, the right salesperson makes the call, the service technician makes the repair call, etc.: these are all important tasks to be done after the show is over if you are going to receive the full benefit of your investment in time and money. And this won't happen by accident. You will need a system.

9. *Evaluate Costs vs. Profits.* Total all the costs associated with going to the show. Calculate all the profits generated from orders written at the show *and* all orders written from leads generated at the show. If the show generated a profit, put it into your permanent planning schedule. If it did not generate an immediate, traceable profit, drop the show from your list and bring up the next one down the list. Remember, all of the shows got on your list by judgment in the first place and nobody makes every call right.

Three Factors that Truly do Make Doing International Business Different

1. *Markets are different.* Once upon a time, some academics touted theories that it was possible to develop global products and services and to sell them with global methods because a global village was developing. That has proven to be wishful thinking. Coca Cola, a truly global brand if there ever was one, sells dozens and dozens of different formulations of sweetness and carbonation in different shaped bottles around the world. The San Miguel beer sold in the Philippines is not the same as the San Miguel sold in Spain and the San Miguel sold in the United States is different from both of them.

The advice that has emerged from the last twenty years of international business development is simple, direct and correct: "Think global, act local." It should be followed.

Okay., this guide has helped you to think global, but how do you learn to act local? And there is only one answer. You have to go there in person and look for yourself. Do not go as a member of a tour group of any kind. All you will see is other Americans. Admittedly, being in a foreign country for the first time, where you may not speak the language, and don't know anybody can be pretty intimidating. But you can do it. And it will get comfortable fast.

Start by reading several good guide books about the country you plan to visit. Houghton Mifflin Company, 222 Berkeley Street, Boston, MA 02116 publishes an excellent series of introductions to individual countries under the title, "Insight Guides—Chile, etc." Then visit your local ITA office and ask them about its "Match Maker" program and ask them to help you set up some appointments with distributors of your kind of products or services as a place to begin. Distributors are always looking for new sources of supply and most will be happy to talk to you. Ask them who else you should talk to, and ask them to help arrange appointments. You will be pleasantly surprised by the graciousness that most Americans receive overseas (on the assumption that you haven't behaved like the Ugly American!)

One Australian management consultant who had lived in the United States for a long time described perfectly how NOT to make this visit! He said the typical Australian company goes about international business by making a photocopy of its price list and sending it with a middle-level sales manager to Los Angeles. When the manager gets off the airplane in Los Angeles, he looks around and says, "Geez, this place is really big!" Then he checks into a hotel and waits for someone to call him. When he hasn't had any calls by the end of the week he goes back to Australia and reports, "There isn't any business for us up there!"

2. *Distances are Large and Time Zones are Different.* While fax messages and E-Mail are extremely helpful in shrinking distances around the world, the fact of the matter remains that distances around the world are large. No matter how you figure it, London is still ten hours away from Los Angeles; Tokyo is also ten hours away and Santiago, Chile is sixteen hours away. When it is noon in Los Angeles, it is 6:00 A.M. the next day in Sydney and 9:00 P.M. that same day in Stockholm.

What this means is that doing business around the world requires very careful planning. When there is a problem, or a misunderstanding, or a potential new customer, in the next county, you can jump in your car and be there in a few hours or a few minutes. This is absolutely impossible when the problem or opportunity arises in another country. So the only protection is extra careful planning.

3. *Nationalism is a Real Thing.* Not only are markets different (see #1 above), the way that people do business from country to country is also different. There truly are national characteristics and you will have to

understand a lot of them if you are going to be successful. If you take a business card from a new Japanese acquaintance with one hand and put it in your pocket with only a passing glance, you will have created a great offense. If you schedule an appointment in Spain between 2:00 PM and 4:00 PM, you will be meeting with yourself because the other party will be somewhere asleep.

This is just one more reason for you to get on that airplane and go to visit the new country where you are trying to build a new business. In the meantime, Roger E. Axtell has written two books that will help you in dealing with nationalism. One is *The Do's and Taboos of International Trade* and *Do's and Taboos of Hosting International Visitors*. Both are published by John Wiley & Sons, Inc., New York, NY.

Three Important Decisions in Building an International Business

Three decision areas are the same in building a domestic business as they are in building an international business, but they are more critical in the international sphere because there are so many more ways to make mistakes because of #1, #2 and #3 above.

1. *Selecting the Best Markets for Your Products or Services.* There is no one procedure that will lead you to select the best markets overseas anymore than there is one domestically, but here are a couple of ideas to begin with. (Remember that we are looking for whole countries here.) Look at the leading countries for U. S. exports now. While this is not very sensitive to your particular products or services, the whole export process will probably be easier for you since so many other people are already doing the same thing. These countries are the main destinations for U. S. merchandise exports now.

You can update this list by ordering the current *Chartbook—Composition of U.S. Merchandise Trade* from the U. S. Government Printing Office.

Another idea is to find which countries are already receiving large imports of similar, or the same, kinds of products you want to export. The best information here will come from the United Nations. (See Information Sources above for the UN address.)

Neither of these will work for services. In that case, try to identify the demographic characteristics of your domestic customers (you should know this already—see Section 9). Then search through the OECD countries for high concentrations of these characteristics. (See Information Sources above for the OECD address.)

Finally, trade shows and exhibitions are a good place to go to watch and listen (and wait for inspiration to strike).

2. *Selecting the Best Distribution System.* A good argument could be made that this is the single most important decision to be made about international business because it may well be crucial to your long-term success, and because distribution decisions are so difficult to change. One way to think about this decision is like finding an affordable, workable, comfortable position of the continuum below:

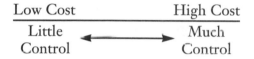

At the left end of the spectrum is "indirect" exporting. You simply locate an interested "manufacturer's export agent," or an "export commission agent," or an "export merchant." You simply sell your products to the selected entity and deposit the check in your bank. However, you have absolutely no say in how your products are handled in the overseas markets.

Moving slightly to the right, you might elect "direct marketing." Here you would assign someone(s) in your company to handle all of the export business. In effect, you would create a separate profit center in your business with the objective of developing an international business. This would cost more because that person, or those people, would be on the payroll whether or not your international business is profitable.

At the other end of the spectrum, you could set up your own manufacturing, warehousing, distribution, and sales office in your selected country. Obviously, this would be expensive, but it would give you the most control.

In between those extremes are a whole host of alliances, joint ventures, licensing agreements, etc. with more or less cost and more or less control.

As you think about this decision and try to balance your needs for control and deal with the reality of cash flow, bear this fact in mind. If you are really successful with your new business in the new country, you will want to control everything! It happens everytime! Therefore, consider this fact in your planning and do not make any arrangement that will prevent you from eventually taking control of your entire business.

3. *Getting Paid and Making a Profit.* Getting paid is relatively easy. First, you do not demand cash in advance from your new overseas customer. That would most likely kill your fledgling effort on the spot. On the other hand, you do not ship goods on account until you have extensive experience with your overseas distributors.

The way you deal with getting paid is a document(s) called a "letter of credit." Almost all international trade between companies is paid with letters of credit which will be explained to you by your bank's international department. (If your bank does not have an international department, you will have to get a new bank. Anything less will cause you endless problems.) This is what happens: your customer goes to his bank in the foreign country and obtains a letter of credit in the amount the two of you have agreed upon. His bank then sets aside enough money from his account to pay for honoring the letter of credit. His bank then forwards to your bank the letter of credit (a promise to pay your bank from his bank) along with a set of documents that describe the conditions of a successful sale. You then ship the merchandise. When you submit documents to your bank that prove you have fulfilled all of the requirements of the letter of credit, your bank credits your account.

If you are thorough in the details and if you get good help from your bank, you will have no trouble getting paid. Making a profit, however, is a different thing. The fundamental problem is that doing business overseas is almost always more expensive than doing business at home. That means you will have to pay particular attention to pricing and to costs. Exhibit 12-1 is a very typical profit and loss statement for an international business. Study it carefully.

What Exhibit 12-1 should tell you is that you *must* understand your costs completely before you undertake building an international business. The second thing that it should tell you is that pricing will be critically important. As you consider that fact, remember two realities of business anywhere: 1) Pricing is an art, not a science. 2) Price is what somebody will pay for something.

Exhibit 12-1

A Typical International Pricing Structure for Manufactured Goods

FOR ONE UNIT

Variable Costs

Materials	30%
Labor	30%
Total Cost of Goods Sold	60%
Gross Margin	40%

Fixed Costs

Plant and Equipment	10%
Administrative Costs	20%
Total Costs	90%
Profits Before Taxes	10%
Selling Price At Your Plant	100%

International Business Costs

Shipping, Warehousing, Insurance, Handling, etc. (10%–15%)	115%
Sales Representatives (5%–10%)	127%
Distributors (20%–30%)	165%
Tariffs and Customs	????

Marketing Planning Page 12-1

READINESS TO BEGIN AN EXPORT BUSINESS

Are You Ready To Export? Here are a series of questions that will help you decide whether you are ready to build an export business, and if not, what will you have to change to get ready?

1. Do you know how an international business would fit into your existing marketing plans?   YES [ ]
                                                                        NO [ ]

Comments: _____
_____
_____
_____
_____

2. Do you have a solid, long-term commitment from your top management to develop an international business?   YES [ ]
                                                                        NO [ ]

Comments: _____
_____
_____
_____
_____

3. Are you willing (able) to modify your products or services to meet regulations or cultural preferences of other countries?   YES [ ]
                                                                        NO [ ]

Comments: _____
_____
_____
_____
_____

Marketing Planning Page 12-1

Readiness to Begin an Export Business *(continued)*

4. Are you willing (able) to print labels, service materials, warranty messages, and the like, in the various languages of the countries involved? YES [ ]

 NO [ ]

Comments: _____

_____

_____

_____

_____

5. Are you prepared to provide readily available service for your products?

 YES [ ]

 NO [ ]

Comments: _____

_____

_____

_____

_____

6. Have you really considered the international market potential of each of your products and services, and concentrated on the best potential? YES [ ]

 NO [ ]

Comments: _____

_____

_____

_____

_____

Marketing Planning Page 12-1

READINESS TO BEGIN AN EXPORT BUSINESS *(continued)*

7. Have you studied enough international markets to be confident that you have selected the one or two with the highest probability of success?   YES [ ]

NO [ ]

Comments: _____

_____

_____

_____

_____

8. Are you prepared to develop separate marketing plans for each new international market?   YES [ ]

NO [ ]

Comments: _____

_____

_____

_____

_____

9. Have you carefully decided on your international distribution strategy?

YES [ ]

NO [ ]

Comments: _____

_____

_____

_____

_____

Marketing Planning Page 12-1

READINESS TO BEGIN AN EXPORT BUSINESS *(continued)*

10. Are you prepared to treat your international distributors on an equal basis with your domestic distributors? YES [ ]

    NO [ ]

Comments: _____

_____

_____

_____

_____

11. Arc you willing to assign responsibility for building an international business to one specific person and provide the necessary financial resources for success?

    YES [ ]

    NO [ ]

Comments: _____

_____

_____

_____

_____

12. Are you willing to wait up to three years (if necessary) to see profits from your new international business? YES [ ]

    NO [ ]

Comments: _____

_____

_____

_____

_____

SECTION THIRTEEN

Technology—It Is Changing Everything You Do in Business

OVERVIEW OF SECTION THIRTEEN: A revolution in the way business is conducted is underway around the world. The changes will be every bit as profound as those created by the Industrial Revolution. While nobody in her right mind would be presumptuous enough to describe in detail how this new revolution will play out (see Section Ten on Forecasting), there are enough major pieces in place to provide a general outline of what is happening right now. Section Thirteen reviews the major developments of this new "Technology Revolution."

THIS IS WHERE YOU TAKE A PEEK INTO THE FUTURE

Everything discussed up to this point has been tested, tried, and proven to be successful by hundreds of companies and thousands of managers all around the world. But at exactly this point in time, much of what has been described in this guide is about to change, and change in some extraordinarily exciting ways. The coming test of successful managers will lie in their ability to negotiate the path from the best present practice, as described here, into a new and uncertain future. And the engine driving that change is simply technology, communications technology primarily but not exclusively.

It is not hyperbole at all to say that managers at the end of the twentieth century are facing a revolution in the way business gets done that will be every bit as dramatic, wrenching and dislocating as the beginning of the Industrial Revolution itself. The changes are coming in the way we produce goods and services, in the way we store them, in the way we distribute them, in the way people work and in the way that we communicate with customers, and in the way that all of these developments re-structure the nature of a business.

The balance of this section will attempt to describe the most important aspects of the coming changes and to show how some businesses are actually adapting successfully to these changes. A REALLY IMPORTANT POINT HERE! Return to Section Ten and review the comments about our ability to successfully forecast the future.

CHANGES IN HOW WE PRODUCE GOODS AND SERVICES

Until approximately the beginning of this century, everything that was made anywhere in the world was made one at a time, usually by one person. Volume of production had absolutely no effect on costs. If it took a potter one hour to make one pot, it took two hours to make two pots. That was "craftsman production."

As this century began, a number of people, most notably Henry Ford and Alfred Sloan, began to experiment with a new way to make things. The results of their work have generally been called "mass production." And the impact that mass production had on production costs was literally amazing. An automobile, for instance, that required 750 man-hours of labor under craftsman production required only 93 man-hours under mass production.

Those rapidly falling costs led to rapidly falling prices, and to the steadily increasing standard of living in the developed world.

But the process of mass production also had a built-in cost, and that was re-work at the end of the production process to correct defects and errors that were introduced during the production process. In a typical U. S. manufacturing plant, 23% to 25% (or more) of the cost of the finished product is accounted for by re-work to correct defects. However, as long as costs, and prices, were falling rapidly, re-work was a cost that could be afforded.

In the early 1950s, two Japanese managers, Eiji Toyoda and Taiichi Ohno, decided that re-work was no longer affordable and began a decades-long effort to develop a new way to make things. The results of their work are now generally known as "lean production" (sometimes called "world class production").

The major characteristics of lean production are these:

- Workers are trained in many skills and work in teams. There are no foremen.

- Each team does its own housekeeping, tool repair and quality checking.

- Each team is given a block of tasks to perform and it is responsible for continually trying to figure out how to do the job better.

- Every worker has a "stop cord" to stop the entire production process the instant a defect is discovered. When that happens, it is the responsibility of every member of the plant to work on that problem until it is solved.

- Lean production requires extraordinary levels of coordination and cooperation between product design, manufacturing, engineering, assembly line workers, parts suppliers, marketing people and dealers.

Lean production has also had a striking effect on costs. As recently as 1986, a mid-size sedan assembled in General Motors' Framingham, Massachusetts factory took 41 man-hours while a mid-size sedan assembled in Toyota City, Japan (where Toyoda and Ohno worked) took 18 man-hours. But reduced assembly costs are only a part of the pay-out of lean production. A fully functional lean production process produces products that require no rework!

That means that lean production processes produce products (and the growing evidence says it applies equally to services) of the highest possible quality. And if you have forgotten the importance of quality as a competitive factor, review Section Two for the hard evidence.

The important idea here is that under mass production conditions (where most managers working today learned their jobs), the objective is to find the lowest possible level of quality that customers will accept because raising quality levels adds to costs. Under lean production conditions, however, *the objective is to find the highest possible level of quality because raising quality levels reduces costs*.

Motorola, Inc. was one of the first U. S. companies to grasp this exceptionally important idea, and put it into practice. That is the primary reason so many other companies benchmark themselves against Motorola. But it is not the only company to put lean production to work for itself. Emerson Electric, Merck Pharmaceuticals, and Caterpillar are also devoted to lean production. Federal Express and the Ritz Carlton Hotels have shown that the ideas of lean production are applicable to service businesses as well. In fact, lean production is probably the single most important factor that allowed Ford Motor Company to avoid bankruptcy in the late 1980s and early 1990s.

For an excellent discussion of lean production, its development and implementation, see James P. Womack, Daniel T. Jones, and Daniel Roos, *The Machine That Changed the World*, (New York: Macmillan Publishing Company, 1990).

Also note that "lean production" has attracted an incredible amount of misguided and misunderstood attention from management consultants and assorted gurus during the past fifteen years. They rushed into the U.S.'s competitive problems with solutions like quality circles, just-in-time delivery, continual improvement, etc. Universally, their efforts failed. What they all apparently failed to understand is that they were only looking at little parts of lean production and mistaking it for the whole thing.

CHANGES IN HOW WE DISTRIBUTE THINGS

There is probably no more dramatic example of the changes coming in distribution than Federal Express' Tracking Software. This service allows you to track the whereabouts and progress of any item shipped with Federal Express, including delivery information and the name of the person who signed for the shipment, right from the computer on your desk, at any time of the day or night. Further, you can do the same thing from FedEx's home page on the Internet [http://www.fedex.com].

In addition, FedEx Logistics Services can replace your existing distribution and storage system for time-sensitive items with its own system. For example, medical products companies keep their inventory physically at FedEx locations and when a doctor orders, say, an artificial hip replacement, it is shipped directly from FedEx to the operating room. Orders can be received as late as midnight and still be delivered by 10:00 AM the next day. Orders can be entered by phone, fax or EDI (electronic data interchange—more on EDI in a minute) twenty-fours a day.

This means that your inventory storage costs are completely variable, your distribution system is open twenty-four hours a day, and your service level is unequaled. Further, FedEx is so confident in the level of service it provides that it has an unconditional money-back guarantee.

CHANGES IN THE WAY WE STORE THINGS

When someone buys a box of Tide detergent at the new Wal-Mart store in Aliso Viejo, California, the package is passed over the scanner at the checkout counter. So far, so good. Nothing unusual in that, you say. Right, but what is unusual (but rapidly becoming usual) is that the information about that individual sale is transmitted instantly to Wal-Mart headquarters in Benton, Arkansas where it is transmitted instantly to Procter & Gamble's headquarters in Cincinnati, Ohio, where in turn, it is transmitted instantly to P & G's plant in Sacramento, California where the Tide sold in the western United States is made. In essence, that single retail transaction has triggered the manufacture of its replacement.

P & G then accumulates shipments to Wal-Mart stores in Southern California to achieve the maximum savings in transportation. Production is no longer made into inventory, it is made into actual sales. Inventory disappears and simply exists only while in transit (which is so far unavoidable—but more on that in another minute).

What you have just witnessed is an example of EDI, electronic data interchange, and it is significantly lowering the costs of doing business for its "partners." Here are the recent selling, general and administrative costs as a percentage of sales for selected large retailers:

Wal-Mart	15.8%
Circuit City	19.0
Vons Grocery Co.	21.0
KMart	22.2
Federated Dept. Stores	33.3

And before you decide that EDI is just a game for big companies, consider The Cedar Works, Inc., a Peebles, Ohio manufacturer of cedar bird feeders and mail boxes, with sales of $18 million. It has been on-line via EDI with Wal-Mart since 1990. In addition, Cedar Works is on-line with ten other major retailers including Home Depot and Target Stores.

EDI produces significant savings in placing and processing orders faster and more accurately. It also allows customers to carry smaller inventories and still reduce out-of-stocks. But when the customers share point-of-sale, inventory and forecasting information with their suppliers, the savings possibilities really become interesting.

Consider the case of G & F Industries, a Sturbridge, Massachusetts manufacturer of plastic molding and parts, with sales of $20 million. Its biggest customer is Bose Corporation, the high fidelity speaker company. Since 1991, G & F has had a full-time employee based at Bose's headquarters (P & G has a small army of employees stationed in Benton, Arkansas). This employee has complete access to all the information available to any Bose buyer and has *the authority to place orders with G & F on Bose's behalf*. He accesses Bose's inventory needs for the upcoming six-week period and orders product shipped directly from G & F to Bose exactly when it is needed. Not only that, he has the same access to Bose plants in Ste. Marie, Quebec, Carrickmacross, Ireland, Hillsdale, Michigan and San Luis, Mexico. G & F now schedules production for Bose's operations world-wide and inventory is now a relic of the past.

Costs come down, quality of service goes up. The lesson of lean production appears again and again. General Electric is so convinced that information sharing will be the primary way to do business in the future that it has established a complete division, GE Information Services. Specifically its function is to assist companies in handling information to reduce inventories, reduce cycle times, shorten the time from when an order is placed until payment, and to improve customer service and satisfaction all around. You can get more information about GE Information Services by calling 1-800-560-4347.

Also notice that technology is permitting small companies to compete on equal footing with the biggest companies. This is an idea we will return to again and again.

Note: The normally supersecretive Procter & Gamble is so impressed with the gains from information sharing with Wal-Mart that it is presently attempting to convert all three hundred major grocery chains in the U. S. to the program. And Procter & Gamble is so impressed with the way information sharing is working that it will eliminate its entire retail sales force starting in 1996. An important part of your thinking about information sharing with your customers and suppliers should be a re-definition of the activities that your sales force is responsible for in the customer satisfaction process.

CHANGES IN THE WAY WE TALK
TO CUSTOMERS—DATABASES

The development of the railroads in the United States in the late 1800s allowed magazines to reach a big enough audience to make publishing profitable. In turn, J. Walter Thompson, a pioneer in the advertising business, persuaded some of those magazines to sell their mass audiences to his advertising clients. In this way, mass audiences and mass circulation was born. It has continued right through radio and television to today without much real change. Any one medium attempts to build the largest mass audience of a particular type (say, women 24 to 49), and re-sell that audience to advertisers. Then advertisers prepare a single message for every one in that audience, a mass message for a mass audience.

Advertisers try to find mediums with audiences that have high percentages of their customers and potential customers. (See Section Eleven for that discussion.) Regardless of how hard advertisers try, mass audiences have exactly the same shortcoming as mass production, considerable waste. That is because lots of people who are not interested in your message receive it and you pay for every one of them.

Technology is rapidly ending this mass message to a mass audience paradigm. Computers are now big enough, fast enough, and cheap enough to allow businesses of all sizes to build databases of information *about individual customers*.

In the United States, there is considerable agreement that the foremost database builder and user is the Vons Grocery Company in Arcadia, California. It operates approximately 350 Vons and Vons Pavillions food stores in southern California and Nevada. A customer enters the database by filling out the familiar check authorization application card. Each customer is then issued a Vons Value Plus Club card. To receive additional discounts on their purchases, Vons Value Plus Club members show their card to the checkout clerk prior to checking. A swipe of the card produces automatic discounts on selected items of interest to *that particular customer and only that customer*. And each visit to the store builds a profile of the purchases of that individual customer.

Vons also works with individual manufacturers to build offers of exceptional value for individual customers. It has issued four million cards to date and membership is growing 25% a year. Manufacturers pay Vons to print and deliver their coupons for them. In addition, Vons gets to keep the whole 8¢ handling fee that is usually split with a fulfillment house. Club members have weekly grocery bills at Vons that are two-and-a-half times larger than non-club shoppers at Vons.

In addition to going a long way to eliminate waste in delivering coupons and customizing communications with individual customers, the Value Plus Club is an extremely powerful tool for building customer loyalty programs. Here are two examples from programs that Vons ran in 1995.

Example One

Vons offered its Club members an opportunity to receive a free turkey for Thanksgiving. Each customer who purchased $300 at Vons between September 27 and October 31 received a gift certificate in the mail good for a free turkey. Each customer's total accumulated purchases were recorded on each register receipt.

Example Two

The Vons Companies, Inc. allocated $750,000 to schools that participated in its "CheckOut for Children" program. First, a Club member filled out an enrollment form for the school he or she wished to support. Then every dollar of purchases made by the Club member was automatically credited to the school of choice. The program ran from September 21 until December 10. The $750,000 was divided among schools that received a minimum of $20,000 in purchase credits. And everything was automatic. Neither the customers nor the schools had to keep any kind of records.

Think about these two examples and then go back to Section Nine and review the ideas about short-term behavioral change. Aren't these perfect examples of how to do it?

One of Vons strategic goals is to increase its private label business (16% in 1995) to 20%. Having records of the purchases of individual customers allows Vons to experiment with store private label coupons to identify the product categories with the most private label potential.

And the next generation of Value Plus Club cards will contain a memory chip that will store data such as the cardholder's birthday. A truly "smart card" from a truly "smart company."

A good technical introduction to database development and management can be found in Robert R. Jackson, and Paul Wang, *Strategic Database Marketing* (Lincolnwood, IL: NTC Business Books, 1994).

Samsonite Corporation, the world's largest luggage manufacturer, also maintains a database on its customers, actually three databases, but it uses the information quite differently. Since Samsonite is a manufacturer and sells its products through retailers, it wouldn't make much sense for Samsonite to use its database to sell directly to consumers and end up competing with its own retailers.

Instead, Samsonite uses its databases to profile its customers, product by product, and to study their likes and dislikes about the products so it can make product improvements. It also uses the answers to lifestyle questions to search for new product opportunities.

One of its databases is built on product registration cards which include an inducement to send it in (see Section Nine). These cards include purchase details, demographic and lifestyle questions. In 1995, the database contained information on one and half million customers. A second database is built around calls to Samsonite's 800 number which is featured in all its advertising. The third one is built around "bingo" cards, those magazine inserts that allow the reader to request more information.

At Mi Amore Pizza & Pasta in Lompoc, California, Gary Mead maintains a database on the 8,500 customers who visit his store and telephone for home delivery (in a town of 11,000), and uses it to develop a one-to-one personal relationship with his customers. Any customer who hasn't purchased in the last sixty days receives a discount coupon by mail as an incentive to return. Every Christmas, the database produces a list of the best customers and Gary sends them a personally signed card. He is experimenting with cross-selling products to selected individuals in the database. He bought the business in 1991 and in just four years, tripled the volume to over $1,000,000. Not bad for a pizza store in a small town!

As you can see, size is not the determinant of successful competition here; imagination is the crucial factor, and anybody can have that.

A CHANGE IN THE WAY WE TALK TO OUR CUSTOMERS—CD ROMS

Compact discs, those small, round, shiny pieces of plastic that Sony introduced to the world in 1984, have revolutionized the music business. In 1984, total recorded music sales in the United States were roughly $4 billion dollars divided about equally between LPs and cassettes. In 1994, the recorded music business in the U. S. hit $12 billion in sales and $8.5 billion was in CDs, $3 billion in cassettes and the remainder in LPs.

Sony and others then expanded the use of CDs by recording video games, and another new business was created.

Now imaginative managers are using CDs in another new way to reach customers one at a time. For one example, Toyota Motor Sales has developed a CD-ROM (Compact Disc—Read Only Memory) that is interactive, i.e., the user can control the information displayed. It contains absolutely marvelous graphics, music and narration. The three main areas of content are 1) Toyota's community involvement in great detail, 2) specifications on all of Toyota's automobiles and trucks, and 3) advice on dealer locations. You can get your own copy by calling 1-800-GO-TOYOTA.

Here are just two ways that Toyota can use its CD-ROM to act as a sales person making a personalized, individual, in-home sales call: 1) Sending them to current Toyota Camry owners, for example, about the time that they will buy a new car to encourage repeat purchasing; 2) Sending them to current Nissan Maxima owners about the time that they will buy a new car to encourage brand switching.

So if you have a database on your existing customers, and on your competitors' customers, CD-ROMs give you an unequaled opportunity to develop a sales presentation that the customer can tailor to his or her interests for the tiniest fraction of what it would cost to send a live sales person to make the call. For industrial products and services, where it is frequently difficult to even get an appointment, CD-ROMs offer some even more important advantages.

Using CD-ROMs In Other Applications

A company called MarketPlace Information Corporation has developed a CD-ROM that contains over ten million Dun & Bradstreet records on U.S. businesses, government agencies and non-profit organizations. Each record contains the name of the company/organization, address, telephone number, name of the owner/president/manager, annual sales volume, number of employees, SIC code classification, etc. You can subscribe to MarketPlace's service on an annual basis and it sends you a new, up-dated CD-ROM every quarter. In an interesting twist, you only have to pay for the records you actually use because of a "metering system" built into the CD-ROM.

MarketPlace can be used to develop direct mail lists tailored to the exact specifications of your business. It can be used to print labels and/or envelopes. It can be used to analyze potential business volume in geographic areas or in SIC coded industries. The data can be manipulated and used in a number of additional ways. Here is one example of how MarketPlace's CD-ROM puts an enormous resource right on your desk top.

Abigail Abbott, Inc. is a small employment agency headquartered in Tustin, California. It has branch offices in Brea, Cerritos, Lake Forest, Newport Beach and Seal Beach, California. The agency decided that its real strengths lie in supplying temporary employees to medical offices and facilities, and to computer/high tech companies. The first step in its business building program is to analyze its existing customer base, office by office, to determine the trading area of each office. Those trading areas are then specified in terms of zip codes. That is, each office has a contiguous piece of geography that accounts for 65–70% of that office's business and that piece of geography is described by a zip code range.

The next step is to determine the exact SIC codes that represent its target market. For example, 8011 Offices and Clinics of Doctors of Medicine, 8021 Offices and Clinics of Dentists, 8031 Offices and Clinics of Doctors of Osteopathy, etc. Then a cross tabulated list is developed for each Abigail Abbott office, zip code plus SIC code. The list is displayed from largest employer to smallest employer and is purged for existing customers because the idea is to develop an introductory offer for new clients.

A direct mail package is prepared and sent to all potential customers on the list. Those accounts with enough employees to generate substantial revenues are assigned to specific Abigail Abbott account executives for personal follow-up sales calls. All other potential accounts on the list are followed up with at least one telephone call. The data from the personal visits and the telephone calls are entered into a database that classifies each potential client in terms of potential gross income, probability of a sale, primary competitor, etc.

At long last a very little company has access to all of the sophisticated data, analysis, sales planning, tracking and evaluation that used to be the sole province of very large companies with substantial resources to invest in developing this kind of information.

For more information, call MarketPlace Information Corporation, 46 Totten Pond Road, Waltham, MA 02154, at (800) 590-0065, or find it on the Internet at [http://www.mktplace.com/home1001].

A CHANGE IN THE WAY WE TALK TO OUR CUSTOMERS—THE INTERNET

If what we have been discussing so far can be described as state-of-the-art, what we must now turn our attention to is somewhere beyond simply state-of-the-art. Perhaps it could better be described as state-of-development. But first, the briefest bit of history.

After World War II, the Pentagon wanted to develop a communications system that would always work no matter where bombs landed. University computer departments and computer research labs responded by developing a network of telephone line interlinked computers that could send messages to each other in an endless variety of pathways. Then scientists started using this network to communicate with each other and it was called the ARPANET. But to use it, you had to be conversant with an incredibly arcane programming language called UNIX. Not many people were, so not many people used it. Still, the Internet grew to be a large interconnected computer network linking people and computers all over the world, via telephone lines, satellites, and other kinds of telecommunications systems.

In mid-1993, some subparticle physicists at the European Laboratory for Particle Physics developed a language that all computers and most people can understand. It is called hypertext. This development, in turn, led to the development of one part of the Internet, based on hypertext, called the World Wide Web. And it is the World Wide Web that interests us here. But the problem is that it is growing so fast (10% a month!?!) that anything specific that can be said about it right now will be long out of date by the time you read this. *Economist* magazine estimated that in July, 1995 there were 20 million users on the Internet and that by July, 1996, a reasonable estimate would be 30 million. Whatever the number turns out to be, the important thing about the Internet is that it gives you the ability to reach any customer, anywhere in the world, who has a computer and modem and an Internet connection. It truly has the potential to allow you to talk to your customers one at a time on an affordable basis.

So, while it is not possible to predict the future of the Internet as a resource for your business, it is reasonable to examine some of the ways that the Internet, and more specifically the World Wide Web, is being used right now.

But first it will be necessary to sort out the hype about the "information highway" and the reality of the situation. As 1996 began, there were two reliable sources of information about computers, computer usage and the Internet. One is The CommerceNet/Nielsen Internet Demographics Survey which was released October 30, 1995. You can purchase a copy from CommerceNet by calling (415) 617-8790 or from A. C. Nielsen at (813) 738-3125. Or you can get an Executive Summary on the Internet at [http://www.commerce.net/]. Another source is the Times Mirror Center for The People & The Press study, "Technology in the American Household: Americans Going Online . . . Explosive Growth, Uncertain Destinations." This one was released October 16, 1995 and you can get a free copy by calling (202) 293-3126. Both studies have large sample bases (Nielsen—4,200 interviews; Los Angeles Times—4,005 interviews) that were selected randomly and the results can be comfortably projected to the entire population. So what did they find out about the Internet?

Just How Big Is the Internet Market?

Nielsen found that 17% of persons 16 years and older in the United States and Canada have *access* to the Internet. That represents 37 million people. His researchers also found that 11% (24 million) have used the Internet in the last six months, and 8% (18 million) have used the World Wide Web in the past three months.

The *Los Angeles Times* study shows that 18 million U. S. households have a home computer equipped with a modem (compared with 11 million in 1994), but 8 million households have never used their modems. In addition, 14 million U. S. households go on-line from home and that 11 million reported going on-line from some place other than home (school, work, etc.). Only 8% has ever gone online in any way and only 3% of Americans has ever signed onto the World Wide Web.

Do They Use the Internet?

Nielsen found that average online users used the Internet five hours and 28 minutes *a week!* Total Internet usage equals the total playback time of all rented video tapes!

Do They Use the Internet to Buy Anything?

Nielsen says 14% of all adults in the U. S. and Canada have purchased something using the Internet (2.5 million people). The *Los Angeles Times* reports that 8% of all U. S. households have purchased something on the Internet in the past month.

Who are Those People on the Internet?

The majority are male (Nielsen—66%; *Los Angeles Times*—men are twice as likely to go online as women). Further Nielsen says 25% of the WWW users have incomes above $80,000, work in the professions or are managers, and 64% of them have graduated from college. The *Los Angeles Times* says 38% of those who go online are between 18 and 29 years old and that 41% are 30 to 49 years old, so 79% of those going online are between 18 and 49. They also say that 57% of those online have graduated from college and that 57% have incomes over $50,000.

What Does All of that Mean?

First, it is pretty big. A reasonable estimate based on the data above suggested that a North American market of some 20 million households is in the ballpark. Online users are primarily men (although certainly not exclusively), they are very well educated, they are relatively young and they have very high incomes. Twenty million bright young people with very high incomes that can be reached individually is a pretty attractive market for a lot of businesses. Here is how some of those businesses are doing business on the Internet and the World Wide Web.

WAREHOUSE WINES & LIQUORS CORPORATION, STAMFORD, CONNECTICUT This $12 million wine and liquor merchant uses a home page on the WWW to promote special products and to make credit card sales. In 1995, it racked up sales of $1.2 million on the Internet. In its store in Stamford, an average sale is $40, on the Internet it is $250. And it seems to be plus business since many of its Internet customers live in New York and New Jersey, and one even lives in Tokyo. You can reach this company with your order at [http://www.netaxis.com/wine/wine.html].

HOT HOT HOT, PASADENA, CALIFORNIA Perry and Monica Lopez have a small retail shop that sells hot sauces and foods, and they have been using a home page on the WWW to expand their sales since 1994 [http://www.hothothot.com/hot]. They began by selecting 125 of the 450+ products that they carry to sell on the Internet and they organized them by heat level, country of origin and ingredients. Then they worked with a professional home page developer to create a home page that they could afford. One year into the project, they get 1,000+ visits to their site daily, an average of ten orders a day (including, usually, one from overseas) which will total about $60,000 in 1995.

FORE PLAY GOLF, PASADENA, CALIFORNIA Scott Lohman has a golf shop in Pasadena, California. He was looking for a way to boost sales when he found the Internet and its possibilities for worldwide business. The first thing he did was to make arrangements with all of the leading golf equipment manufacturers to drop ship his orders directly to his customers. Then he developed a home page [http://www.4play.com/sports/4play] that has a lot of information of interest to golfers. The real payoff is the part of the home page where customers can search for any brand name golf equipment that they are interested in buying. They receive information on the product and its price, and the same thing for a whole range of similar equipment. Scott Lohman's business on the Internet is now much larger than the business at his store.

PEAPOD, INC., EVANSTON, ILLINOIS Andrew and Thomas Parkinson discovered the Internet as long ago as 1990. Their company takes grocery orders over the Internet and delivers them right to the customer's home. Ten thousand customers in Chicago and San Francisco regularly send their detailed grocery orders over the Internet to Peapod's headquarters. When Peapod receives the order, it is forwarded to the participating grocery chain store closest to the customer's home. Peapod's partner in Chicago is Jewel/Osco and in San Francisco it is Safeway.

Customers pay a $29.95 start-up fee, a monthly service fee, and they pay a flat $6.95, plus 5% of the total order price, to receive Peapod's electronic shopping/home delivery service. It has an amazing 80% retention rate. Consider that America Online manages to retain about 70% of the people who try its service and only $9.95 a month is at stake. In an interesting twist on the typical online user being male, 75% of Peapod's customers are women.

Peapod's 1995 sales exceeded $20 million. However, high start-up and high fixed costs have prevented it from making a profit as of this writing. However, the brothers Parkinson are convinced that as soon as they acquire a big enough base of customers, the fixed costs will be covered and profits will roll in in a major way.

ENGINEERING SIMPLICITY, INC., IRVINE, CALIFORNIA This company searches for government design and construction projects that are coming up for bid in the southwestern part of the United States. The major categories that it monitors are Retrofit Engineering, Transportation, Water and Wastewater, Municipal Project Management and Troubleshooting. Subscribers to the Simplus Project Finder are allowed to search for upcoming projects by type, dollar amount and location. They then can receive detailed reports on every project of interest in the entire area. Engineering Simplicity's home page is [http://www.simplus.com].

AUTOSCAPE™, INC., LOS ANGELES, CALIFORNIA This company maintains a huge database on virtually every automobile sold in the United States, new and used. Users of this online service [http://www.autoscape.com] first select a manufacturer that they are interested in and then the specific model of interest. They then receive an online evaluation, text and photos, of that model covering design, features, options, safety, and technology. The user can then get advice on the closest dealers. Autoscape™ provides this service free to users by charging participating dealers an annual fee of $5,000. You judge for yourself how well it is doing by visiting Autoscape's™ home page and counting the participating dealers.

SECURITY FIRST NETWORK BANK, LEXINGTON, KENTUCKY On Wednesday, October 18, 1995 a small savings and loan bank in Kentucky was the first bank to conduct true online banking services. Starting that day, Security First's customers anywhere in the world could pay bills, make deposits and view their account balances, among other things. You can view its range of services at [http://www.sfnb.com/].

CLAITOR'S LAW BOOKS AND PUBLISHING DIVISION, BATON ROUGE, LOUISIANA This $2.7 million publisher became the only vendor of Louisiana parish histories (and federal tax law books) on the Internet on August 8, 1995. You can find them at [http://www.premier.net/~CLAITORS].

MARCUS & MILLICHAP REAL ESTATE INVESTMENT BROKERAGE, PALO ALTO, CALIFORNIA This mid-sized real estate broker uses its Internet WWW to show its listing to potential clients all over the world. You can check out its current listings at [http://www.mmreibc.com].

ELECTRONIC GOURMET GUIDE, NEWPORT BEACH, CALIFORNIA Thomas Way takes a different approach to doing business on the Internet. He "publishes" a large collection of news about food and wine, recipes, cookbook reviews, safety tips and just plain talk about food. His income is generated by the advertising he sells at the EGG [http://www.2way.com/food/egg/].

THE INTERNET AND YOUR BUSINESS: WHAT HAPPENS NEXT? You have just reviewed ten successful (or soon-to-be-successful) businesses doing business on the Internet. They range from medium-sized to small to tiny. All of them share the powerful advantages offered by the Internet. They all appear to be as big as any Fortune 500 company and they have the ability to serve their customers on an individualized basis (which most Fortune 500 companies cannot do) anywhere in the world. It seems likely that you will want to give some serious thought about how you could use the Internet in your business. If so, the first thing to do is think seriously about what you might be able to accomplish for each/or all of your brands by having a presence on the Internet. Marketing Planning Pages 13-1 through 13-4 on pages 337–340 are designed to help you organize your ideas.

If you think that there might be an opportunity for you on the Internet, the next step is to decide how you are going to develop your home page. Your local software store has several programs to help you here. Scott Lohman (ForePlay) and Thomas Way (EGG) developed their own.

The other way to do that job is to engage the services of a professional Website developer. Delta Internet Services, 731 East Ball Road, Suite 204, Anaheim, CA 92805 is one of a number of companies that can help you design a custom site for your business. It developed the home pages for Engineering Simplicity discussed earlier in this Section. Kerry Garrison, Director of the Delta

Design division of Delta Internet Services, says there are five relatively simple steps involved in developing a custom home page for the World Wide Web.

1. The developer reviews all of your printed materials, i.e., sales brochures, letterheads, advertising, etc.

2. You and the developer discuss and agree on the objectives you are trying to accomplish online. Then the two of you agree on a budget to accomplish those objectives.

3. The developer prepares a "rough" set of pages for review and discussion. Based on the review, revisions are made.

4. The developer sets up a site on the WWW for your home page.

5. A test review is then conducted and further refinements are made.

You then go live on the Internet and you are in business.

If you would like to talk to Delta Internet Services about this process, you can reach them at

Tel: (714) 778-0370

Fax: (714) 778-1064

eMail: sales@delta.net

and you can review Delta Internet Service's Internet site at [http://www.delta.net/].

Business Information on the Internet

Another extremely valuable aspect of the Internet is the huge amount of business information available to you. Here are three central locations that serve as excellent places to start to understand the wealth of information available:

1. The Institute of Management and Administration [http://starbase. ingress.com/ioma/]

2. The U. S. Small Business Administration [http://www.sbaonline.sba.gov]

3. Lexis-Nexis Small Business Advisor [http://www.openmarket.com/lexis-nexis/bin/sba.cgi]

Michael Kuretich is a Senior Associate with the independent environmental testing company of Barr & Clark, 23505 Crenshaw Boulevard,

Torrance, CA, 90505 (telephone: (310)517-0805). He searches the Internet for upcoming projects requiring environmental testing anywhere in the world. He recently was successful in winning a contract in Malaysia that he says he would never have learned about in any other way.

There are also dozens of marketing research services online. One company that provides extremely useful market data on the Internet is USA DATA. It provides demographic data market by market. It will sell you a really wide variety of reports on very specific market segments and will do it even by county or zip code. This is a great source of information for the questions asked in Section Five, the Market Review, and in Section Nine, Marketing Intelligence. To find out more about USA DATA, Inc., 330 East 38th Street, Suite 37A, New York, NY 10016, call Michael Hoffman at (212)789-3541 or send him e-Mail at [info@usadata.com]. Its home page can be found on the Internet at [http://www.usadata.com/] .

FINAL THOUGHTS

As we discussed in detail earlier, forecasting the exact future of the effects of technology is a no-win game. But ignoring its effects on your business is even more risky. As you think about rapidly changing technology and your business, you might do well to consider the factory in Boynton Beach, Florida where Motorola makes its world famous pagers. Orders flow into the plant from all over the world via telephone on an 800 line, e-Mail, on the Internet, or by fax. The orders are generated by Motorola salespeople and directly from Motorola pager resellers. The order is for anything the customer wants, i. e., one blue one that plays the Star Spangled Banner, seven yellow ones that go "ding ding," and eight blue ones that just beep.

The incoming information is translated into digital form and sent to the assembly line. Pick-and-place robots immediately assemble the parts needed to fill that particular order. These materials are transported to a work station where a human assembler puts the pagers together, a process that requires eighty minutes at the most. Depending upon the customer's location and the time of the day, customers can receive their order the same day. Otherwise, all orders are delivered the next day.

Do you understand why so many companies benchmark against Motorola?

Marketing Planning Page 13-1

INTERNET OPPORTUNITIES FOR BRAND A

Who would be your target customers? _____

_____

_____

_____

What would attract them to your home page? _____

_____

_____

_____

What exactly would you sell? _____

_____

_____

_____

How will you get the order? (online? 800 number? fax? ??) _____

_____

_____

_____

How will you get paid? (credit card? check? bill customers? electronic money? ??)

_____

_____

_____

Marketing Planning Page 13-2

INTERNET OPPORTUNITIES FOR BRAND B

Who would be your target customers? _____

_____

_____

_____

What would attract them to your home page? _____

_____

_____

_____

What exactly would you sell? _____

_____

_____

_____

How will you get the order? (online? 800 number? fax? ??) _____

_____

_____

_____

How will you get paid? (credit card? check? bill customers? electronic money? ??)

_____

_____

_____

Marketing Planning Page 13-3

INTERNET OPPORTUNITIES FOR BRAND C

Who would be your target customers? _____

_____

_____

_____

What would attract them to your home page? _____

_____

_____

_____

What exactly would you sell? _____

_____

_____

_____

How will you get the order? (online? 800 number? fax? ??) _____

_____

_____

_____

How will you get paid? (credit card? check? bill customers? electronic money? ??)

_____

_____

_____

Marketing Planning Page 13-4

INTERNET OPPORTUNITIES FOR BRAND D

Who would be your target customers? _____

_____

_____

_____

What would attract them to your home page? _____

_____

_____

_____

What exactly would you sell? _____

_____

_____

_____

How will you get the order? (online? 800 number? fax? ??) _____

_____

_____

_____

How will you get paid? (credit card? check? bill customers? electronic money? ??)

_____

_____

_____

Pulling It all Together to Develop a Winning Strategic Marketing Plan

OVERVIEW OF SECTION FOURTEEN: This Section provides a number of suggestions about how you can organize your own company's strategic marketing planning system so that it will provide the maximum value to your company.

HOW TO DEVELOP YOUR OWN STRATEGIC MARKETING PLANNING SYSTEM

You now know a great deal more about your products and services, your customers, your competitors, your markets and the environment in which you operate than when you began this book. Now it is time to turn all of that information and insight into a strategic marketing plan that you can actually use to grow your business. To do that, you need four things: 1) a system for organizing what you know and what you have to do; 2) a method for converting those tasks and plan into a financial landscape; 3) a schedule for specifying when certain events are expected to take place; and 4) a system for reviewing the progress being made against the plan so you can make the necessary adjustments. (In fact, #2 and #3 are quite closely interrelated and it is hard to do one without the other.)

#1 Organizing What You Know and What You Have to Do

The most important aspect of getting real value out of your strategic marketing planning is how you organize what you know and what you have to do to develop and execute a successful strategy. And there is no one right way to do this job.

Beyond question, the most important part of the strategic marketing planning process is the analysis and thinking that go into it, but the tangible product is the "plans book." And the plans book plays a very important role in the success of your strategy. It explains to everyone involved where the business is today, where you think it should be going (and why), how you expect to get there, and, most important, what part each member of your group is expected to fulfill.

If the plans book contains too much detail, it is easy to lose the real strength and direction of the analysis and the strategy. But if it is too "thin," the understanding that you want to communicate may be lost. As a result, every company develops a plans book format that best fits its own needs. And that format can change over time as shortcomings become apparent and as new opportunities arise.

Therefore, what follows is how four different companies organized the information in their strategic marketing plans. See exhibits 14-1–14-4. Take whatever makes sense to you and develop your own system.

As you can see from these four marketing plan examples, there is no one "right" or "best" way to structure your marketing and business plans. Whatever format you decide upon, the primary purpose is to keep your focus on the best opportunities to grow your business. And don't worry about making mistakes, you can always change the format next year to incorporate what you learned this year.

#2 Planning the Financial Landscape

When #1 (Organizing what you know and what you have to do) is accomplished, developing the supporting financial detail is relatively simple. Any good spreadsheet system will help you do this part. If all else fails, an accounting book from your local business supply store will work. Your job is to describe your marketing strategy and plan in numbers and you do that by creating a profit & loss statement suited to your business. You will want to prepare this financial description on an annual basis, a quarterly basis and a monthly basis at least. If events really move fast in your business, you may want to break it down into weeks.

To begin, average the data for the past three years, by weeks if necessary, by months, and by quarters. Use those numbers as a foundation to reflect the seasonal variations in your business. Then superimpose your plans onto that base. Each of the examples of marketing plans shows financial data in some form in some place, but the emphasis is certainly different from company to company.

#3 Setting Up a Schedule

This is also pretty straightforward. You simply need a calendar that shows days and weeks and months. You begin by writing in the dates when you plan to have events take place. Then you start backing up and identifying the dates by which certain things must be done if your plans are to be executed on time. This, in turn, helps you assess the financial impact of your plans.

#4 A Monitoring System

All that is required here is a schedule of dates for reviewing the plan number against the actual numbers as they develop. At an absolute minimum, this should take place on a quarterly basis. Bi-monthly reviews are better. If events in your business move very rapidly, you may want to do this review on a monthly basis. You can make this job much less onerous and much more productive if all of the people involved always have access to the information in #2 above. And don't forget to review your assumptions about the environment at least annually.

Exhibit 14-1

A LARGE CONSUMER PRODUCTS COMPANY
ANNUAL STRATEGIC MARKETING PLANS

I.   Business Profile and Current Assessment (3–4 pages)

A.   Business Profile

A concise narrative describing the business as it would appear to someone unfamiliar with the business. It should include the following items:

- Product lines and services
- Target markets
- Market share positions
- Production facilities
- Sales methods
- Distribution channels

B.   Overall Current Assessment

A brief summary of the marketing strategy of business now (based on actual existing behavior).

A concise assessment of the current situation in:

- Products and services
- Market segmentation
- Geographic coverage
- Quality levels
- Competitive position
- Production facilities
- Distribution
- Technology

A summary of key performance measures (last three years)

- Market shares
- Sales volumes
- Profits
- Investment
- Cash flow
- Return on investment

A concise assessment of the attitudes/position of other important parties.

- Unions
- Distributors
- Key suppliers

Exhibit 14-1 *(continued)*

II. Environmental, Industry and Competitive Assessment (3–4 pages)

A. The Environment

Major trends and/or assumptions that can have a significant impact on the business (no more than four or five).

- Economic
- Technological
- Demographic/social/cultural
- Political
- Environmental

How will these trends in the environment affect

- Markets and segments
- Competitors
- Industry structure
- Costs
- Suppliers

B. The Industry—An Overview of the Market and its Structure

What need does this industry fill?

- Service
- Value added

Market fundamentals

- Investment required
- Ease of entry and exit
- Profitability
- Technology
- Long term outlook

Crucial factors for success

- Internal
- External
- Predictability

C. Competitors

Individual, concise competitive assessments of three or four major competitors.

- Strengths and weaknesses
- Market shares and trends
- Quality levels

Exhibit 14-1 *(continued)*

- Financial performance
- Position with customers
- Production facilities
- Technology
- Past, present and most probable future strategy

III. Proposed Strategy

A. Objectives

Concise statements on where the business is expected to go in total and by product/service line.

- Growth
- Market shares
- Costs vis-a-vis the competition (sales, advertising/promotion, production, distribution)
- New products and/or services
- Quality
- Position with the customer
- Summary of financial goals

B. Marketing Strategy

Broad strategy statement of how the brand(s) is positioned vis-a-vis the competition and in the market. Identification of specific programs which are intended to execute the strategy and move the business ahead.

- Rationale for each program
- How it will be measured
- Personnel assigned
- Budget required
- How it will fit into ongoing operations

C. Unresolved Issues

Exhibit 14-2

A Small Hotel Chain Marketing Plan Outline

I. Introduction. Set the background for the overall plan. Identify specific, measurable objectives, i. e., open a new hotel in Atlanta, increase system-wide occupancy by ten percentage points in June, July and August, etc. Identify major problem areas.

II. Marketing Position in the Market. Describe precisely the consumer benefit that distinguishes our hotels from our competitors.

III. Update. Identify all changes in facilities and services that have occurred in the past year and are planned for next year.

IV. Overview of the Environment. Describe briefly any major developments in the external environment that might impact the business or the competition.

V. The Competition. Briefly identify the primary competition in each market, specifying number of rooms, what is new in its facilities, pricing, or marketing strategy.

VI. Marketing Data

A. Identify the top five geographic areas producing transient business, with percentages of total room nights compared to past three years.

B. Briefly describe the guests at each hotel in demographics, expectations and reasons for staying with us.

C. Identify specific market segments with the percentage each one contributes.

VII. Marketing Strategy by Market Segment

A. Groups

1. Objectives: Identify what you specifically wish to achieve in this segment.

Exhibit 14-2 *(continued)*
---

2. Strategy: Identify how sales, advertising and public relations will work together to reach the objectives.

3. Sales Activities: Divide by specific market segments.

   a. Corporate

   b. Associations

   c. Incentives

   d. Travel Agents

   e. Tours

   f. Other

   Under each category provide a narrative description of your specific planned activities including timing and personnel responsibilities.

4. Sales Materials: Identify all items to be included in the budget.

5. Direct Mail: Briefly describe each planned mailing project including objectives, message and content. Will this be a new piece or an existing one?

6. Research: Indicate any planned projects and explain their purpose.

B. Transient

   1. Objectives: Identify what you specifically wish to achieve in this segment.

   2. Strategy: Identify how sales, advertising and public relations will work together to reach the objectives.

   3. Sales Activities: For each segment—

      a. Consumer

      b. Corporate

      c. Travel Agents

      d. Wholesale/Airline/Tour

      e. Packages

      f. Government/Military/Education

      g. Special Interest/Other

   4. Sales Materials: Identify all items to be included in the budget.

   5. Direct Mail: Briefly describe each planned mailing project including objectives, message and content. Will this be a new piece or an existing one?

   6. Research: Indicate any planned projects and explain their purpose.

Exhibit 14-2 *(continued)*

C. Food & Beverage

1. Objectives: Identify what you specifically wish to achieve in this segment.

2. Strategy: Identify how sales, advertising and public relations will work together to reach the objectives.

3. Sales Activities: For specific market segments—

    a. Restaurant and Lounge, external promotion

    b. Restaurant and Lounge, internal promotion

    c. Catering

    d. Community Relations/Other

4. Sales Materials: banquet menus, signs, etc.

5. Direct Mail: Briefly describe each planned mailing project including objectives, message and content. Will this be a new piece or an existing one?

6. Research: Indicate any planned projects and explain their purpose.

VIII. Advertising

A. Describe the objectives of each advertising campaign planned.

B. Briefly describe the contents of the advertising and identify the key benefit to be advertised.

C. Identify media to be used by location and type.

D. Indicate the percent of the advertising budget allocated to each market segment.

IX. Community Relations.

A. Describe objectives of community relations programs and explain how they support the marketing strategy.

B. Specify what proportion of the community relations programs will support each market segment.

X. Summary. Conclude with a brief statement describing the major challenges of the next year and how they will be met.

Exhibit 14-3

A SMALL CONSUMER PRODUCTS COMPANY MARKETING STRATEGY FOR FY____

MARKET REVIEW

This section summarizes key trends and developments in the market during the past 12 months.

1. Market Growth. Total industry sales reached XX million cases in the fiscal year ended July 31, XXXX. This is up 5.3% over FY XX. Next year's sales are estimated to be XXXX.

Fiscal Year	Industry Sales (thousands of cases)	Year Change
19__	XXXX	5.3%
19__	XXXX	5.0%
19__	XXXX (forecast)	5.1%

2. Regional Variations. Growth in the Southeast and Southwest continue to be much stronger than in the rest of the country and now accounts for 62% of total sales.

Regions	% of Sales	% of Population	Category Development Index
N. E.	8%	22%	36
S. W.	32%	20%	160
S. E.	30%	18%	167
N. C.	20%	28%	71
Pacific	10%	12%	83
U. S. total	100%	100%	100

Exhibit 14-3 *(continued)*

3. Shipments. Sales for FY__ are currently estimated to close out the year at XXXX cases. While this is an increase of 29,000 cases over FY__, it is a shortfall of 98,000 cases against the FY__ plan. The primary reason for this shortfall appears to be a failure of the fourth quarter dealer loader program.

	1st Qtr	*2nd Qtr*	*3rd Qtr*	*4th Qtr*
FY__ Plan	XXX	XXX	XXX	XXX
FY__ Actual	XXX	XXX	XXX	XXX
Difference	YYY	YYY	YYY	YYY

4. Competitive Shares: In FY__, we lost 1.1 share points, Competitor Two lost a little less, -0.8% and the All Other category lost -0.5%. Competitor One appears to have gained all of these lost share points. See attached Exhibit for detailed analysis by region.

U. S. MARKET SHARE

	FY__	*FY__*	*Share Change*
US	27.7%	26.6%	-1.1
Competitor One	32.5%	35.0%	+2.5
Competitor Two	15.3%	14.5%	-0.8
All Others	24.5%	24.0%	-0.5
Total	100.0%	100.0%	

5. Distribution: No major changes have occurred in FY__ for us or any of our competitors.

6. Competitive Advertising and Promotion:

   a. Expenditures: Both Competitor One and Competitor Two continue to outspend us on a per case basis. In particular, Competitor One remains a dominant force in the market. Two significant competitive developments have occurred in FY__.

   (1) Competitor One has resumed advertising on daytime part network television and it has made a major increase in its promotional activity in a niche market in the S. E. region.

Exhibit 14-3 *(continued)*

(2) Competitor Two has shifted out of national magazines and now spends almost exclusively on local spot television in the top 50 markets.

b. Creative: No major changes have taken place in the basic creative strategies of the major competitors during FY__. Competitor One appeared to experiment with a new "Improved Flavor" campaign in Atlanta during the third quarter. It does not appear to be a significant improvement in its combination, and no change in its share or sales level has been observed in the test area.

c. Promotion: The primary emphasis for all of the major competitors in this market was on deep trade promotions in FY__. There were two exceptions of note.

(1) Competitor Two shipped two-for-one packs nationally during September. (Analysis of the results is not completed at this date.)

(2) Competitor Two used a mystery shopper program in the black markets in the S. E. It appears to have been quite successful and may have limited its share loss significantly in FY__ .

7. Product Development:

a. Competitive Product Tests: A blind taste test conducted by our Marketing Research Department indicates that Competitor One has made major improvements in its texture and flavor. These improvements now give it parity with our products on every determinant attribute. It is believed that this is a serious change in the competitive environment.

However, Competitor Two remains at a large disadvantage in appearance, texture and flavor.

b. Product Improvement Programs: Consumer tests of the vitamin-added new formulations have been completed and the consumer response was stronger than any product we have ever tested. The vitamin-added versions have been submitted to the FDA for approval. No problems are foreseen and approval is expected by the first quarter FY__. Plans are currently being developed to test market these products in the S. E. during the second quarter of FY__ , with a full national roll-out during the third quarter of FY__. Details are attached.

Long-term stability tests of the new Alpha formulations are currently underway. Definitive results will not be available for at least eighteen months.

8. Additional Activities: A specially commissioned marketing research study of the black market indicates that household consumption may be as much as two

times greater than we had previously thought. In addition, multiple-pack purchases are extremely popular in this market.

SUMMARY—PROBLEMS AND OPPORTUNITIES

The material reviewed above leads to the following conclusions:

1. *Market Growth* The growth of the total market exceeds both population growth and food-at-home sales growth, so it is believed that a continued major effort in this market is clearly in support of the company's overall corporate strategy. It is believed that the new vitamin-added products give us a chance to take the leadership position away from Competitor One and blunt its recent quality improvements.

2. *Media Strategy* The FY__ decision to shift our advertising dollars into national magazines and spot television in selected markets appears to have been effective. Our advertising awareness level is 10 percentage points higher than one year ago while our competitors' levels are unchanged. This media strategy will be continued in FY__.

3. *Creative Strategy* We continue to be thought of as the best tasting product in the category (and the most expensive) by heavy users of the product category. Therefore, no changes are proposed.

4. *Niche Market* New research findings and the apparent success of Competitor Two in this market suggest strongly that we must develop a stronger approach to this market.

5. *Advertising Budgets* Our serious disadvantage in per-case spending levels (due to Competitor One's extensive media buying leverage) is believed to be the primary factor in our market share loss and in our failure to meet the FY__ sales plan. Accordingly, it is recommended that a heavy-up spending test in selected markets be conducted when the new vitamin-added products are available.

6. *Packaging* Both our research and Competitor Two's actions indicate that there is a real opportunity in the black market for multiple packs. However, it is believed that some method must be found to limit such multi-packs to very specific geographic areas.

MAJOR COMPETITIVE THREAT

The marked improvement in the quality of Competitor One's product and the success of Competitor Two in the black market are believed to be major competitive threats to our position.

Exhibit 14-3 *(continued)*

MAJOR BUSINESS OPPORTUNITY

The primary business opportunity is believed to lie in the new vitamin-added products, if sufficient advertising funds can be authorized. A secondary opportunity is believed to lie in our new appreciation of the size of the niche market.

GENERAL BUSINESS OBJECTIVES FY__

1. The strategies proposed for FY__ are based on the following forecasts.

	FY__	*FY__*	*% Change*
Total Industry Sales (in cases)	XXX	XXX	+5.1%
Our Sales (in cases)	XXX	XXX	+9.0%
Our Market Share	26.6%	27.6%	+1.0 points
Advertising/Promotion Budget	XXX	XXX	+36%
Expenditure Per Case	$0.72	$0.90	+25%

2. The new vitamin-added products will be approved and test marketed, and a heavy-up advertising test will be conducted. In addition, a fresh approach to the black market will be developed.

MARKETING STRATEGY FY__

The activities and programs described below are designed to support the General Business Objectives of the Business for FY__.

1. Total advertising and promotion expenditures for FY__ will be increased substantially in response to the competitive threats from 1) Competitor One's improved product quality, and 2) Competitor Two's success in the black market.
2. The increased advertising and promotion budget will be allocated in approximately the following way.
   a. Five percent of the total budget ($XXX) will be held in the general reserve against the possibility that the planned volume objective cannot be attained. A recommendation concerning the disposal of this fund will be made at the end of the 3rd quarter.

    b. An additional five percent of the total budget ($XXX) will be allocated for the marketing research costs involved in the heavy-up advertising test, additional consumer testing of the vitamin-added products, and a developmental program targeted toward the niche market and built around multiple-packs.

    c. The remaining ninety percent of the total budget ($XXX) will be divided equally between media advertising and consumer promotion.

        (1) Primary emphasis in the media advertising will be to announce the new vitamin-added products among all users of the product category.

        (2) Heavy sampling and couponing will be designed to force trial of the new vitamin-added products and to reinforce perceptions of our high quality level.

3. Consistent with current practice, the advertising budget will be allocated so as to provide some support in all regions of the U. S., but with extra weight against the S. E. and S. W. regions where category development indices are highest.

4. In view of the apparent failure of our FY__ dealer loader program, the FY__ trade promotion budget is limited to one free goods offer (one free with nine) in the first quarter and a 15% off-invoice allowance co-incident with the introduction of the new vitamin-added products.

5. In recognition of the possibly high potential in the niche market, a special "buy one-get one free" coupon will be dropped in selected zip code areas in ten major markets. In ten different major markets, we will advertise on the two highest-rated radio stations in the market for three months. Sales results will be monitored in all markets.

SUMMARY

The basic market continues to exhibit good growth characteristics and it is believed that it is in the company's best long-term growth prospects to continue to be a vigorous competitor in this market. Our creative strategy and media strategy appear to be working satisfactorily and no changes are anticipated. While our recent market share decline is worrisome, it is believed that additional advertising and promotion spending can halt this share erosion and a heavy-up advertising test is being planned to verify this idea.

A major competitive threat is anticipated from recent quality improvements in Competitor One's products. It is believed that the vitamin-added formulations will not only blunt this competitive threat, but (in conjunction with increased advertising and promotion spending) will provide a realistic opportunity to take the lead in this market. National roll-out is expected to be completed during the 4th quarter of FY__.

A special opportunity in one niche market seems to be available to us. Two test programs are planned to learn how best to serve this market.

Exhibit 14-4

A MID-SIZED BANK MARKETING PROGRAM PLAN

1. Background

   Summarize what market conditions/situations led to this program and/or how it relates to the product's annual marketing plan.

2. Program Summary

   Brief summary description of the program (including scope, content, etc.)

3. Business/Marketing Objectives
   a. Quantitative: Specific, numeric, measurable goals for the program (e. g., $ sales, # sales, #inquiries, etc.) If available, provide past performances for comparison.
   b. Qualitative: Non-numeric goals (e. g., increased employee involvement, etc.)

4. Marketing Strategies

   Planned action to achieve the objectives above. Discuss the product, pricing, promotion, delivery, field incentives, advertising, public relations, etc. Discuss specifically what role advertising will play and the specific advertising objectives.

5. Target
   a. Definition: Demographics, psychographics, financial relationship, etc.
   b. Frame of Reference: What does the target already know about the category, our product and the competition? What is it concerned about? What is its primary problem? How does it shop for the product?
   c. Purchase Motivators: What factors drive the purchase selection (one brand vs. another)? Why would someone buy from our bank? Why would someone not buy from our bank?

6. Competitive Frame

   What category are we competing in? Who are we primarily competing with (i.e., where will we source our volume to meet the objectives above)? Where do we stand vs. this competition? How do we compare to this competition on the Purchase Motivators above?

7. Point(s) of Difference

   The factors that most distinguish us from the competition and will motivate purchase of us. Which factor is the most meaningful/motivating?

8. Communication Objectives

    What we want the target to think and do as a result of the advertising. Be specific and focused.

9. Creative Strategy

    What we must communicate to motivate the target to think and do what we want. Expressed as follows;

    [Product] is better than [Competition] for [Target] because it [Buying Motivator] as a result of [Support for Buying Motivator].

    The Competition and Target are summarized from the information in Sections 5 and 6 above.

    The Product is written as it will be described in the advertising (e.g., "[Bank] Home Equity Loans and Lines of Credit").

    The Buying Motivator is the one essential factor that, when communicated, will produce the desired response. It must be singular and focused. Almost always expressed as a benefit, it can be a feature if the benefit is self-evident.

    The Support provides the reason(s) to believe the Buying Motivator and explains it. There may be more than one reason, but they must be listed in priority order and should include only the information to be communicated in the copy.

10. Tonality

    The basic character conveyed by the advertising.

11. Executional Guidelines

    Indicate copy mandatories (e. g., legal/corporate requirements, 800#, linkage to corporate theme, etc.).

12. Offer Details

    Provides additional details of how the offer (if any) is structured and will work. The information is for background purposes and unless it is included in the Support or Executional Guidelines Sections above, it will not necessarily appear in the copy.

13. Timing

    Specify timing for the program (include documentation of product seasonality, if available), and key milestones.

14. Budget

    Specify the budget for the program in detail.

ONE POSSIBLE WAY TO USE YOUR COMPLETE MARKETING PLANNING PAGES

The strongest point of this section is that each company has to develop a planning system and method that best suits the personnel, competitors and customers of that particular company. However, successful companies do that job within an overall framework that looks moderately similar from company to company. What follows is one possible way to structure a marketing strategy and planning system around the Marketing Planning Pages you have been completing as you progressed through this guide. Make sure that you add all of the additional material that is important for your particular situation.

I.   Introduction
     Mission Statement (Marketing Planning Pages 8-1 and 8-2)
     Customer Advisory Board (Marketing Planning Page 9-13)

II.   Market Analysis
      The Product Life Cycle (Marketing Planning Pages 3-1 to 3-8)
      Recent History of the Market (Marketing Planning Pages 5-1 to 5-4)
      Market and Brand Development Indices (Marketing Planning Pages 5-5 to 5-8)
      Market Share Strategy (Marketing Planning Pages 2-1 to 2-4)

III.   Competitive Position
       Customer Value Competitive Analysis (Exhibit 2-1)
       Business Factor Ratings (Marketing Planning Pages 4-1 to 4-6)
       Other Competitive Analysis Materials

IV.   Environmental Analysis
      Economic Environment (Marketing Planning Page 7-1)
      Technological Environment (Marketing Planning Page 7-2)
      Demographic/Social/Cultural Environment (Marketing Planning Page 7-3)
      Political Environment (Marketing Planning Page 7-4)
      Ecological Environment (Marketing Planning Page 7-5)

V.   Customer Analysis
     Customer Profile (Marketing Planning Pages 9-9 to 9-12)
     New Customer Cost Analysis (Marketing Planning Pages 9-1 to 9-4)
     Profitability by Customer Type (Marketing Planning Pages 9-5 to 9-8)

VI.   Developing Marketing Strategy
      Defining The Market (Marketing Planning Pages 6-5 to 6-8)
      Using The Served Market Concept (Marketing Planning Pages 6-1 to 6-4)

Customer Value Strategy (Marketing Planning Pages 2-6 to 2-9)
Creative Strategy (Marketing Planning Pages 11-12 to 11-15)

VII. Sales Force Plans
Customer Importance vs. Selling Effort (Marketing Planning Pages 10-1 to 10-4)
Market and Brand Development Indices (Marketing Planning Pages 5-5 to 5-8)
New Customer Cost Analysis (Marketing Planning Pages 9-1 to 9-4)
Budgets

VIII. Advertising Plans
Creative Strategy (Marketing Planning Pages 11-12 to 11-15)
Demographic Profile (Marketing Planning Pages 11-1 to 11-4)
Using Newspapers (Marketing Planning Page 11-5)
Using Magazines (Marketing Planning Page 11-6)
Using Television (Marketing Planning Page 11-7)
Using Radio (Marketing Planning Page 11-8)
Using Outdoor (Marketing Planning Page 11-9)
Using Direct Mail (Marketing Planning Page 11-10)
Using Cable TV (Marketing Planning Page 11-11)
Budgets

IX. Sales Promotion Plans
New Customer Cost Analysis (Marketing Planning Pages 9-1 to 9-4)
Profitability by Customer Type (Marketing Planning Pages 9-5 to 9-8)
Sales Promotion Programs (Marketing Planning Pages 11-16 to 11-19)
Budgets

X. Financial Plans
Sales Forecasts (Marketing Planning Pages 10-5 to 10-8)
Quarterly and Monthly Forecasts (Marketing Planning Pages 10-9 to 10-12)
Forecast Profit and Loss Statement

XI. Timetable

XII. Special Projects
Readiness to Export (Marketing Planning Page 12-1)
Internet Opportunities (Marketing Planning Page 13-1 to 13-4)

XIII. Contingency Plans

Index